Form and Idea in Modern Theatre

Form and

Idea in

Modern

Theatre

by John Gassner

Sterling Professor of Playwriting

Yale University

THE DRYDEN PRESS · NEW YORK

FOR
Caroline and Sumner

FOREWORD

THE DEVELOPMENT OF PLAYWRITING AND STAGE PRODUCTION since the nineteenth century has been characterized by efforts to put into effect various concepts or "ideas" of theatre. The leaders in these efforts—whether romanticists like Hugo, naturalists like Zola, or latter-day opponents of realism—have made theatrical history with strongly urged ideals and truculent formulations. Even the votaries of show business, indifferent though they may be to generalizations, have not been impervious to the programs of successive *avant-gardes*. The pragmatists have usually appropriated (if also misapplied and vulgarized) the very aims they have professed to scorn.

Today, questions concerning the kind of theatre we have or ought to have crop up frequently, even in the press that covers Broadway presentations. The reviewers are apt to join the academicians in giving thought to the esthetics of the stage. This is especially the case whenever Broadway realism displays its threadbare tatters without colorful patches of "entertainment" or whenever an experiment in theatrical stylization proves particularly inviting or tantalizing. Thus, in one respect or another, matters of "form" and "style" have ceased to be exclusively esoteric considerations.

One would have to be singularly obtuse, however, to conclude from this that the stage, especially the American stage, is approaching well-defined objectives under the direction of leaders who manifest a clear understanding of its present situation. A clarification of that situation is still needed, and this cannot, I believe, be achieved without glancing at the paths hitherto followed by those who have sought to modernize dramatic art in conformity with some idea or ideal. The discussion therefore follows a largely historical sequence, although it is somewhat qualified by the supplements entitled "Some Further Observations."

In my overview, the modern theatre appears as an enterprise strongly marked by instability, eclecticism, and a mélange of genres. Early in the nineteenth century, the theatre emancipated itself from conventionality with much romantic bravado only to accept, after a while, a new form of bondage in submitting to the ultrarealistic requirements of verisimilitude and illusionism. A second revolt against the constraints of convention was therefore in the making by 1890 even while realism, the first major phase of modern dramatic art, was winning victories for the modern spirit. Departures from realism soon became numerous and produced new and overlapping phases of modernism. The theatre has swung from extreme to extreme around an indistinct core of opportunistic commercial enterprise. There has been no resting point for playwrights and devotees of the stage ever since realism reached its apogee about half a century ago. At best, it may be said that the multiplication of formal experiments since 1890 has resulted in an uneasy coexistence of poorly developed and haphazardly reconciled alternatives. A state of crisis has been chronic during the greater part of the century.

We cannot fail to realize that the future of our stage depends greatly upon the possibility of turning the present chaotic coexistence of realism and nonrealistic stylization into an active and secure partnership. A reconciliation of the polarities of realism and theatricalism is indeed inherent in the very nature of dramatic art, and so I close this book with a section, entitled "The Duality of Theatre," which is an examination of the theatrical experience itself.

JOHN GASSNER

July 1956

ACKNOWLEDGMENTS

I OWE THE GENESIS OF THIS BOOK TO THE KIND INVITATION OF Alabama College to deliver the biennial Dancy Lectures, which was accompanied by exemption from the usual requirement to speak on a Southern subject—a requirement I could not have met with even a fraction of the knowledge such previous Dancy Lecturers as Lewis Mumford and Dumas Malone brought to their subjects. For the exemption, which enabled me to roam across considerable space as well as time, I am indebted to the Dancy Lecture Committee. And for the gracious hospitality of Alabama College I am particularly grateful to President and Mrs. F. E. Lund, Professor and Mrs. Walter Trumbauer, and Professor Eva Golson.

In accordance with a requirement of the Dancy Fellowship, a statement by Professor Trumbauer, the chairman of the Dancy Lecture Committee, follows:

The contents of this volume were originally prepared and delivered by the author at Alabama College in November 1953 as the seventh series of Dancy Lectures. We are pleased that these lectures are now presented to the reading public. They provide a comprehensive panoramic view of the developments in drama and theatre since the last century.

No one can speak with more authority on form and idea in the drama and the theatre than Mr. John Gassner, who eminently combines the virtues of historical scholarship with the practical acumen of the artist-producer. Further commentary on this work, or on a critic so well and so widely known, would be supererogation.

For whatever has been accomplished in this book-length version of the lectures I am especially grateful to my wife, Mollie Gassner, and my publisher-friend Stanley Burnshaw.

J.G.

CONTENTS

Theatricalism and Crisis

4

The Duality of Theatre

ILLUSTRATIONS

1

The Modernization of
Dramatic Art

THE REALISTIC PHASE

To discern causes is to turn vision
into knowledge and motion into action.
—GEORGE SANTAYANA, The Life of Reason

1

ONE DOES NOT UNDERTAKE TO DISCUSS FORM IN ANY ART WITHOUT qualms, and when the art under consideration is theatre there is the added complication that we are concerned with *two* arts, dramatic literature and stage production. Nor is stage production at all a simple matter, for it involves all the arts of the theatre— acting, music, the dance, scenic design, stage lighting, costume design, and architecture—that is, the kind of playhouse occupied by the actors and their audience and the kind of stage upon which the performance takes place. (See pp. 51-54.) All these arts, separately or in varying combinations, are involved in dramatic modernism, so that it becomes necessary to touch upon developments in different arts. Moreover, such terms as "form" and "idea" can become extremely troublesome when used in connection with these developments.

Without delving into the esthetic absolutes suggested by "form," it is necessary to resolve initial ambiguities by establishing some arbitrary definitions. By "form" I mean the distinctive *structure* of a play and the distinctive *texture* of the writing—that is, the style in which it is written. I also use the term more loosely to signify an over-all type or style of theatre. Moreover, I relate the forms of modern drama to certain "ideas of theatre"—that is, to certain conceptions of theatrical art and certain expectations from it. By "idea" I do not mean subject matter, but the view of theatre apparent in the play or the production (or in both), and the special esthetic aim pursued in the work aside from the general one of interesting, entertaining, or stirring an audience. This idea, moreover, is to be thought of as more or less consciously held and deliberately served in playwriting and play production. It is held consciously by leaders of various types of theatre (for example Hugo, Ibsen, Zola, Antoine, Stanislavsky, and Shaw) and tacitly by less analytical persons as well as by the sedulous apes of fashion whose number is as great in the theatre as in any other art. Ideas, in the popular sense of subject-matter—namely, the ideas that constitute philosophy, sociology, topics of discourse, arguments, even propaganda—cannot, of course, be excluded from our purview. It is often difficult to distinguish between an artist's view of theatre and his view of life, society, politics, or religion. It is certain, for example, that Ibsen's idea of a realistic theatre and Zola's idea of a naturalistic one had affiliations with nineteenth-century social criticism and nineteenth-century enthusiasm for science, respectively. Nevertheless, I employ "idea" to mean something larger than a mere topic or opinion; I use the term to denote some specific way of conceiving the nature and use of theatre, which in turn determines or helps to determine dramatic form and the stage presentation.

As for the use of the term "modernity" in this discourse, a chronological approach is the best means of simplification. The generally accepted view that drama and theatre became distinctively "modern" during the last quarter of the nineteenth century is adopted here. The advent of modernity can be equated with the rise of realistic drama and stage production under the leadership of Ibsen, Zola, Shaw, Antoine, and Stanislavsky. The appearance of realistic technique and style was the first phase of modernism in drama. It is essential to realize that modern realism is not distinguishable in every instance and every respect from the art of theatre before 1875. Endeavors to make stage illusion stronger by using solid settings and abbreviating or removing the forestage made headway earlier in the century. And a trend toward realism that was foreshadowed by Elizabethan middle-class tragedy as well as by such eighteenth-century pieces as George Lillo's *The London Merchant* and Lessing's *Miss Sara Sampson* culminated in a variety of problem plays by Dumas *fils* and Émile Augier and in studies of middle-class Russian life by Alexander Ostrovsky. Indeed, the most durable examples of realism before the vogue of Ibsen came early: Nikolai Gogol's social satire *The Inspector-General* appeared in 1836, *Maria Magdalena*, Friedrich Hebbel's tragedy of middle-class values, in 1844, and Turgenev's "Chekhovian" drama of provincial stalemate, *A Month in the Country*, in 1849. Even the extremes of naturalism, without benefit of formulation by Zola, can be traced as far back as 1836, the year in which the short-lived genius Georg Büchner wrote his powerful play *Woyzeck*. Our chronological distinction is based on the fact that all such dramatic efforts before the last quarter of the century were sporadic.

Chronology, however, must be supplemented by the observation that realism by itself does not define dramatic modernism, because a second aspect, one of nonrealistic stylization, has been important in the modern theatre almost as long as realism has. Dramatic modernism consists of a succession and then an interweaving of strands that may be called Ibsenism and Wagnerianism, realism and symbolism, objective naturalism and both subjective and objective antinaturalism. (Subjective antinaturalism was manifested in expressionism; objective antinaturalism in epic theatre as formulated and presented by Erwin Piscator, Bertolt Brecht, and those who created "living newspapers," such as

Power and *One-third of a Nation,* during the climactic years of the New Deal in the 1930's.) Even romanticism has been woven into the fabric of modernism. Romantic drama, rejected as outmoded by pioneers of the 1870's and 1880's, came to be considered "modern" again after Rostand wrote *Cyrano de Bergerac* in 1897. And not only Rostand but Maxwell Anderson, whose popular historical plays recall both Shakespeare and Schiller, and other writers, such as Yeats and Paul Claudel, who combine romanticism with symbolism, belong to the modern theatre. Their work, far from being dismissed as old-fashioned, has been acclaimed as actually representing progress in the theatre. And although claims on behalf of these playwrights can be questioned, one may at least concede that their work, even when reminiscent, has been less moth-eaten than many up-to-the-minute, quasi-journalistic plays written in the realistic mode.[1] Whether judged by content or by style, the post-1914 verse dramas of Yeats are certainly immeasurably more remote from the mid-Victorian age than, let us say, *Pollyanna,* vintage 1916, and *Abie's Irish Rose,* vintage 1922. Indeed, as I shall show, a seminal concept of modern theatre was embodied in the very romantic movement that had to end before the modern theatre could establish itself. In the process of nostalgically looking back to the Shakespearean stage, the early-nineteenth-century exponents of romanticism were actually looking forward.

It may be said, then, that in concerning ourselves with "modern" theatre we are dealing with a phenomenon the nature of which will not be apparent until dramatic form and, especially, the period's ruling views of theatre have been examined. We cannot know *what makes our theatre specifically modern* without such an examination. Nor can we understand the contemporary

---

[1] I am not concerned here with distinctions between early-nineteenth-century romantic drama and the latter-day neo-romanticism, although the latter has been generally restrained in style and tempered by psychological, social, or political realism. A comparison of *Cyrano de Bergerac* and *Hernani,* or Anderson's *Mary of Scotland* and Schiller's *Maria Stuart,* would reveal this much.

theatre's seeming stalemate, or properly appraise the development of new forms as a means of breaking that stalemate.

The Idea of Freedom of Dramatic Form

The first ruling idea of modern theatre, and the one that is still dominant and most productive, although also conducive to some anarchy, is the idea of *freedom*. Its emergence was associated with the revolt of romanticism against the rigors of neoclassicism. Under the influence of romanticism, the theatre became an open rather than a closed, strictly conventionalized art. Romanticism sharply challenged the belief fostered by neoclassic critics that there are rules to which the theatre must adhere. Laws that had been especially insisted upon after 1650— rules concerning the importance of "decorum," the idea that tragedy may deal only with the fate of princes and nobles, and the primacy of the so-called unities of time, place, and action— were banished from the theatre. Romanticism introduced the principles of flexibility, adaptation of form to content, and intellectual and artistic independence which modernism, whether realistic or nonrealistic, has cherished, if not always kept inviolate.

These principles, first affirmed in the Germany of Lessing and Goethe after 1765, were reaffirmed in France between 1827 and 1830, especially by Victor Hugo. His romantic play *Hernani,* staged in 1830 amid rioting in the theatre, signalized the end of the domination of the theatre by arbitrary rules. And as the production of *Hernani* in 1830 occurred in Paris, then and for many years afterward the cultural capital of Europe, the event was of international importance.

The French theatre was the last stronghold of neoclassicism in Europe. Far from overthrowing the traditional style, the French Revolution and the Napoleonic regime had supported it.

Both the leaders of the Revolution and the supporters of the monarchy identified themselves with classicism: the former with the ideals of the Roman Republic, the latter with the glories of the Augustan age of Rome. The same observation may be made concerning the plastic arts, whose outstanding leader, Jacques Louis David, favored classic lines in his portraits, such as the celebrated one of Madame Recamier, and both classic form and subject matter in his historical paintings. The strong resistance to romanticism in painting is described in Élie Faure's treatment of David and his times;[2] among many passages on this subject is the following:

> For a quarter of a century, Antiquity has been before the minds of men. That way lies Virtue, and there also is Beauty. André Chenier [the period's most distinguished playwright as well as poet] dedicates hymns to David, in whose works Robespierre recognizes the physical expression of that which he himself represents in the moral world; and it is to David that the Convention intrusts the work of organizing Republican aesthetics on the model of the austerity, the pomp, and the stoicism of Rome. (p. 238)

The reaction against the decadent *ancien régime* of the Bourbons was moralistic as well as political, and republican probity was identified with Roman virtue. Cartesian rationalism, reinforced by ideals of Roman stoicism, erected barriers to romantic aims. This was especially the case in institutionalized art such as the theatre, which was partly subsidized by the state and partly dependent on the support of the moralistic middle classes before, during, and after the Napoleonic period.

Thus the dogma of the antique retained its hold on painter, playwright, and actor alike. Neoclassicism literally had a stranglehold on the theatre until the memorable evening of February 25, 1830, when Victor Hugo's youthful left-bank supporters, bearded, long-haired, dressed in the clothing of all ages but their own, and led by Théophile Gautier, wearing his rose-colored vest,

[2] *History of Art*, Vol. IV: *Modern Art* (New York: Dover Publications, 1924), pp. 236-253.

smothered the neoclassic opposition determined to hiss *Hernani* off the boards of the Théâtre Français.

Three years earlier, moreover, Victor Hugo, then twenty-six, had formulated a view of drama in which it was maintained that the theatre was free to present every subject and to employ any form or style. In the flamboyant introduction written in 1827 to his not particularly good play *Cromwell,* for which he had been unable to win a stage production, Hugo argued that life alone, life in its infinite variety, should be the playwright's model. In an age of "liberty," Hugo maintained,

> let us take the hammer to theories and poetic systems. Let us throw down the old plastering that conceals the façade of art. There are neither rules nor models; or, rather, there are no other rules than the general rules of nature, which soar above the whole field of art, and the special rules which result from the conditions appropriate to the subject of each composition.[3]

Hugo was arguing for his own brand of romantic drama, of course. For example, he made a strong plea for the place of the grotesque in art, since he made lavish use of this element himself in such plays as *The King Amuses Himself* and *Ruy Blas.* The element of the grotesque had come into favor with the rise of romantic literature, and its exploitation before and after Hugo's time is a familiar characteristic of romanticism. As late as the turn of the century Edmond Rostand was to get some of his best effects of pathos and irony from the length of Cyrano's nose. In the preface to *Cromwell,* however, Hugo recommended the use of grotesque characters and situations for the purpose of conveying "reality." He rejected as unnatural the absolute separation of comedy and tragedy that had been insisted upon by neoclassicism. He called for a combination of the sublime and the grotesque, which, he declared, should "meet in the drama as they

[3] Barrett H. Clark (ed.), *European Theories of the Drama* (Crown Publishers, 1947), pp. 374-379.

meet in life and creation." In support of this view Hugo cited the example of Shakespeare, calling attention to the confrontation of Romeo and the apothecary, Macbeth and the witches, Hamlet and the gravediggers, Lear and the Fool. In the name of nature and truth (which also led him to favor the use of local color), Hugo asserted a principle of freedom for dramatic art that is central to modern theatrical developments. When he proclaimed his defiance of "the customs officers of thought," he signalized a general loosening of critical bonds that had already been partly accomplished in Germany and England and that was long overdue in France. He did not, indeed, introduce the "idea of freedom" into the theory of drama; he had been anticipated, half a century before, by the German playwrights of the "storm and stress" school, who opposed neoclassicism by exalting "inner form" and by propounding the principle of unity in the individual atmosphere or, so to speak, in the soul of the play, in contrast to logical, external unity.[4] With support from Rousseauist enthusiasms and revolutionary political tendencies, the principle of a thoroughly free, rather than ruled and regimented, theatre was bound to prevail in Europe. Hugo's summary of principle, however, was historically the most important, and it became cardinal doctrine that has been constantly reaffirmed by the modern experimentalists.

Today the flexibility of dramatic and theatrical conventions is recognized everywhere. Although there has been no lack of censorship of a moral or political nature to curtail the freedom of dramatic expression, no esthetic principle has curtailed experimentation except when some reactionary regime, as in Hitler's Germany and Stalin's Russia, has assailed experimentation as a symptom of artistic decadence. The modern theatre has been the most experimental, and therefore the most varied, in history. From a view of the theatre as an institution that exists primarily for the preservation of some cultural norm (the mythos and ritualism of the city-state or *polis* in Athens, the sense of order and *bon sens* in

[4] See Siegfried Melchinger, *Dramaturgie des Sturms und Drangs* (Gotha, 1929), pp. 93-99.

the Paris of Louis XIV) we have arrived at the idea that theatre is the showplace of every conceivable display of ingenuity.

The sociological aspects of this conception of theatre need not detain us here after we have conceded that our theatre has reflected the instability of modern civilization. Nor need the question of content concern us greatly here. There can be no doubt that, despite the instances of moralistic or political censorship in the Victorian and post-Victorian periods, the modern stage has taken more liberties than at any time before in history. It has been truly the museum, forum, and marketplace of opinions, speculations, and aberrations. But although this freedom of content is obviously important, it has not been the major factor in the development of specifically modern modes of drama. That development has been a matter of form rather than content, except, of course, in so far as the struggle for form has been motivated by the need for a special means of expression. Content dictated dramatic structure, for instance, when English poets adopted choral drama for expressing an elegant religiosity, or when Marxist playwrights used "mass chants" and demonstrational devices in plays for the purpose of teaching the "class struggle." It is the effect of the idea of freedom on form that is of primary interest in the present inquiry. And justifiably, I believe, as it is not the "modernity" of the content that we can extract from a play that will distinguish the work from a Greek drama. There is no dearth of "modern" thinking about war and sex in *The Trojan Women* and *Hippolytus,* plays concerning whose distinctively classic form there can be no question. An even more obvious example is Robinson Jeffers' adaptation of *Medea,* which retains Euripides' subject without in the least constituting Greek choral drama. So close is the relationship of content to form that the difference between the two Medea plays is enormous; the story is the same but the life of the two works—which includes the meaning and the experience alike—is not at all the same.

Hugo's preface to *Cromwell* is a springboard for modern dramatic art because one of the manifestations of his idea of a free theatre was the rise of realism and naturalism, which effected a far more radical transformation of dramatic form than the wildest romantic drama, which was merely Shakespearean or pseudo-Shakespearean in structure and texture. Moreover, realism in playwriting and stage production was to be followed after 1880 by a variety of styles, such as symbolism, expressionism, theatricalism, constructivism, and surrealism, each accompanied by some program for a new dispensation.

These styles followed one another with increasing rapidity, and came to jostle each other not only in the small theatres playing to a cultural élite, but in all the marketplaces of commercial showmanship. Consequently, the modern stage became at once the battleground of multifarious, sometimes vituperative, factions and the parade grounds of a "live-and-let-live" eclecticism unmatched in any earlier period of theatre. Today, it is not unusual for Broadway to display in a single season a number of prosaically realistic plays, a romantic verse drama such as Anderson's *Anne of the Thousand Days* or Christopher Fry's *The Lady's Not for Burning*, a surrealistic effort such as Gertrude Stein's *Four Saints in Three Acts*, and numerous musical comedies of indefinable character. And the drama critics, as well as the playgoers, do not even blink at this profusion of styles until they reach surrealism, which is apt to disconcert them not because of its departure from realism, but because of its incomprehensibility. They would not dream of requiring playwrights and producers to adhere to any single dramatic convention. Demands for conformity in matters of dramatic form have been made only where totalitarian systems of government have prevailed, as in Germany and Russia. (In Germany, the National Socialist regime, between 1933 and 1945, declared all modernist art decadent. In Russia after 1935, the Stalinist dictatorship in the arts demanded conformity to an orthodox blending of elementary realistic technique with Socialist doctrine—a so-called "Socialist realism" in the arts.)

We are even likely to encounter an amalgamation of two or more different styles of composition in the very same play; the result, far from disturbing us, usually gains our approbation. Arthur Miller's *Death of a Salesman* contains scenes that belong to the most thoroughly realistic type of drama, but they alternate with recollected and hallucinated scenes that are more or less expressionistic in treatment. It is also to be noted that both the acting and the stage design of the 1948 Broadway production directed by Elia Kazan and designed by Jo Mielziner showed this alternation of styles. Miller's hero, Willy Loman, was characterized naturalistically. But Willy's remembered brother Ben was "stylized" by the actor who played the part. Ben's speech and stage movement were exaggerated, and an unnatural briskness and automatism characterized the performance; Brother Ben was Willy's unrealistic, indeed distorted, notion of a hard-driving, infallible, and invariably successful tycoon. The actor impersonating Ben was also eerily sudden and abrupt in making his entrances and exits; he gave the impression that he was a revenant in Willy's disturbed mind. Details of Willy's suburban home, such as the bedroom and the parlor, were rendered with an effect of cramped and unlovely realism; but the house itself was skeletonized and placed on a platform, and the stage space in front and at the sides of the structure was left scenically neutral. This space served as a backyard, as a restaurant, as a portion of a hotelroom, and, finally, without any scenery whatsoever, as the cemetery in which Willy is buried. The same setting, altered only by the lighting, was sometimes realistic, sometimes stylized and formal, but always fluid enough to let reality and dream intermingle.

In the modern theatre, indeed, there has been so much blending of effects that the question of which part of a play is "real" and which is "unreal" is sometimes meaningless. The question has hardly any meaning, for example, when asked about such plays as Strindberg's *There Are Crimes and Crimes* and Pirandello's three theatrical treatments of the subject of reality, *Right You Are (If You Think So!)*, *Six Characters in Search of an Author*, and *Tonight We Improvise*. Georg Kaiser's *From*

Morn to Midnight (once its cashier-hero runs away from the secure tedium of his job and home) presents reality and fantasy commingled in a new reality—that of the cashier's disorientation in a world already illusory enough without the superimposition of the character's fantasy. John Howard Lawson's *Processional* presents a picture that is both real and fantastically exaggerated into a sort of "jazz symphony" of society. "Which part is real and which is fantasy?" has little meaning, too, when asked about O'Neill's *The Hairy Ape:* first, because the play was intended by its author as a parable on the pathos of man's present stage in the evolutionary process that has separated him from the animal world but has not yet allowed him to attain complete humanity; and secondly, because even the most exaggerated of the scenes, the Fifth Avenue episode, is not presented as the dream of the protagonist.

To illustrate a mingling of genres and of angles of presentation, we can turn to an essentially simple play, Ferenc Molnar's *Liliom.* The present writer has encountered people in university departments of literature to whom *Liliom* is a difficult drama: it is considered "unclear" by them because the fantastic part is not differentiated from the "real" part (that is, the first four scenes) by being presented as the dying Liliom's dream or delirium. These critics of the play would have been put at ease only by a distinction between a character and his fantasy such as that which exists between the realistic and unrealistic scenes in *Beggar on Horseback* and *Lady in the Dark,* or between the "frame" in *The Emperor Jones* and the fleeing man's fantasies. Unfortunately for such critics, the posthumous portion of Liliom's career is not at all the dream of any character in the play.

A certain degree of sophistication concerning the nature of theatre has been required of us even by moderate ventures in dramatic modernism. We are expected to realize, in considering plays as different in numerous respects as *Liliom* and Brecht's *The Good Woman of Setzuan* and Giraudoux's *The Madwoman of Chaillot* (or, for that matter, *The Hairy Ape* and Wilder's *The Skin of Our Teeth*) that there is no meaningful difference between reality and fancy in a theatrical demonstration or imaginative construction. Everything in Molnar's play has *equal reality* as an element of the author's theatricalized argument, which may be stated as follows: "Liliom is the sort of individual who, if he were to go to the anteroom of heaven, would encounter just another police court. If he behaved in character after his death, he would steal a star out of the sky for his daughter; but if he were to meet her, he would be sure to lose his temper and strike her as he used to strike her mother despite his love for her—he would make the same mess of things he had made while alive." But, of course, this elementary retelling of the theme would only sentimentalize and weaken the impression of a work that is essentially a *jeu de théâtre* rather than a Sunday-school lesson.

A freedom that the stage had not enjoyed before except in Elizabethan times was bound to result in the mingling of formal elements which, even if not invariably gratifying, has helped to make modern drama and theatre stimulating. Even pastiche came into vogue, as did a mode of drama that was, if not pastiche, something close to it. There is a provocative mingling of the sacred and profane, for example, in *The Cocktail Party,* which in its mixture of the supernatural with British drawing-room comedy might give the impression of being the joint effort of Paul Claudel and Noel Coward. And there have been other alliances and misalliances in dramaturgy as striking as those which appear, for radically divergent purposes, in Eliot's *Murder in the Cathedral* and Brecht's *Caucasian Circle of Chalk.* The first-mentioned, and to us more familiar, work is composed of elements as varied as a chorus of Canterbury women, a Christmas Morning sermon, a fantasy of ghostly tempters, and a series of public addresses by Becket's murderers. Some of Brecht's and Piscator's "epic theatre" productions and our American "living newspapers" of the 1930's have had the qualities of a *collage.* Even the principle of esthetic unity has been challenged in the relentlessly iconoclastic modern theatre.

The idea of freedom in modern theatrical creation is an over-all principle, and the concept of a theatre shaped by the needs of expression rather than by the claims of tradition has been hospitable to both realistic and antirealistic art. It was this freedom of expression that sparked the naturalism of Zola, the critical realism of Ibsen, and the expressionism of Strindberg, during the last two decades of his life. Inevitably, then, the possibilities of dramatic art became enormous, and it is easy to understand why ours has been the most eclectic period in stage history. Eclecticism, of course, can be a vice as well as a virtue, and it has been accompanied by extreme instability in the modern theatre. Indeed, the theatre of our day may be condemned for its artistic flabbiness as much as it may be commended for its flexibility.

Modern experiments have become outmoded too rapidly, and we may well regret the quick obsolescence of such modernistic ventures as expressionism and surrealism. These required patient nursing if they were to prove their value as something more than expressions of eccentricity or calculated sensationalism. Only realism, both as a form of drama and style of performance, ever had the opportunity to develop its potentialities sufficiently.

Moreover, few modern playwrights have moved steadily toward consummation of their artistry by developing skill and depth in a single dramatic mode, as did Sophocles, who never abandoned the classic choral form, or Shakespeare, who never abandoned the free-flowing Elizabethan manner of playwriting. The course of a few authors is representative of the careers of many of their colleagues. Strindberg first earned an international reputation in 1887-1888 as a naturalist with such plays as *The Father* and *Miss Julie,* then embarked upon the perilous course of an expressionist playwright a decade later in such plays as *To Damascus, The Dream Play,* and *The Ghost Sonata.* In between, he wrote more or less symbolist plays and historical dramas. He also returned to extreme naturalism, in 1902, with his appallingly sordid drama of domestic hatred *The Dance of Death.* It may be said of Strindberg, as of many of his twentieth-century successors, that he never lighted upon a single mode which could satisfy his need for self-expression. O'Casey abandoned realistic dramaturgy after having given the century two of its dramatic masterpieces, *Juno and the Paycock* and *The Plough and the Stars*. He turned to expressionist drama with *The Silver Tassie*, tried his hand at choral poetic drama with *Within the Gates*, and made experiments in dramatic form in every succeeding work. O'Neill provides still another example of fluctuation. He gave the American stage many of its most powerful realistic plays, such as *Beyond the Horizon*, *Anna Christie*, and *Desire Under the Elms*, although he enriched his realism with the symbolist use of such elements as the sea, "dat ole davil sea" that stands for malign fate in *Anna Christie*. Never satisfied with realism, however, O'Neill resorted to expressionistic fantasy and distortion in such plays as *The Emperor Jones* and *The Hairy Ape*, and to other kinds of stylization, including the use of masks, in his later work.

We can observe the same fluctuations even in the still incomplete careers of our best-known recent playwrights. Arthur Miller wrote *Death of a Salesman* after having succeeded with the tightly knit, thoroughly realistic social drama *All My Sons*; Tennessee Williams followed the poetic naturalism of his *Streetcar Named Desire* with his extravagantly symbolical *Camino Real*.

The Idea of Environment

So much for the "new freedom" so memorably promulgated by Hugo. We must note, however, that experimentation first became canalized in a single direction—that of realism, or, as it was generally called on the European continent, naturalism. (See pp. 66-70.)

Freeing the theatre from all convention, propounded at first for the practical purpose of freeing it from neoclassic regulations, is a romantic ideal that cannot possibly be realized. All theatre is a tissue of conventions, including the convention of naturalness. But in the theatrical world, as in the literary, we find romanticism paving the way for realism as well as for the later neoromantic and antirealistic styles that followed on the heels of triumphant realism. The idea of a "free theatre" inevitably became the concept of a theatre that was to reflect reality: having been liberated from subservience to neoclassic convention, the stage was to be free to follow "nature" or "truth," and indeed was considered to have an obligation to do so. Hugo implied an allegiance to this conception in his preface to *Cromwell* when he rejected the neoclassic ideals of "the graces," "good taste," "selectivity," and "ennoblement," and instead wanted art to "set about doing as nature does, mingling in its creations . . . darkness and light, the grotesque and the sublime . . . the body and the soul, the beast and the intellect." [5] He wanted the stage, in short, to reflect reality.

The romantic movement in the French theatre dribbled out . :thin a decade of its beginnings. Hugo's victory in the theatre in 1830, when his adherents routed the conservatives in the so-called "battle of *Hernani*," was followed by the vogue of Eugène Scribe's formula for the speciously realistic "well-made play." The theatre was pre-empted by a species of intrigue-drama from which neither such French writers of problem plays as Dumas *fils* and Émile Augier nor even Ibsen, as late as the time of writing *A Doll's House,* could quite win divorcement. But the movement toward realism seems in retrospect to have been inevitable as nineteenth-century Europe became increasingly industralized and as its outlook grew more materialistic, scientific, and sociological.

All that was necessary by 1850 was for dramatic realism to become crystallized as a form of drama and a style of play production—that is, as a style of acting, décor, and *mise en scène* or staging. This is what occurred after 1875, and two ruling concepts made this possible—the idea of illusionism (that the theatre must provide the illusion of reality on the stage) and the idea of en-

[5] "Preface to *Cromwell*," in Clark, *European Theories of the Drama,* p. 369.

vironment. The first idea is an old one which developed in the Italian court theatres of the Renaissance. The second, that of the stage as an environment, was relatively new in the theatre. Without it, we could not have had the dramatic realism that has modernized the stage. First of all, nothing in the.second half of the nineteenth century could have strengthened the illusion of reality more than the use of the box set and the replacement of painted scenery by solid objects and workable doors and windows. Secondly, nothing at that time could have contributed more to a theatre concerned with contemporary issues than a presentation of environment as a conditioning element and as a reality to be reckoned with, opposed, or changed by the individual.

If we return to the preface to *Cromwell*, we observe that when Hugo claimed a place for the grotesque in the theatre he opened the floodgates to every kind of tabooed material, including the most sordid. Ultimately, freedom for the drama came to include the freedom to present pictures of seedy characters, low life, gross appetites, disease, and all the conditions of living associated with poverty and even degeneracy. The credo of naturalism which developed in France during the 1870's justified the representation of these conditions and the inclusion of tabooed material on the ground that the theatre should show the truth. But however much the playwright's exploitation of the grotesque affected the content of modern drama, it did not have any relation to the development of dramatic form. It was the concept of environment, or, more specifically, the idea of the stage as an environment, rather than as simply or mainly a platform for acting, that effected fundamental changes in dramatic art.

Hugo referred to local color as something more than pretty nature painting: "People are beginning to understand in our day that exact localization is one of the first elements of reality." [6] He added that "the place where this or that catastrophe took place

[6] Clark, *European Theories of the Drama*, p. 376.

becomes a terrible and inseparable witness thereof." But he actually lagged some three quarters of a century behind the concept of environment as evolved by the French encyclopedists and *philosophes* of the eighteenth century. Montesquieu, in writing his influential study *The Spirit of the Laws,* gave environment a greater role than that of serving as a setting for men's action. In Montesquieu's opinion, environment was not merely a background but a *condition* of human activity, a condition to which the very forms of government tend to conform. As long ago as 1758, moreover, the *philosophe* Denis Diderot had already acknowledged the importance of social position, its obligations and circumstances, as a factor in human life that should be allowed to play a role in the drama. Thus the idea of environment, given ever-greater prominence in the nineteenth century by sociologists and revolutionists as well as by such advanced critics as Hippolyte Taine, inevitably became a decisive factor. In the theatre, the stage setting, which had been treated as magnificently irrelevant to the actor's performance or only operatically valuable in baroque and rococo theatres, was now regarded as essential to the meaning of the play.

The growing use of the concept of environment is well illustrated by the numerous comments of the leaders of our nineteenth-century modernism. That pioneer play producer the Duke of Saxe-Meiningen, standing at the threshold of modern theatre, saw a function in the objects on the stage, declaring that it was "always an advantage to have an actor touch a piece of furniture or some other near-by object naturally. That enhances the impression of reality." Antoine, writing in 1903, was emphatic in sharing this view, declaring that "we must not be afraid of an abundance of little objects, of a wide variety of small props. . . . These are the imponderables which give a sense of intimacy and lend authentic character to the environment the director seeks to re-create." The cluttered setting implied in this comment is enough to drive a lover of simplified design such as Craig to desperation. But not Antoine, who went on to say: "Among so many objects . . . the performers' acting becomes . . . more human, more intense, and more alive in attitudes and gestures."

Antoine also counted on ceilings in relief and visible beams to provide "the impression of solidity and weight which was unknown in the make-believe painting of the old stage sets," and he believed it to be important "to fashion complete doorframes and window frames." An interior on the proscenium stage should be designed with "its four sides, its four walls" in mind (as in the world outside the theatre), "without worrying about the fourth wall, which will later disappear so as to enable the audience to see what is going on." And Antoine went so far as to declare that he found it indispensable to *first create the setting and the environment*, "without worrying at all about events that were to occur on the stage." For him it was "the environment that determines the movements of the characters, not the movements of the characters that determine the environment." And he could not even claim novelty for his views, since his patron Emile Zola had announced as early as 1873 that modern drama would delve into "the twofold life of the character and its environment." [7]

Such statements introduced a point of view encountered with increasing frequency after the founding of Antoine's epoch-making Théâtre Libre in 1887. We find in them a sturdy allegiance to reality as the middle-class civilization of the late nineteenth century conceived it to be. It was, distinctly, a reality of human beings feeling and acting in places and with objects about which there could be no mistake: the characters were specifically located and specifically occupied with material realities in a material world.

We may contrast this view—although it could be humanistic as well as materialistic—with the classic opinions of the leaders of antirealistic design or stylization. For example, there is Adolphe Appia's remark, in 1904, that

the human body does not seek to produce the illusion of reality *since it is in itself reality!* What it demands of the *décor* is simply to set in relief this reality . . . we must free

---

[7] Preface to *Thérèse Raquin*.

staging of everything that is in contradistinction with the actor's presence. . . . Scenic illusion is the living presence of the actor.

And we may take note of Gordon Craig's desire, expressed in 1911, to cover the actor's face with a mask "in order that this expression—the visualized expression of the Poetic spirit—shall be everlasting," as well as Craig's longing for acting wholly free from human "egotism" and for performances possessing "the fire of the gods and demons, without the smoke and steam of mortality." [8]

Environment came to be presented as a source of conflict in many modern plays. It was already present as the very matrix of middle-class tragedy in Hebbel's early play *Maria Magdalena,* written in 1844. In *A Doll's House,* the milieu was the dramatic factor; a provincially limited society has kept Nora ignorant of the world outside her home and is thus partly responsible for her leaving her husband. In *Ghosts,* environment imposed conformities upon Mrs. Alving that had kept her tethered to an unfaithful husband, and the unfortunate results of her compliance are demonstrated with consummate pathos and irony in the denouement. In Henry Becque's *La Parisienne,* the amorality of Parisian society is the paramount consideration; the comic action consists entirely of the married heroine's assumption that her extramarital relations are entirely correct, harm no one, and actually enhance her husband's position. Becque's Clotilde considers herself not only a devoted wife but a right-thinking woman. "You even pass for a free thinker," she reproves her lover Lafont, "and no doubt would get along famously with a mistress who had no religion at all."

In some modern plays, environment even assumes the role of a diffuse or concentrated antagonist. In Hauptmann's *The Weavers,* the economic situation of the cottage weavers of Silesia is the central fact, and the depression of their wages caused by the

[8] All of the quotations in this paragraph are from *Directing the Play,* ed. Toby Cole and Helen Krich Chinoy (Bobbs-Merrill Co., 1953), pp. 71-135.

introduction of machinery is the precipitating force in their conflict with an employer who is himself a victim of economic forces unleashed by the Industrial Revolution. Chekhov noted the corrosive effect of provincial life in several of his plays. Environment is so important a factor in *The Three Sisters* that Fate is identified with stagnation in a provincial town. And, not surprisingly, it was Ibsen who set the modernists an almost classic example when he pitted the reformer Dr. Stockmann against an entire Norwegian town in *An Enemy of the People:* Dr. Stockmann wants to expose the contaminated condition of the waters of a bathing resort; the town, which derives considerable income from those who come to the resort in search of health, suppresses the idealist.

Details of setting thus became decisive and playwrights began to count upon stage settings to convey the conditions of life that were the subject of a play and that sometimes played the role of destiny. Without a sordid environment, for example, Gorki's famous play about derelicts and social outcasts *The Lower Depths* would lose its meaning and force, as would O'Casey's *The Plough and the Stars,* which requires us to "experience" life in a Dublin slum if we are to comprehend the author's viewpoint.

That a ruling idea rather than the availability of technical means was decisive in the rise of modern realism is proved by the fact that the ability to create illusion had been demonstrated again and again in Renaissance and Baroque stage design. The tendency of illusionism was toward realistic scenery and, as the settings were built and painted behind the proscenium arch, they could have suggested an environment. But the modern concept of environment as a dynamic element of human experience had not yet developed. Environment had little, if any, significance to most playwrights before the last quarter of the nineteenth century—that is, before the application to playwriting of the naturalistic idea of environment as a determinative factor. And the actor, who had no responsibility for the content and philosophy of a play, was even less likely tö succeed by himself in developing the implications of Renaissance-born illusionism. Feeling most at home on a platform, not yet willing to isolate himself psychologically from the public, the prerealistic actor treated the stage setting as mere *background* by playing in front of the scenery and by playing to the audience.

The maintenance of the pre-illusionistic acting tradition of direct communication with the spectator made it impossible to establish a true sense of environment. In this respect the actor collaborated with the prerealistic playwright, who kept his characters in communication with the spectator by employing soliloquies and asides as the easiest way to convey information and express sentiment. In turn, the Renaissance and post-Renaissance stage designer exercised great talent in inventing spectacles in which he used tricks of architectural perspective that would have been ridiculous if the actors had actually played inside the set, instead of at some distance in front of it. And his spectacles, of course, would have been utterly incongruous if they had been associated with productions resembling modern realistic drama. They were used instead for court masques, pastorals, and opera that grew grander and grander. The astounding settings of the Bibiena family of baroque designers in Italy and Austria were not intended as décor for any dramatic genre represented by *Ghosts* and *All My Sons*.

As a means of achieving architectural perspective, the floor was raked, or tilted, up toward the back; acting on such a plane could not have been conducive to either comfort or naturalness in performance. The perspective of the series of flats or side-wings also diminished rapidly; the shallower the stage, the more rapid the reduction of size. Actors playing inside such settings might have found their eyes on a level with a second-story window or balcony painted on a flat, and the resulting illusion of giantism might well have startled an audience. And indeed, the stage became increasingly shallow after the eighteenth century. In the heyday of baroque perspective scenery the stage space was at least as deep as the auditorium, if not one and a half times as deep; it eventually became equivalent to not much more than one half of the auditorium. Lee Simonson writes in *The Stage Is Set* (p. 266) that "once the average stage became so shallow that an actor moving twelve or fifteen paces up stage had the sky at his elbow, the entire structure on which the illusions of scene-painting were based collapsed." In order to make scene shifting easy it also became necessary to paint furniture and stage properties on the canvas flats; it is hardly necessary to point out that such painted two-dimensional scenery was unsuitable for the creation of an environment for the performer, and that it also made impossible the creation of an *illusion of environment* for the spectator.

Finally, it is not to be forgotten that prerealistic scenery was usually changed during the action in the presence of the audience, rather than behind the proscenium curtain as was done after the advent of realism. Indeed, the mechanical changing of scenery was often an important part of the "show," so that illusionistic scenery served the purposes of spectacle rather than drama. The result was artifice rather than realism, theatrical jugglery rather than the establishment of environment. In Paris in the early eighteenth century there was actually a show at the Salle des Machines in the Tuileries that consisted entirely of displays of scene-changing by stage machinery.

Obviously, in these conventions there is reflected a conception of theatre radically different from that of the age of Stanislavsky. And this conception was also sustained by the prerealistic conventions of acting based on the principle—a thoroughly theatrical one—that the actor's first prerogative is to exhibit himself and display his skill. Nor is there any reason to suppose that the audience felt it imperative for him to lose himself in his role. Like his predecessors, the old mimes and virtuosi of the *commedia dell' arte,* he stood out as a *performer* rather than as a character. At his best, in the tempestuous acting of a Rachel Felix or an Edmund Kean, the actor developed character, but by giving primacy to "temperament" and the "passions" he *theatrical-ized* it and thus managed to display his virtuosity and uniqueness. Typically, the actor was a star rather than a member of an ensemble. It was especially difficult for the pioneering modernists to destroy the prerealistic "star system" that was prevalent everywhere except in the Duke of Saxe-Meiningen's company, the Meininger, before Antoine founded his Théâtre Libre in 1887.

In brief, the prerealistic theatrical orientation, carried over from the pre-Renaissance platform stage, thrust the actor forward to win far more admiration than conviction, even when he ran the gamut of the emotions discoverable in his role. And to forego admiration was the hardest demand that realism and naturalism ever made of the old-fashioned actor or actor-manager like Sir Henry Irving, who resisted dramatic realism long after he began to play in "solid" realistic settings. Not surprisingly, Irving usually turned even these into *coups de théâtre*. He accomplished this not only by giving the scenery spectacular qualities but by subordinating every element in the production to his personality. Thus arose the contradiction that still appears in many quasi-realistic productions. The scenery provides an environment (in the physical sense), but the actor nullifies its value by thrusting into the limelight the glamorized personality of star actress or matinee idol. The actor, who is presumably in a realistic environment (in the box set consisting of three "walls" formed by lashing together a number of flats), manages to turn the set into the semblance of a platform for himself. And more often than not, the result is a tremendous box-office success. It would be a mistake, of course, to assume that the average audience cares a straw whether the rules of realism are observed or violated.

The style of acting introduced by realism not only called for natural behavior and speech, but for the observance of what came to be called the "fourth-wall" convention—the assumption that the open space framed by the proscenium arch is the fourth wall of a room. Consequently, the actor is not supposed to see the audience; the playgoers are simply not supposed to exist. The actor can turn his back to the spectators whenever the action requires such a position. Furniture can be placed right at the footlights. In fourth-wall staging every effort is made to disguise the fact that the stage is a platform for players and to create the illusion that it is a true environment, separate from and independent of the auditorium. (See pp. 54-64.) Common sense has dictated discretion in the practice of realists, of course. It was considered sufficient to suggest the new convention instead of following it to the letter. For example, the actor can call attention to the fourth wall by turning his back now and then for a moment only. The important point has become, indeed, not what the actor does, but what he refrains from doing—what he does to avoid violating the illusion of reality by blandly playing and reciting to the public.

Historians may assure us that the aim of reproducing actuality on the stage was associated with the practicality of the middle class, whose rise was a major factor in nineteenth-century civilization. Supposedly, a good bourgeois soul was made to feel as secure by "solid" settings and practical windows and doors (with real door knobs in productions of Tom Robertson's plays in the 1860's) as by the designation of prayers for business success in a Gideon Bible. But there are also simpler explanations for the naive realism in the work of the pioneering stage companies. Their leaders were motivated partly by the desire to counter the extreme artificiality of the commercial theatres and partly by the enthusiasm of discovery. Thus, the discovery of realism led Antoine to hang chunks of real meat in a butcher-shop scene, and the desire for perfection of detail caused the Moscow Art Theatre to take two years for the production of *Hamlet* and to rehearse a dramatization of *Crime and Punishment* 150 times.

The Moscow Art Theatre, especially, was dominated at first by the passion for detail and the fourth-wall fanaticism that characterized naturalism. There was a museum quality about the décor of the first production, Alexis Tolstoy's historical drama *Tzar Fyodor Ivanovich,* for which the actual costumes of the periods were used. According to one writer's reminiscence, "During the presentation of Chekhov's *The Cherry Orchard* the spectators can detect the genuine aroma of fresh ripe cherries. A real wind blows the curtains . . . beating of hoofs on a wooden bridge." [9] And the elaborate preparations for *The Lower Depths* (such as Mme Chekhov's odd effort to "live" herself into the part of Natasha by getting a common prostitute to room with her) are recounted in detail by Stanislavsky's associate Vladimir Nemirovich-Danchenko in *My Life in the Russian Theatre*.

It is a mistake, of course, for either friends or foes to underestimate the importance of the element of imagination for the training of the actor in the ultimately evolved Stanislavsky "system." (No system, indeed, but a flexible method for the personal work of actor and teacher.) Michael Chekhov, whose notes were used by the New York Group Theatre in their training program, tried hard to prevent misinterpretations of his master's method. In these notes, made in 1922 while he was a member of the Second Moscow Art Theatre Studio, he reminded himself that "to portray life without an element of fantasy is to make a photographic copy, not to recreate it." The actor was to work just as hard to develop his imagination as his powers of concentration, and imagination was to be defined as "the union and combination of diverse elements into a whole which does not correspond to reality." At the same time, however, Chekhov made plain his advocacy of Stanislavskian realism in acting by observing that "the materials of imagination are always taken from life. . . . Imagination consists in associating known objects, uniting, separating, modifying, recombining them. . . . He [the actor] must learn to draw on life, study, seek out the most diverse aspects of it, create for himself conditions in which he will be exposed to manifold expressions of it—and not wait until life by chance thrusts some striking scene under his nose." [10]

Stanislavsky, after discarding his early emphasis on *external*

<hr>

[9] Alexander Chramoff, "Moscow Art Theatre," *The Liberator* (February 1923), pp. 15-20.
[10] A. M. Chekhov, "Stanislavsky's Method," *New Theatre* (November, 1935), pp. 6-7.

realism, began to evolve a realism of performance that is essentially an *inner realism* of character creation. Stanislavsky expected this to be developed through methods of training that would enable the actor to react as he would if he were actually the character rather than the player. Stanislavskian training, which involves the use of sensory and emotional stimuli by the actor, is a separate subject that cannot be considered here in detail. Its basis is not simply the idea of environment, but rather that idea of "truth," of fidelity to life, which is the over-all principle of realism. But this training for performance, which has proved useful even for poetic drama and fantasy as a means of creating the illusion of reality, was generically associated with the entire movement which made the fourth-wall convention desirable, if not indeed imperative. If it was considered important to maintain the illusion of a "real" environment, such illusion could be valuable only if the acting also conveyed reality. (See pp. 54-64.)

It is to be noted, too, that the pioneers of the realistic theatre laid great stress on ensemble playing, and that an ensemble creates a sort of environment for the main characters. Under the star system the leading actor had inevitably been a showman surrounded by secondary stock characters upon whom he shed his luster. (It was customary, for instance, for nineteenth-century stars to travel as far west as San Francisco by themselves, or with one or two associates, to make quickly rehearsed guest appearances with local companies that they had never seen before.) Ensemble acting was not considered important for bravura showmanship, whereas in good ensembles the actor who played the chief role was genuinely a part of his human environment. The development of good ensemble playing had other advantages, of course; mainly, it ensured a unity of acting in the stage production that could be favored even by artists who were not particularly devoted to realism and naturalism. Thus the management of stage crowds by the celebrated Duke of Saxe-Meiningen, an important part of his effort to integrate all details of a production, had a tremendous influence, even though his Meiningen Company performed Shakespearean and Romantic drama from 1874 to 1890. But realism at Antoine's Théâtre Libre and Stanislavsky's Art Theatre benefited especially from the stage-struck princeling's passion for ensemble. To coordinate performances is to create an environment even when there is virtually no scenery on the stage; people *are* environment.

Realism and the Illusion of Reality

So much for the effect on the stage of the idea of environment. The effect on dramatic form, which has already been introduced in general terms, is even more important. Before the end of the nineteenth century it was understood that only behind the imaginary fourth wall could the theatre consistently present the *lambeau d'existence,* the fragment of life, demanded by Zola, or the *tranche de vie,* the slice of life, required by Zola's disciple and Antoine's staunch supporter Jean Jullien (see pp. 66-70). Playwrights were soon expected to observe the fourth-wall convention as strictly as actors and stage producers; and once this doctrine had come into vogue, various changes in dramatic structure and texture ensued.

In the first place, soliloquies and asides became obsolete in the realistic theatre. Playwrights did not at first follow the logic of the fourth-wall convention to its conclusion. Even Ibsen used soliloquies in his early realistic work; there are at least four in *A Doll's House.* And Tolstoy employed soliloquies as late as 1886 in his otherwise intensely naturalistic peasant tragedy *The Power of Darkness.* It soon became apparent, however, that soliloquies and asides were not only generally unrealistic but actually breached the fourth wall. "Asides" can have a theatrical justification only when addressed to the audience, which the realistic actor was expected to ignore as nonexistent; and soliloquies are a means by which a stage character explains himself to the public. Only when the soliloquy was psychologically motivated— that is, when it was presented as a credible manifestation of the disturbed mental state of a character—could the author escape the charge of violating realism.

After 1840, moreover, the increasing use of the solid box set caused changes of scenery to be difficult, slow, and expensive. Romanticism, in defying the neoclassic principle of the unity of place, brought back the vogue of the multi-scened play. The romanticists returned to Elizabethan play structure. A loosely organized play was, therefore, in vogue in the early part of the last century, and even late romantic plays such as Ibsen's *Brand* and *Peer Gynt,* written in the 1860's, are diffuse. The use of solid settings, however, made a return to unity of place desirable. A major reason for the butchering of Shakespearean plays by such actor-managers as Sir Henry Irving and Sir Herbert Beerbohm-Tree during the last quarter of the century was the vogue of the realistic setting. In order to escape the necessity of shifting scenery frequently and thus slowing up the production, the actor-managers transposed scenes, eliminated some, and fused others. This meretricious practice came to an end only when producers adopted suggestive scenery, used unit sets, or returned, as did William Poel, after founding the Elizabethan Stage Society in 1894, to methods of staging resembling those of the Elizabethan theatre.

In the writing of the new-fashioned realistic plays after 1875 there was, indeed, virtually a return to neoclassic structure. There arose the tightly knit play for which a single setting, or at most two or three changes of scene, would be needed. Realistic plays became masterpieces of compression. Strindberg pared down the action to psychological crises; Ibsen telescoped the crises of a life story by exposing them only in some grand climax of reckoning and revelation. The main structural feature of Ibsen's plays during the middle period of his career and afterward is the presence of *retroactive* action.

This method is actually classic; it was used constantly in the drama of the fifth century B.C., where it effects great economy in playwriting. In *Oedipus the King,* for example, the story starts many years after Oedipus killed his father and married the widowed queen Jocasta. A plague has broken out in Thebes and the hunt has begun for the unknown individual who, according to the Delphic oracle, has brought this curse upon the city. The Greek play starts close to the climactic point at which Oedipus will discover that he himself is the man whose presence pollutes Thebes. The action moves rapidly to the king's discovery that the man he actually slew long ago was his father, and that the woman to whom he has been married for many years is none other than his mother. The audience is shown only the last stages of the unraveling of the unfortunate hero's destiny.

Compactness distinguishes the structure of *A Doll's House, Ghosts,* and many other realistic plays written after 1880. *A Doll's House* begins when a bank clerk, who is about to be dismissed by Nora's husband, threatens to expose her forgery of a signature on a promissory note; past action is here projected into the present. *Ghosts* begins when Mrs. Alving is about to open an orphan asylum in memory of her late husband. The play deals with a series of closely related events, primarily revelations, which demonstrate Mrs. Alving's tragic folly in having obeyed the dictates of convention many years before. This, in brief, is the retrospective method of playwriting, which gave the modern theatre the taut dramatic form usually identified with realism. One might say, then, that the freedom of dramatic art advocated by Victor Hugo first led to a tightening, rather than a relaxation, of dramatic form. The neoclassic unities of time, place, and action which Hugo and other romanticists routed from the theatre around 1830 came to be more or less restored half a century later as a result of the ascendancy of realistic drama.

Whether the result has been advantageous or disadvanta-

geous is the crux of many a discussion about the state of contemporary drama. There is always danger that the compressed
realistic play will become dismally dull. Mediocre playwrights
have succumbed to that danger ever since Ibsen's time. Nevertheless, the gain in dramatic tension is apparent in many plays by
Ibsen, Strindberg, and certain of their successors. If most products of the realistic dramatic method fall considerably below the
dramatic excellence of *Macbeth* or *Hamlet,* there are surely other
reasons for failure than taut realistic construction; lack of sustained poetic and tragic power is very often to blame. In their
own ways *Macbeth* and *Hamlet* are also tightly knit plays, and
many of the works of Shakespeare's contemporaries, who lacked
his poetic power and his ability to create absorbing characters,
fall to pieces precisely because they are haphazardly assembled.

We may agree with William Archer, even without sharing his
smugness about realism,[11] that realistic dramaturgy resulted in
better rather than worse playwriting on the whole. The tight
dramaturgy associated with the fourth-wall convention certainly
did not inhibit playwriting as much as has been alleged. It could
not suppress the imagination and poetic sensibility of writers
who possessed them to begin with, even if realism *per se* did not
encourage the development of the creative imagination. The environment in *A Streetcar Named Desire,* for instance, was realized by Tennessee Williams atmospherically as well as realistically, and his observance of the rules of realistic credibility did
not interfere at all with his penchant for poetic dialogue. He
simply motivated "poetry" in the dismal surroundings and the
sordid plot. A febrile and overcompensating poetic dialogue was
"natural" to his Blanche Du Bois, daughter of the Southern gen-
try, ex-teacher, and pretender to vanished glories. Nor did the
observance of the fourth-wall convention prevent Elia Kazan, the
director of the Broadway stage production, from using tawdry,
naturalistic exterior and interior scenes imaginatively without a

[11] *The Old Drama and the New* (London, 1922).

change of setting. Present-day stage directors and scene designers have no difficulty in showing several levels of a house or several rooms of an apartment simultaneously, or in getting the action of a multi-scened play to flow freely from place to place in almost Elizabethan fashion.

Modern realism, however, has other important characteristics in addition to compressed play structure. Compression cannot serve as the sole criterion of realism, for the neoclassic drama exhibits an even greater degree of condensation. Tight construction, besides, has been frequently violated throughout the modern period. It has been violated, although not wantonly, in such modern realistic chronicles as Gerhart Hauptmann's *Florian Geyer* (1894), Arnold Bennett and Edward Knoblock's *Milestones* (1912), Noel Coward's *Cavalcade* (1931), and Robert Sherwood's *Abe Lincoln in Illinois* (1938); in some naturalistic "slice-of-life" sequences, such as Arthur Schnitzler's *Anatol* and *Reigen* (*La Ronde*); and in some notable group dramas such as Hauptmann's *The Weavers* and O'Casey's *The Plough and the Stars*. The severe limitation of action frequently attributed to Ibsen's example and influence (most recently by Walter F. Kerr in his vigorous book *How Not to Write A Play,* published in 1955) is not in itself either a virtue or a defect. It is a virtue only in so far as the condensation of action provides an intensified field of observation and thought. The limitation of action in realistic drama can represent a legitimate fusion of form and content.

"Tight" realistic dramaturgy has differed from artificially taut melodrama as well as from the drama of plot intrigue and calculated suspense that Scribe and his followers made known as the *pièce bien faite,* the well-made play. The naturalist program, in particular, was severely critical of that kind of tightness. Realists, from Ibsen, writing in his middle period in the 1880's, to Galsworthy, in the first quarter of our century, avoided it. Shaw excoriated plot contrivance when he wrote dramatic criticism in the 1890's, and alert critics have been wary of it wherever they have detected it. Realistic drama attained a high degree of concentration by organic means, not by means of tricks and devices. Whenever condensation has not been inherent in the character drama or in the substance of the argument, the good realistic playwright has not felt constrained to adhere to rules of neat packaging. O'Casey, for instance, provided a tight structure in the family drama *Juno and the Paycock* and a loose one in *The Plough and the Stars,* the national drama of the Easter Rebellion; and, so appropriate is the structure in each play, it would be difficult to determine which is more "correct" or "dramatic."

In realistic theatre, it is true, there has not been the structural variety that characterizes the best examples of condensation in other types of drama. The limited action of the characters in Greek plays was supplemented by the action of the chorus and enriched by the poetic ambience of both the choral and nonchoral passages of drama written, as it happens, by three of the world's great dramatic poets. Greek dramatic form bears no resemblance to the dramatic form represented by the trim little play set in a living room or bedroom that abounds indeed in the realistic theatre but which should not be wholly identified with realism. A tragedy by Racine is not concentrated in the same way as *Ghosts* or Strindberg's *Miss Julie; Phèdre,* to take a familiar example, benefits from dramatic extension by the poetry or rhetoric of Racine's *tirades,* the amplitude of his dialogue, the semiritualistic formalism of his Alexandrines, and the propulsion of passion that carries us clear out of the workaday world. The talented realist has indeed been prompted to look for means of dramatic extension and enrichment. Whether or not he has found them, he has not identified his ideal of realism with condensed dramatic structure *per se.*

Realism began early to encourage other developments. Many modern plays have a collective rather than an individual hero. Hauptmann's weavers, Gorki's derelicts in *The Lower Depths,* and O'Casey's Dublin slum dwellers in *The Plough and the Stars* are group protagonists. No matter how vividly the individuals of the group may be distinguished from one another, they are most important to the meaning of these plays as members of a group. By way of contrast, it might be noted that in *Henry IV* we are concerned with the actions of Falstaff and Prince Hal as individuals; in *King Lear,* with the destiny of Lear as a unique character whose fate is merely paralleled by that of the Earl of Gloucester. In *The Weavers,* on the contrary, it is the collective action of the Silesian workers that matters most. Until the rise of the modern theatre, the hero of an action was almost invariably an individual.

The difference between the individual hero and the group protagonist becomes, in a profound sense, a difference in dramatic form. First, there is a sharp change of focus when the drama concentrates on the group, rather than on the individual, as the initiator or the object of an action. When this occurs the stage becomes a moving camera closing in now on one person, now on another, and then moving back to include the entire group as protagonist or participant. A play, such as *The Plough and the Stars,* that has a group protagonist may be metaphorically called a symphony in contrast to the concerto-like play in which an individual hero is merely supported by other characters.

It is also true, however, that when the camera pulls back, the single actor dwindles in size. When the group is the hero, the individual thus loses stature. When stature is so lost, the creation of standard tragedy becomes difficult, if not impossible. If we consider a collective drama a tragedy, then it may be necessary to redefine the latter term. Such dramas, unlike classic tragedies, are not concerned with the representation of the catastrophic career of a character who stands measurably above his fellow men and falls down to destruction impressively.

This need to establish a new definition does not trouble the present writer; if a literary term such as "tragedy" does not fit new works, it should be extended or other, more suitable, terms should be invented. It is the specific work, not the descriptive term, that matters. The Greeks displayed more common sense in this connection than have some modern scholars and critics. They did not withhold the designation "tragedy" from such works as Sophocles' *Philoctetes,* a tragicomedy, and Euripides' *Helen,* a romance, even though these plays do not end in disaster for the protagonist. Nor does it seem to have occurred to the classical world to call into question Euripides' great drama *The Trojan Women* because it concerns the collective fate of the women of conquered Troy.

Nevertheless, we cannot deny that modern authors employing a mass-hero have tended to reduce the dimensions of individual characters. (One may cite Hauptmann's *The Weavers* and *Florian Geyer,* Ernst Toller's *Man and the Masses,* and even Gorki's *The Lower Depths* among the plays in which this is evident.) And the granting of primacy to environment has reduced the stature of the individual even in other plays in which there is no collective hero. One of the most conspicuous shortcomings of modern playwriting has been the insignificance of the individual. Even when characters have been drawn in the round, they have often lacked the capacity for independent action that would have made them representative of humanity's greatest potentialities. Many characters have represented men rather than Man. In consequence, modern realistic drama has proliferated in the valleys instead of ascending to the heights of experience.

Like the scarcity of great poetry, the scarcity of high tragedy in modern drama is a serious limitation. A strong deterrent to the development of tragic art has been the treatment of environment as a prime determinant of human conduct and destiny. As dramatic characters have lost distinction, moreover, their capacity for expressing themselves in distinguished language has dwindled proportionately. Prose is the suitable language for such characters. In earlier ages, of course, the greatest playwrights were also the greatest poets. Since 1875, in the main, poets have been one breed of men and playwrights another.

The state of modern realistic playwriting would be depressing indeed but for a number of compensations. There have been gains in the plausibility and intimacy of dramatic composition. Also, a sympathetic interest in the common man has brought into the theatre the often vigorous and colorful prose of common speech. And as Shaw's plays have shown, the discussions given a place in the theatre by modern realists can rise to eloquence when a talented author's partisanship reaches white heat.

The deluge of commonplace writing in the thousands of plays that have appeared since the 1870's should not cause us to underrate the powerful prose, often verging on poetry or constituting a sort of prose poetry, that some modern realists have brought to the theatre. It is well to bear in mind that in the past there have been large quantities of miserable writing in verse drama, too. Marlowe, Shakespeare, and Ben Jonson were surrounded by a host of mediocre playwrights, and there is no reason to believe that the forgotten playwrights who competed with Aeschylus, Sophocles, and Euripides in fifth-century Athens were distinguished dramatists. Racine had genius, but other writers of neoclassic French tragedy after 1650 are now virtually forgotten. An age and an art form are properly judged by their best products, not by their worst.

The disappearance of rhetorical devices, inessential and not infrequently injurious to the drama, also brought a general improvement in playwriting. Under the restraints imposed by the fourth-wall convention, characters are not allowed to address the public in fustian. Nor are they supposed to speak for effect unless they are naturally eloquent, as are Synge's and O'Casey's Irishmen, or unless they are "motivated," as when they try to convince or stir up other characters in such modern plays as *An Enemy of the People, Saint Joan,* and *Abe Lincoln in Illinois.* Elizabethan drama provides striking examples of the opposite type of dramatic utterance—speech that is not realistically motivated. The writers of the Elizabethan and Jacobean ages favored rhetorical virtuosity either with or without dramatic motivation, and they also had acquired the habit of figurative writing from the overuse of analogy in philosophy and pseudo science.[12] George Chapman, in his dedication of *The Revenge of Bussy D'Ambois,* maintained that "elegant and sententious excitation to virtue and deflection from her contrary" are "the soul, limbs, and limits of an authentical tragedy." Ben Jonson, referring to his own tragedy *Sejanus,* called for "gravity and height of elocution." Realism emphasized the scrupulous construction of a play, by means of character-determined and otherwise plausible action, as strictly a dramatic and unitary work rather than as elocutionary pyrotechnics or a parade of haphazardly assembled episodes.

Ibsen was the first modern playwright to demonstrate that powerful dialogue could be written in the realistic mode. Henry James characterized Ibsen's art pointedly when he wrote that Ibsen "arrives for all his meagerness at intensity." Describing Ibsen's "rare mastery of form" in *John Gabriel Borkman,* James wrote, "Well in the very front of the scene, lunges with extraordinary length of arm the Ego against the Ego, and rocks in a rigour of passion the soul against the soul." [13] James, writing about *Little Eyolf,* a distinctly minor work, showed a great realistic writer's awareness of environment when he referred to Ibsen's "confined but completely constituted world, in which, in every case, the tissue of relations between the parts and the whole is of a closeness so fascinating." [14] In Ibsen's cramped world, compressed action struck sparks of intense dialogue precisely because in that world so little was left to do and so much was left to say.

[12] See David Klein's *Literary Criticism from the Elizabethan Dramatists* (New York: 1910); Clemen's *Shakespeares Bilder* (Bonn: 1936), pp. 278-285, 306 ff.; and Hardin Craig's *The Enchanted Glass* (New York: Oxford University Press, 1936, Chap. 3), and *Wit and Rhetoric in the Renaissance* (New York: 1937).

[13] See Henry James's review of *John Gabriel Borkman* in *The Scenic Art,* ed. Allan Wade (New Brunswick: Rutgers University Press, 1948), p. 293.

[14] *Ibid.,* p. 289.

Ibsen first showed the possibilities of his method of creating a drama of climactic disclosures and realizations in *A Doll's House*. Toward the end of the play, Nora makes her husband, Torvald, sit down across a table from her in order to "talk things over." Why has the threat of scandal wrecked their marriage? The exchange of views which follows is memorable. When he asks her, "Have you not been happy here?" she replies, "No; only merry." And she explains ". . . our house has been nothing but a play-room. Here I have been your doll-wife, just as at home I used to be papa's doll-child. And the children in their turn have been my dolls. I thought it fun when you played with me, just as the children did when I played with them. That has been our marriage, Torvald." And she leaves Torvald with a terse Euripidean line. Torvald hopes that they will come together again when, as she has put it, "the miracle of miracles" will happen. He asks, "We must so change that—?" She answers that they must so change *"That communion with us shall be a marriage"* (italics added).

Much can be said about the variety and range possible to realistic dialogue. But here it is necessary to note only that memorable dialogue, as contrasted with merely fine writing, is mainly the attribute of a special kind of realism associated with character probing and with provocative drama of ideas. If we do not sufficiently recognize this fact, it is because we tend to identify realism with any sort of play in which prose is spoken and in which the situations represent the commonplaces of everyday living.

That kind of playwriting, practiced by second-rate writers before and after Ibsen, is, indeed, realism, but it is not modern realism in any meaningful sense. Shaw used the term "discussion" to define the new dramaturgic element that distinguishes modern realism. This "new" element can be associated with arresting details of exposition (such as the medical details in *Ghosts* and in José Echegaray's *The Son of Don Juan*) to enforce the making of a value-judgment. But it should not be forgotten that realism was valued by its proponents, not for any absolute merits al-

leged to be possessed by realistic dramaturgy, but for its useful-
ness in providing insight into men's minds.

"Formerly," Shaw wrote in *The Quintessence of Ibsenism*,[15]
"you had in what was called a well-made play an exposition in
the first act, a situation in the second, and unravelling in the
third." He was describing plotty plays of intrigue such as those
written by Scribe and Sardou and still being written today.
"Now," Shaw explained, "you have exposition, situation, and discussion."

For Shaw the modern drama actually began when Nora compelled her husband to sit down and discuss their marriage. Ordinary plays of intrigue, melodramas and crime dramas—the "commonplaces of the Newgate Calendar," to use Shaw's apt phrase—
are not distinctly *modern*, even though many are written in
our day. "Up to a certain point in the last act," Shaw wrote, "*A
Doll's House* is a play that might be turned into a very ordinary
French drama by the excision of a few lines and the substitution
of a sentimental happy ending for the famous last scene." But
when Nora and Torvald sat down to examine their relationship,
the dramatic form of the so-called well-built play began to be
altered by this extension of complication into analysis. Shaw referred to it as the "addition of a new movement, as musicians
would say, to the dramatic form." [16]

In Ibsen's next drama, *Ghosts*, and in still later plays, the
element of analysis or evaluation arrogated to itself more and
more of the body of a play. As Shaw put it, "the discussion has
expanded far beyond the limits of the last ten minutes of an
otherwise 'well-made' play." Accordingly, he added, "we now
have plays, including some of my own, which begin with discussion and end with action, and others in which the discussion in-

[15] Originally read to the Fabian Society in 1890, published in
1891, and revised and expanded in 1913. In *Major Critical Essays*
(London: Constable & Co., 1932), p. 135.
[16] *Ibid.*, p. 138.

terpenetrates the action from the beginning to the end." [17] And Shaw himself went even further in writing such pieces as *Getting Married* and the *Don Juan in Hell* interlude, in which the discussion embodies the sole action or dramatic movement of the play.

Shaw's analysis can be accepted as substantially correct. If it is possible to suspect him of writing more about his own methods than Ibsen's, this suspicion need not prevent us from recognizing the importance of the element of discussion as a feature of modern realism. It is necessary only to understand "discussion" figuratively as well as literally. "Discussion" should be equated with the manifestation of a critical spirit that helps to shape the modern realistic play and to give it a significance well above that of merely pictorial realism. It is also important to realize, of course, that Shaw's polemical intentions in *The Quintessence of Ibsenism* made him play down Ibsen's exceptional ability to create absorbing characters. The younger Dumas had dealt with social problems before Ibsen and had congratulated himself for doing his "duty as a man" as well as his part "as a poet." Not only did Ibsen "out-think" and "out-challenge" Dumas *fils*, however, but he "out-created" him. The Scandinavian masterbuilder gave life to characters who have outlasted all the creations of the writers of problem plays. Indeed, a new character-realizing rather than conventionally histrionic, "show-stopping" kind of acting was called into being for the kind of realism Ibsen led his contemporaries in introducing into the theatre. Ibsen, moreover, managed to get along as a dramatist without the crutch of intrigue which Scribe and his followers considered indispensable, and in so doing set modern authors a valuable example. Even *A Doll's House* is actually free from intrigue, in spite of Krogstad's effort to blackmail Nora, which is used only to help teach Nora that her doll's house has cardboard walls. (*The Pillars of Society*, written two years before *A Doll's House*, was Ibsen's last intrigue-drama.) It is not in one way only, but in many respects, that Ibsen, whom Archer called "the creator of men and women, the

[17] *Ibid.*, p. 136.

searcher of hearts, the weaver of strange webs of destiny," [18] proved the power of the drama of ideas. And it has since been demonstrated repeatedly that social situations, in particular, can provide engrossing drama when they are presented largely through discussion or argument. The best part of Miller's *All My Sons,* for instance, is not the establishing of Joe Keller's guilt which constitutes the plot, but the "discussion," by means of both argument and dramatic action, of the fallacy of exclusive family loyalty. Miller's play, we may add incidentally, also proves that undistinguished lines can have emotional power in the context of strong dramatic situations—a power that seems continually to surprise literary critics but would not at all have surprised Aristotle, who recognized the primacy of action.

Inevitably, however, one turns to Shaw himself for a lesson in how magnificent, as sheer writing, discussion-dramaturgy can be. The reader of English can get at Shaw's writing directly rather than in translation, and, after all, Shaw was one of the masters of English prose. He made discussion incandescent and exciting throughout his work, being more resolved than even William Blake not to "cease from mental fight." He had great comic genius, of course, but he did not need his native eloquence for comedy; he needed it for trying to build a Fabian Jerusalem in England's no longer entirely green and pleasant land. Hence the great passages: Father Keegan's "three-in-one" speech on the country of his dreams "where the State is the Church and the Church the people," the tent and trial scenes in *Saint Joan,* Don Juan's apologia in *Man and Superman,* and Undershaft's credo in *Major Barbara.* Shaw's writing was not hobbled as Galsworthy's was by the self-imposed "naturalistic" requirement of copying the speech of floundering characters. A typical and extremely frustrating Galsworthian conversation is the following, between the Parson and the escaped convict in *Escape:*

[18] In the preface to Vol. I of the standard translation of Ibsen's plays.

MATT: Wonder what Christ would have done.

PARSON: That, Captain Denant, is the hardest question in the world. Nobody ever knows. The more you read those writings, the more you realize that He was incalculable. You see—He was a genius! It makes it hard for us to try to follow him.

Someone once asked, "What is the prose for God?" The best rejoinder comes from the London critic Kenneth Tynan: "'What is the prose for God?' cries one pundit, quoting from Granville-Barker and forgetting that the answer to the question is on almost every page of the Bible." Mr. Tynan goes on to say what every sensible man in the theatre must think, "Nobody wants to banish the luxury of language from the theatre: what needs banishing is the notion that it is incompatible with prose, the most flexible weapon the stage has ever had, and still shining new." [19] There is no prose for God when Galsworthy's characters are speaking,[20] but there is prose for God in the utterance of Shaw's characters.

That psychological conflicts can also be conveyed with great force through discussion and argument was demonstrated in the province of psychological drama by Strindberg and his successors. Strindberg's gripping treatment of female vampirism in *The Creditor* consists almost entirely of discussion. And nothing is more forceful in his sex-duel tragedy *The Father* than the verbal skirmishes between the Captain and his wife when they strip their souls bare. It is in the culminating argument toward the close of the second act that both the dramatic conflict and the dialogue rise simultaneously to a shattering climax: here the action is thought and the thought is action. To what heights the mere statement of the issue rises, how completely the conflict be-

[19] "Prose and the Playwright," *The Atlantic Monthly* (December 1954).
[20] All the more regrettable in view of Galsworthy's attractive writing in *The Apple Tree* and *The Indian Summer of a Forsyte* when he did not feel that he had to be "natural," like his characters, rather than "natural" like himself.

tween husband and wife becomes a flame of language, may be observed in the Captain's last words in that discussion. Speaking of the dissatisfaction they both came to feel in marriage when he had allowed Laura to sap his strength, the Captain says:

> . . . like the rest of mankind, we lived our lives unconscious as children, full of imaginations, ideals, and illusions,—and then we awoke. That would have been well enough. But we awoke with our feet on the pillow, and he who waked us was himself a sleepwalker. When women grow old and cease to be women, they get beards on their chins; I wonder what men get when they grow old and cease to be men. Those who crowed were no longer cocks, but capons, and the pullets answered their call,[21] so that when we thought the sun was about to rise we found ourselves in the bright moonlight amid ruins, just as in the good old times. . . . It had only been a little morning slumber with wild dreams, and that was not an awakening.

In contradiction, then, to glib generalizations to the effect that modern realism has caused the quality of dramatic dialogue to deteriorate, it can be maintained that dialogue has actually been strengthened by being made inviolably functional. Verse may have been largely banished from the theatre, but dialogue far from taking a secondary part, has become if anything more truly dialogue, whether or not it is extractable for quotation as "literature." Dialogue itself became drama again in the realistic theatre, as it is in the best work of Sophocles, Shakespeare, and Racine, instead of being confounded with embellishment.

It is above all necessary to realize that this question of dialogue, which has led us to Shaw's conception of "discussion" as

[21] Elizabeth Sprigge's translation, *Six Plays by Strindberg* (Doubleday Anchor Books, 1954), p. 42, here reads: "In this false dawn, the birds that crowed weren't cocks, they were capons, and the hens that answered their call were sexless, too."

the new element, has to do with an important change in dramatic form. The change from prerealistic playwriting consisted principally of a concentration upon the issues in which characters are involved, whether these be sociological, as in *A Doll's House,* or psychological, as in *The Father.* Modern realistic form became distinguishable from every kind of pre-Ibsenite dramaturgy employed by writers who proclaimed their allegiance to "reality."

Thus the form changed in response to the "idea," even while the idea itself was in flux. Whether playwrights held that human behavior was determined by environment and considered themselves rigorous naturalists, or merely maintained that environment affected conduct, they tended to adopt methods of presentation that produced a change in dramatic form. Drama as an acted-out adventure or intrigue came to be displaced by drama shaped and expressed as experience. Regardless of whether a play created under the banner of revolutionary realism resembles Shavian discussion, Ibsenite disclosure and demonstration, or "Chekhovian" stasis, the dramatic form was, so to speak, organic. The play invariably manifested characteristics of informality, spontaneity, unexpectedness, or disregard for mere theatrical effect. "Plot," if at all conspicuous in the work, was always the servant, never the master, of psychological or social reality. The new dramatic form represented, to a greater or lesser degree (usually to a lesser degree in popular pseudo- and semi-Ibsenite drama such as Sudermann's *Magda*) the liberation of dramatic action from the dominance of plot. Action was brought more or less into conformity with the norms of experience. Life is usually independent of intrigue, suspense, and the other trumperies of dramatic contrivance that strike us as so ridiculous in the dialogue of Victorian melodrama. And naively or not, sincere realists and naturalists of the second half of the nineteenth century had set out to imitate "real life."

Mimesis, fortified after 1875 by a thoroughly realistic technique and attuned to modern sensibility, whether mechanistic, skeptical, reformist, or revolutionary, became the dominant principle. The aim was to make dramatic art as *untheatrical* as possible. No one with any experience in the theatre, of course, expected it to be entirely untheatrical; but for purposes of propaganda or in the zeal of advocacy the fact that the theatre was, after all, *the medium of the playwright and the actor* was conveniently dismissed. Thus, to call something "theatrical" in playwriting or acting was tantamount to denouncing it as meretricious, just as it was enough to call a play one didn't like "contrived." The embattled realists who fought for a new order in playwriting and play production were fed up with empty showmanship. The question for them was not how much a drama was like "theatre," but how much it was like life. Dramatic art that had only the stage for its frame of reference had disgraced itself so greatly with jejune plays and "ham acting" that it could not command the respect of forward-looking men who had good reason to regard with envy the towering achievements of the nineteenth-century novel. Experience of reality was action enough for them, and such experience embraced the entire social and intellectual activity of the modern world. Modern dramatic realism was exploratory and critical, analytical and rebellious.

If realism carried mimesis to greater lengths than had earlier forms of theatre, this was not because the realistic stage performed greater miracles of scenic illusion than had the stage of the Bibiena family. Mimesis had a different function for the pioneering realists who had in view neither plot nor spectacle, regardless of the degree of illusionism or verisimilitude in a production. Verisimilitude, for them, was a means for furthering a meaningful experience, just as plot was regarded as merely the means for sustaining an action of social or psychological character. We may remark indeed that the example of the realists was followed in some respects by postrealistic playwrights. Modernism as advocated by Ibsen and Shaw has this in common with the symbolist drama advocated by Maeterlinck and Andreyev:[22] it is

[22] Maeterlinck, *Le Tragique quotidien* (1896), in *The Treasure of the Humble,* reprinted in Clark's *European Theories of the Drama,* pp. 412-413. Also, Maeterlinck's preface to Vol. I of his collected works (Brussels, 1901), of which there is an extract in Clark, pp. 414-416.

not primarily plot drama. It has this in common with imaginative work such as, let us say, *The Madwoman of Chaillot:* it favors the play of mind, for which Ibsen, Strindberg, and Shaw had, indeed, a special aptitude. Nor is the critical or analytical mode of realism as remote as has sometimes been thought from that ultra-intellectual technique which constitutes Brechtian "epic realism"; for, after all, what is *Ghosts* but an intensely ironic demonstration, though in a non-epic context, that the wages of Victorian virtue may be death? And did not that pillar of Victorian society Mrs. Humphry Ward, Dr. Thomas Arnold's novelist granddaughter, call *Ghosts* "a piece of moral vivisection . . . fit only for an audience of doctors and prostitutes." [23]

Maeterlinck wrote a tightly drawn, completely self-contained drama when he composed his symbolist mood-piece *Pelléas et Mélisande.* Even Ibsen's realistic masterpieces are not much tighter or more self-contained than this play; the difference is one of tone, texture, and dynamics. Giraudoux' *The Madwoman of Chaillot* is a *jeu d'esprit,* but no more so than many a play by Shaw. Also if Maeterlinck's symbolist plays are mood-pieces, so are the plays of Chekhov, who is considered a supreme realist or naturalist. Nor is the present writer convinced that Brecht's *Mother Courage,* a celebrated "epic drama," is basically or radically different from O'Casey's *The Plough and the Stars,* an exemplary realistic or naturalistic drama. The former has formal features that the latter does not have. The difference in effect, however, is not as great as one might expect after reading Brecht's theoretical writings. However, the difference could be great in stage production if, for example, Brecht's Theatre Ensemble in East Berlin played *Mother Courage* and the Abbey Theatre in Dublin played *The Plough and the Stars* in their respective and distinctly divergent styles. But, then, the difference might be quite as marked if the Brecht group performed *The Plough and the Stars* and the Abbey played *Mother Courage!*

There is little doubt that realism was not only the first phase

[23] Elizabeth Robins, *Both Sides of the Curtain* (London: William Heineman, 1940), p. 198.

of modern theatre, but the decisive one. However, protests and rebellion against realistic and naturalistic theatre became frequent and strong after 1890. And the protests have had particular cogency in recent decades for the good reason that the meaning of realism, as exemplified in the work of Ibsen, Strindberg, Shaw, and a few other playwrights, became attenuated in general practice. Realism became primarily descriptive rather than exploratory and critical, or it was critical in a manner that was at best unimaginative or obtrusively propagandistic. The point was reached where continued adherence to the canons of realism in playwriting and production was justifiably regarded as an impediment to creativity.

This brief account of the first phase of modernism might end here. Realism was once a subject of paramount interest, but it is no longer that. Among critics it has evoked more boredom than interest, and its possibilities have been met with indifference rather than elation. In 1921, Ludwig Lewisohn had no reservations in focusing his *Modern Drama* on advances toward realism in playwriting, whereas the latter-day critic Eric Bentley, in his book *The Playwright as Thinker* (1946), rightly placed stress upon the departures from strictly realistic writing after 1890. Realism has been the prominent interest in recent criticism only when the critics' interest was decisively sociological.

We cannot, however, leave the subject at the point of an absolute impasse or surrender. We may or may not regard the sociological reasons for recovering or refreshing our interest in realism as extraneous to dramatic art. But in neither case should we accept the limits set for realism in the nineteenth century by the founding fathers. There were several such limits.

One limit was set by their acceptance of the "picture-frame" development of the stage and the development of the playhouse along opera-house lines. We can realize today that the realists were unnecessarily content with the combination of a court the-

PREREALISTIC OPERATIC ILLUSIONISM *Among the numerous designs by members of the Bibiena family, this celebrated one by Ferdinando Galli di Bibiena (1657-1743) is an example of baroque illusionism on the extravagant scale that made illusionism operatic and "theatrical," as indeed illusionism often was in the seventeenth and eighteenth centuries. The illusionist theatre of Ibsenite realism was, on the contrary, generally characterized by modesty of scale and comparative austerity. It should be borne in mind, of course, that the astounding designs of the baroque scenic artists were not necessarily executed with perfection and that they were rarely as effective on the stage as they are in pictures. The effects achieved by painted scenery supplemented by built-up constructions could be eye-filling without in the least providing modern realism; they provided only illusion.*

POSTREALISTIC DYNAMISM *The New York Theatre Guild's 1924 production of Ernst Toller's expressionistic social drama* Man and the Masses *(Masse-Mensch) was directed and designed by Lee Simonson after the 1921 Jürgen Fehling production at the Volksbühne in Berlin. This rather abstractly rendered mob scene, representing a popular uprising in Germany after 1918, was staged without illusionistic scenery, on a steep ramp made up of steps set against a black curtain. Here the antagonists, the exponent of violence known as "The Nameless One" and the representative of humanitarianism or liberalism called "The Woman," were placed at the extreme ends of the diagonal formed by the mob. This placement of the incendiary at the top, while "The Woman" stood below, symbolized their relative strength at the moment when "The Nameless One" was successfully inciting the mob to violence.* Photograph: Brugière.

STYLIZED REALISM   *A scene from* Bus Stop *by William Inge, produced on Broadway in 1955, illustrates the expressive use of realism, achieved not merely through that simplification of the interior for which the term "selective realism" has been in vogue but through the simultaneous, hence somewhat stylized, presentation of both interior and exterior. Part of the ceiling was omitted in order to show an exterior part of the building at the left and the tree at the right.* A Robert Whitehead–Roger L. Stevens Production directed by Harold Clurman and designed by Boris Aronson. Photograph: Zinn-Arthur. Courtesy of Barry Hyams for the producers.

ENVIRONMENT AND SYMBOL   *Jo Mielziner's permanent setting for the William A. Brady Broadway production of Elmer Rice's* Street Scene, 1929, *illustrates the symbolic possibilities of an ostensibly naturalistic setting. (See also Mordecai Gorelik's analysis on pages 214-215.) The dual functioning of this scenic construction as both environment and symbol would indicate that the blending of a degree of realism with a degree of theatricalism is natural in the creative process. The point at which environment exerts its full power is the point at which the factual may become symbolic as well.* Photograph: Vandamm.

atre and a peephole stage that was evolved after the Italian Renaissance. They were too conservative in restricting their innovations to scenic modifications, to elimination of apron stages, the reduction of ornateness in the auditorium, and the abolition of boxes. Although at first they derived advantages from adopting camera-like illusionism, these began to succumb soon to the law of diminishing returns. It is questionable today whether realism would not have developed more vitally in the first place if producers had not clung so closely to old-fashioned theatre architecture. It is also a question, and a more important one, whether realists of the present and the future could not, and should not, utilize other forms of architecture. This subject will be considered further below (see pp. 51-54).

Related questions are whether the pioneering realists did not take too narrow a view of environment, and especially whether the visual realization of environment is as necessary to dramatic realism as its nineteenth-century proponents thought. Realism can have considerably more freedom in respect to physical environment than was once believed. This topic is considered below under the heading "Environment—Illusion or Realism?" (see pp. 54-65).

A third inquiry concerns the relation between realism and naturalism. Although the subject is familiar and the present writer, for one, can add nothing to our present knowledge, it is nevertheless reviewed in an extended note (pp. 66-70) with the intention of removing some possible confusions (more likely to occur in America than abroad) and determining to what extent the problems of realism can be considered cognate with those of naturalism.

Finally, we may inquire to what degree drama and verse actually had to undergo separation for the sake of realistic theatre and follow separate destinies. This is the subject of the comments entitled "Verse and Verse-Realism" (see pp. 70-76).

SOME FURTHER OBSERVATIONS

Stage Architecture and the Play

Some present-day proponents of central staging or arena theatre are oddly unwilling to acknowledge that there is a relationship between the architecture of the playhouse, or even the architecture of the stage, and the play. They maintain that every sort of play is suitable for central staging. I suspect that this view arises in part from a disinclination to limit the repertoire and thus deprive local audiences of interesting plays. Nor is a discrepancy between the style of a play and the style of its production likely to be detected by the public when the community affords no opportunity for making reliable comparisons. And, of course, discrepancies between the style of the play and the style of the stage production have been frequent even in the most highly professionalized theatre. Sometimes, indeed, the discrepancies have been deliberately cultivated in modern stage practice.

It is nevertheless a mistake to disregard the relationship between architecture and the drama. Our "peephole" stage is obviously not ideal for Shakespearean drama, which needs a platform stage. And it is actually no less incongruous to perform realistic drama in these theatres. Except for some concessions to modern ideas of functional simplicity, most professional playhouses are simply opera houses in which the public is incongruously offered intimate realistic drama requiring psychological acting which probably eludes half the audience, by whom the actors' facial play cannot be seen clearly. Incongruously, too, these playhouses are post-Renaissance and pseudo-Renaissance court theatres now occupied by plebeian playgoers.

Open-air theatres for productions of "pageant drama" or "symphonic drama" (I have in mind such theatres as those on Roanoke Island, N.C., and at Williamsburg, Va.) are admirably suited to the plays they accommodate, since they were built with a special purpose in mind. Arena theatres have been designed for intimacy, a generally laudable objective. But they have not been built in response to the requirements of a particular mode of playwriting any more than they have grown out of a modern cultural matrix.

In the absence of the necessary relation between play and playhouse, curious things can happen. There is the case of Tennessee Williams' *Summer and Smoke*. Not written especially for central staging, the work was nevertheless brought into final shape at Margo Jones's arena theatre in Dallas, where it proved immensely successful and aroused great expectations for a successful translation to Broadway. But the Broadway production in the fall of 1948 at a typical Broadway playhouse, the Music Box, was a failure, although the play, again staged by Margo Jones, had an excellent cast which performed at the top of its bent as well as scenery by Jo Mielziner which drew plaudits from all the newspaper reviewers. Somehow this particular play was, or had become in the course of revision, an ideal arena-theatre play. Brooks Atkinson, while praising the New York production, felt obliged to concede that he had seen the play go better (this, with a less professional cast) in Margo Jones's Dallas theatre. Then, as if to clinch the point, several years later *Summer and Smoke* was produced again, this time in a Greenwich Village arena theatre, Circle-in-the-Square, where it brought stardom to Geraldine Page and great repute to José Quintero, the director. A circle, as in Dallas, or a three-sided stage, as in Greenwich Village, "contained" this novelistic play with its heroine's history of failure and deprivation, whereas the Broadway production forced the action toward the wings and failed to center the heroine on the stage except in the prologue and the epilogue. Centralized staging, in brief, corresponded with the essential character or form of Williams' play.

When the same kind of staging at Circle-in-the-Square was given Truman Capote's Broadway failure *The Grass Harp,* however, it proved to be less effective. It failed to improve the play, which suffered from a tendency toward stalemate after its early sensational show of activity with the flight of three rebellious characters to a tree-house in the woods. It was *development,* not containment, that this particular play needed: when the tree-house scenes were played, there was evident discordance between the temporarily forward-thrusting action and the three-sided rectangular stage. The action of the main characters occupied only a corner of the rectangle, with the rest of the space remaining fundamentally functionless. The main characters, looking down the length of the rectangle, the shape of which called for movement on their part, were constrained by the plot not to move forward, for the play suffered from a deficiency of developing action. (The denouement consisted of the characters' return to the home of the tyrannical woman against whom they had rebelled.) Yet the natural thrust of the long narrow space was a forward one. The rest of the space was used by characters who came on to oppose the occupants of the tree-house, and since the role of the former was altogether negative (and not very interestingly so), the greater part of the rectangular stage was psychologically empty and dramatically useless.

When we add to these illustrations the many others that could be cited, especially the late nineteenth-century efforts to frame stage pictures for Shakespeare, it is evident that we should not neglect the question of the correspondence between stage architecture and the play.

Yet it is precisely this correspondence that has been ignored, because of ignorance, indifference, or expediency, whenever the commercial theatres have produced plays notable for antinaturalistic stylization. The expedients usually resorted to—the addition of a little forestage or apron, the building of a false proscenium behind the permanent proscenium arch, the placing of a few actors in the boxes or the orchestra—are sometimes downright pitiful. Only rarely have special theatres been built for nonrepresentational stage productions—theatres, like Copeau's Théâtre du Vieux-Colombier, which abolish the distinction between the stage and the auditorium, thus eliminating the convention of the fourth wall.

Luckily for dramatic representationalism, the prerealistic picture-frame stage that was developed from the late fifteenth century to the middle of the nineteenth century offered possibilities for the pictorial reproduction of domestic scenes. After 1850, moreover, once the box setting came into vogue, the picture-frame stage, with a "picture" made up of the scenery placed behind the "frame" (the proscenium arch), became a *peephole stage*, with the entire action enclosed in the box. In the second half of the nineteenth century, realists and naturalists found at least one architectural change to be decidedly helpful to representational, truly environmental, theatre; the abbreviated post-Renaissance platform, the narrow stage in front of the proscenium arch known as the "apron," was removed.

Environment—Illusion or Idea?

Because some architectural or scenic effects will be found in every production, it is important to distinguish between mere illusionism and the modern concept of environment. A setting, in itself, is not an environment, nor is a scene an environment, in any true dramatic sense, unless it encloses the characters and the stage action. Moreover, illusion can be created for the works of nineteenth-century realists and their twentieth-century successors only when the acting area is treated as both geographically and psychologically distinct from the area occupied by the audience.

The alternative is to treat the stage and the auditorium as a single environment, and this alternative was adopted by both romanticists and realists of our century. In Reinhardt's staging of *The Miracle,* for instance, the auditorium of the playhouse was treated as a portion of a Gothic cathedral and the stage as the transept and apse. The object was to create more perfect illusion, although it is questionable whether this arrangement induced empathy or resistance in an experienced playgoer, who, like Hamlet, knew that he was being played upon. And in productions of *Waiting for Lefty* in the 1930's, to cite another example, the stage and the auditorium were fused into single environment by treating the theatre audience as an audience of taxicab drivers who were being addressed by union delegates (the actors) on the question of whether or not to call a strike against the taxicab companies. Again, it is questionable whether the regular playgoer felt at all like a taxicab driver.

The creators of modern realism, from Antoine to Stanislavsky, however, would probably have rejected both these examples as stunts and as examples of self-conscious make-believe. The playgoer was being required to make a pretense, and a theatre of transparent pretense is precisely what the nineteenth-century pioneers had set out to destroy in the service of their idea of theatre as a theatre of "truth." The argument could run as follows: It is one thing to ask the actor to play at make-believe; it is his *métier,* and he performs his job seriously and efficiently. It is another thing to require the *spectator* to play at make-believe—that is *not* his métier.

The realist sought to create an environment solely for the

character on the stage, an environment in which he could simulate reality while the audience observed him and achieved various degrees of identification with him. (The identification, I venture to say, was never absolute.) And this was particularly important for the development of critical realism by Ibsen and his successors, whether or not these dramatists were aware that their realism was one of thought (of so-called ideas) rather than of verisimilitude. Only an actual gulf between the stage and the auditorium can sustain the illusion of a distinctive environment. Only a spectator who is physically separated from the stage can function as a detached observer and can partake of the illusion that the stage is an environment. And only the actor who can ignore the audience can consistently treat his stage as an environment rather than a platform on which to play to the audience. Consequently, the consistent realists felt the need to abide by the fourth-wall convention. Without the assumption that a wall separated actors from audience, the theatre could never have become thoroughly illusionistic or, more important, realistic, in the sense of establishing the illusion of a specific, nontheatrical location for the action.

Never, to my knowledge, did the pioneers in realism question the premise stated above, although it does not follow that all of them were aware of the fourth-wall convention or that those who were aware of it understood all of its implications. The more we work in the theatre, however, or reflect upon its workings, the more certain we are to arrive at the conclusion that the decisive question concerns the effect on the actor's performance.

We may present the problem in the form of questions and answers:

Does the actor need a thoroughly simulated environment in order to perform effectively? Experience in the theatre dictates an answer in the negative. The good actor can *imagine* whatever environment is needed for his playing. He does so, in fact, whenever he rehearses without scenery. Just as he does not need a cup and saucer and hot water in order to pretend that he is drinking tea, he does not need an exactly reproduced living room in order to conduct himself as though he were in a parlor.

In that case, why should a simulated environment be considered necessary to his giving a convincing performance? If the actor or actress had the genius of a Garrick or a Duse, a simulated environment would probably not be at all necessary. But Garricks and Duses are few and far between. Moreover, even they would be playing with other, less talented, actors. The question is on a par with the old one of feeling or not feeling one's part—the question of how much real emotion the actor should experience while performing, raised as long ago as 1770 by Diderot in *Le Paradoxe sur le comédien*.

The great Garrick supposedly did not immerse himself wholly in his role: he was likely to jest in the wings after having made a noble exit from the stage. Does this mean that he had not identified himself with the character he was playing, and that he would not do so again a few minutes later? Not at all, says Lee Strasberg, probably the greatest American teacher of acting in our time. We may conclude simply that Garrick "was not strained or forced, that he possessed the muscular relaxation Stanislavsky considers so necessary for acting, that his concentration was excellent when it had to be. He could stop and start easily at will." [1]

We also know that a century later Constant Coquelin, the very first of the Cyranos of the stage, maintained in *L'Art et le comédien* that the actor must "remain master of himself throughout the most impassioned and violent action . . . in a word remain unmoved himself, the more surely to move others . . ." Asked during the long run of *Cyrano de Bergerac* what he thought of, Coquelin replied candidly, *"Souvent je pense à autre chose."*

Even J. T. Grein, founder of that little outpost of realism the Independent Theatre in London, admitted that "overwhelming sincerity" in playing a part may "kill the projection," and his recollection of the conduct of the Flemish actor Victor Driessens in Antwerp is worth repeating:

[1] *Theatre Arts* (May 1950), pp. 39-42.

He was one of those who commanded tears; his voice was moving; his personality monumental. . . . His peculiarity was rarely to be word-perfect. The prompter in front of him knew this, and from his box watched him like a lynx and always managed to give him the right cue. . . . Now once, in the midst of a terrific scene of Victor Hugo's "Bellringer of Notre Dame," the prompter did not catch the speaker's eye. And would you believe, Driessens, in the most dramatic moment, instead of halting, flung at the prompter a furious "Verdomme—what is the word?", caught it, went on, brought the house down. He had not a second's anxiety, he said afterwards; all he wanted to do was to get even with the prompter.[2]

However, neither Coquelin's "I often think of something else" nor Driessens' blast at the prompter proves that every actor can perform without identifying himself with the character he is playing. Coquelin could move in and out of a familiar part with an agility not at the command of a less self-assured actor. The story merely proves that Driessens was so extraordinary an actor that he could get back into his role more rapidly than an ordinary performer.

The realistic setting, which can be selective rather than naturalistically literal, fixes the environment for all the actors. It objectively determines the physical movement and helps to make it natural. Above all, the stage space, when transformed into environment (or when the rehearsing actor expects it to be so transformed), serves as a psychological frame of reference for the performer. This was virtually an article of faith among stage directors of Antoine's persuasion after 1887.

If they could have their way, some scrupulous realists would even turn the offstage areas, the wings of the stage, into an "environment." According to report, the talented director Benno Schneider, in staging the depression-drama But for the Grace of God for the Theatre Guild, had one member of the cast flying an

2 The New World of the Theatre (London: Hopkinson, 1924), pp. 150-151.

imaginary pigeon in the wings during rehearsals. The actor was playing the role of a tubercular youth who spent the greater part of the day flying pigeons on the roof.

The point of the procedure is not, of course, in any passion for literal realism or "actualism" on the part of Mr. Schneider, who, as director of the remarkable Artef group of players during the 1930's, had given New York some provocatively stylized productions; the point is simply that he believed that the actor would have more reality onstage if he had more reality offstage. And it happens that the tubercular youth's offstage environment "on the roof" was an important part of his onstage environment in the slum-tenement apartment beneath it. His home was charged with economic pressures and personal tensions that drove other characters to desperation and a younger brother to crime. The roof environment and the pigeon-flying represented the detachment of the ailing elder brother, who was unable to assist his impoverished family. For hours before entering the action of one of the scenes of the play, he had been looking into the sky and watching the flight of birds; Benno Schneider believed that it was important to make the offstage life of this character an onstage reality.

Granted that one can go too far in this direction, it is nevertheless true that environment can be an action or the equivalent of action, and that anything a character does at any time and anywhere may be supposed to contribute to present and onstage reality. It is also true that actors' inadequacies in performance are often attributable to lack of concentration on the reality of their parts, which involves action in an environment. In discussing the performance of scenes with student actors, for example, I found it necessary to ask them where they (as characters) had come from and what they had been doing before appearing on the stage and speaking their lines. It was necessary to remind them that their life as characters was only fractionally stated in the lines written for delivery by them. What was their life or action between pauses, for example? The answer was only roughly given by the stage business assigned to them in the author's script. How had they lived, functioned, and felt, and in what circumstances had a personal tension arisen, before the scene in which they were performing?

Realism, one may add, can often seem picayune until we refer to the effect on the actor. An elementary, perhaps rather naive, example was described by Seymour Peck in an article about the acting of Arthur Kennedy in Arthur Miller's *The Crucible*. In this play Mr. Kennedy, who had hitherto been playing boys' roles, as in *All My Sons* and *Death of a Salesman*, had to play a mature Puritan farmer. Jed Harris, who directed *The Crucible*, asked Kennedy to dye his blond hair to a dark brown. Mr. Harris is quoted as saying, "I was looking for something that would make him aware of himself in a way he hadn't been before. Dyeing the hair changes people. Take a mousy woman with mouse-colored hair, she dyes it blonde, she may change, expand, she may act like a blonde, she may assume some of the coquetry of a blonde." [3]

Regardless of the conclusions stated above, we must observe one fact: the actor himself can establish environment for the spectator. A sense of place at the Globe was conveyed, at least to some degree, by the level (upper or lower) upon which the action was performed, and the illusion of place was no doubt furthered by the use of some stage properties such as seats, thrones, heraldic banners, and other hangings. But a sense of environment, in the final analysis, could be convincingly conveyed only by the actor—by the way he related himself to stage areas, properties, other actors, and the audience.[4] We can observe the same thing today in the arena theatres. Especially

[3] "Growth and Growing Pains of an Actor," New York *Times Magazine* (Feb. 15, 1953), p. 34.

[4] Shakespeare's plays afford the actor many opportunities to use a variety of means, ranging from an elementary statement concerning the locus of the action to the complex and intensely dramatic means to be found in the first act of *Hamlet* and the second act of *Macbeth*.

in complete theatre-in-the-round, the actor performs on a floor without surrounding walls and with only vague boundaries of environment—conventionally, the area around which the seats of the spectators are arranged. Theoretically, then, theatre-in-the-round should not communicate a sense of environment at all. Yet this sense can be established by the fact that the actors' action occupies a certain space on the floor in the midst of the audience, *provided* that the actors perform as though they were living and acting in a specific, enclosed area. The audience encloses it physically, and the actor creates the enclosure psychologically, by the way he treats the space surrounding the acting area as nontransparent and by his ignoring the audience. The fact that the furniture is usually scaled down a good deal, in order to avoid obstructing the audience's view of the action, makes no difference; the public doesn't come to the theatre to measure the height of the tables, chairs, and couches.

The illusion of environment may be disturbed by the fact that one section of the audience can see another section on the opposite side of the threatre-in-the-round. Therefore, an effort was made in the arena theatre in use at Fordham University around 1950 to place a scrim around the acting area; with proper lighting it was possible for spectators at one side to observe the performance without also seeing the spectators behind the actors. So strong, however, is the power of illusion when the actor does not go out of his way to violate it that most arena theatres have not adopted the scrim. We may count on the actors' treatment of the acting space, combined with the playgoer's will, to produce an illusion. It is to be noted, besides, that "fourth-wall playwriting" has prevailed even during the vogue of theatre-in-the-round staging, and such playwriting has been well sustained without fourth-wall settings. As for nonrealistic presentational playwriting, as in a Shakespearean drama, I have not noticed that it harmonizes better with theatre-in-the-round (although theoretically it should) than with the picture-frame theatre. The reason may be that contemporary performances are usually oriented toward fourth-wall playing, both in proscenium and arena theatres.

It may be noted, finally, that no matter how detailed the realism of environment may have become in the last decades of the nineteenth century, it was bound to be somewhat ineffectual in large theatres because the details were blurred for the playgoers seated in the balconies and in the back rows of the orchestra. This detailed realism was also doomed to be overshadowed by the pictorial naturalism of motion pictures. There could be no doubt about this after 1915, the year in which D. W. Griffith released *The Birth of a Nation*—a motion picture that was to gross about $18,000,000 within the next few years. Showmanship had been straining toward illusionism for nearly a century and a half,[5] and had acquired a realistic direction after 1860 from Tom Robertson, the Duke of Saxe-Meiningen, Antoine, and others. But after 1915 it was patently hopeless for the theatre to expect to equal the capacity of the screen for conveying realistic detail —indeed, not merely visual detail, but emotional accent as well. "Every little series of pictures, continuing from four to fifteen seconds, symbolizes a sentiment, a passion, or an emotion," wrote the New York *Times* critic Henry MacMahon in his review of *The Birth of a Nation;* and there were "more than five thousand pictures" in that film! Obviously, the theatre could not expect to change its setting every "four to fifteen seconds" and still be theatre.[6] Audiences that came to expect this kind of pictorialism were bound to be lost to the so-called legitimate stage even before the high cost of Broadway stage production and the price of theatre seats became factors in the economics of entertainment.

It was apparent, then, at the beginning of the new century that realism of environment on the stage could not be mere pic-

[5] This has been true ever since Garrick had employed the Alsatian scene designer P. J. de Loutherbourg at the Drury Lane in 1771; the latter moderated eighteenth-century conventional stage practices with naturalistic pictorialism, although he used little practicable scenery.

[6] See A. Nicholas Vardac, *Stage to Screen* (Harvard University Press, 1949), pp. 223-225.

torialism. Eventually even a Belasco was to find his match in a Cecil B. De Mille, and the film's canned scenery would soon overshadow the theatre's settings. The point is, of course, that the value of modern dramatic realism was not dependent upon pictorialism, but upon convincing representations of meaningful experience; and environment, too, was fundamentally far less a matter of verisimilitude in details than of *significant* representation.

As for motion pictures, it is obvious that pictorialism could be used to subvert realism as well as to serve it, and that, characteristically, the pictorialism of the mass communication media (films in 1915 and television today) has been naturalistic-romantic rather than realistic. Genuine realism strove, and still must strive, not to *deceive* the playgoer, but to make him perceive.

The environment, as realized illusionistically on the stage, serves the audience as well as the actor. The visual illusion enables the average playgoer to observe the relationship between the individual and his milieu more or less directly. But, of course, the *illusion* of environment which began to be introduced into Western theatre during the Renaissance is less important than awareness of the *effect of environment*. It isn't a floor plan or a combination of flats and levels that makes the difference between, let us say, Ibsen's *Ghosts* and Goethe's *Faust,* but the awareness of milieu as destiny. Mrs. Alving's story is conceivable only under conditions that are primarily environmental or, broadly speaking, social. The *raison d'être* of the play arises from this fact, and a stage production that failed to communicate awareness of it would endanger the author's argument.

The modern idea of environment is a dynamic concept, and it expresses an awareness of kinetic relations between the individual and his society. Environment need not, therefore, be confined to or be dependent upon technical realism. On the contrary, environment has become a factor in modern nonrealistic drama too.

THEATRICAL NATURALISM   *In the last scene of the Elia Kazan 1947 production of Tennessee Williams' A Streetcar Named Desire, the blending of exterior and interior views and the distribution of the play's grimly naturalistic action over five areas constitutes an imaginative,* theatrical *employment of realism. Design by Jo Mielziner.* Photograph: Graphic House. Courtesy of Tennessee Williams and the producer, Irene Selznick.

THEATRICAL PICTORIALISM *Horace Armistead's sketch for the storm scene of the 1955 production of* The Tempest, *directed by Denis Carey, at the American Shakespeare Festival Theatre, Stratford, Conn., illustrates the encompassing of pictorial illusionism by formal and theatrical means. Although it never concealed its theatricality, a production like this one contrasts sharply with the space-stage presentation of Appia and of Craig, which continues to be resisted in its pristine form as too austere for the commercial theatre.* Courtesy of Philip Bloom for the American Shakespeare Festival.

Environment has a dramatic reality, intensely immediate as well as suggestive, in *Riders to the Sea* and *The Playboy of the Western World,* plays presented by Synge to the reading public with strong protests against the realistic school of playwriting. Environment is a dynamic factor in many expressionist works, such as Kaiser's *From Morn to Midnight,* Toller's *Man and the Masses* (*Masse-Mensch*), and George S. Kaufman and Marc Connelly's *Beggar on Horseback.* It is of paramount significance in the epic theatre of Erwin Piscator and Bertolt Brecht, both of whom have consistently deplored naturalism; that is, it is significant as a factor in the dramatic action and the thesis of the play.

Shaw and Realism

First, a clarification. Throughout the present work I refer to Shaw as an outstanding representative of the realistic theatre. I do not believe that Shaw can be pigeonholed as easily as Galsworthy, and I am not in the least disposed to deny the presence of extravaganza, fantastication, and bravura writing in Shaw's plays. But Shaw belongs to realism as a critic by virtue of his having made himself Ibsen's champion in England. And as a playwright as well as critic he belongs to realism because he exemplifies the realistic belief that the theatre is a place for the examination of facts and issues rather than a place for the service of "beauty" and the worship of "universals." Shaw's use of discursive prose is a further reason for classifying him as a realist, as is his fundamental adherence to the fourth-wall convention even in the long speeches of *Getting Married,* the Don Juan episode of *Man and Superman* and the tent scene of *Saint Joan.* His detailed, often rounded characterizations, too, would distinguish his work from that of devotees of antinaturalism. As Eric Bentley has reminded us, the same thing may be said of Shaw that Shaw said of Dickens: that he combined "a mirror-like exactness of character-drawing with the wildest extravagances of humorous expression and grotesque situation." Shaw had no use for the usual "cup-and-saucer" type of British realism except when he could transfigure it with his intellect, as he did in *Candida,* and he rapidly made himself the master of a brilliant dialectical method of instructing the mind while delighting it. It was to implement this kind of realism that Shaw rejoiced in extensive rhetoric, called for "the exciting or impressive declamation I had learned from old-timers like Ristori, Salvini, and Barry Sullivan," and did not hesitate to employ fantasia, in the fourth act of *Man and Superman* and the epilogue of *Saint Joan,* not to mention the whole of *Back to Methuselah.*

The form of discursive drama that became most distinct in Shaw's playwriting is, indeed, intrinsic in the Hegelianism that became so widespread and influential in Europe, both in its idealistic and materialistic aspects. Its implications for drama were perhaps best understood before the advent of Ibsen and Shaw by the poet and dramatist Friedrich Hebbel, who was a devout Hegelian and is best remembered in English-speaking countries for the middle-class tragedy *Maria Magdalena* (1844). "The drama," Hebbel wrote in his diary, "is not to tell us new stories, but to show new relations." He went on to say that modern drama, if it is ever to arise, would have to transcend Shakespearean playwriting and be different from it in the respect "that the conflict of dramatic reasoning is to be not *only within the characters but is to be transferred to the idea itself.*" Not only *"the relations of men to moral concepts,"* but *"the validity of those very concepts,"* is to be debated.[1] A better anticipation and description of ultra-Shavian drama would be hard to find. Of course, there is also more to Shaw's good plays than this element of discussion, and, to be sure, Shaw realized that there was something more than "discussion" in Ibsen's plays when he published his exegesis *The Quintessence of Ibsenism* in 1891 and amplified it for a new edition in 1913. But one thing is certain: Shaw

[1] The italics are mine. I quote from an out-of-print Boni and Liveright Modern Library volume, *A Modern Book of Criticism* (1919), edited by Ludwig Lewisohn.

could have easily agreed with Matisse's statement that in art "l'exactitude n'est pas la vérité," as well as with Picasso's that "art is a lie that makes us realize the truth," without feeling that this made him less of a realist.

The issue of intellectual content versus mere verisimilitude can be similarly joined in the case of Ibsen, who had no reason to consider himself less of a realist when he wrote atmospheric drama and employed some symbolism, as in *The Master Builder* and *John Gabriel Borkman*, than when he wrote *A Doll's House* and *Ghosts*. Nor are we likely to make the mistake of saying that Ibsen is not a realist in any of these plays because he does not allow the action of a play to run on freely. Ibsen is all the more an adherent of critical realism because he has *arranged* events. The coincidences in *Ghosts*, for example—the fire in the orphan asylum erected in honor of Alving, and the discovery of the illness of Alving's son, are related to the revelation that Mrs. Alving's conformity to convention in returning to her husband had been a disastrous error of judgment. Arthur Miller, speaking at Harvard in 1953, referred to Ibsen as one who "squeezed out" the "hidden connections" of events "to the mores, habits, and social institutions of the time—so that a *tension*, a contradiction, immediately appeared." Hebbel's call for the presentation of "relations" was vigorously met by Ibsen, and this readiness to make dramatic associations and dissociations that had been ignored by most playwrights defines Ibsen's realism. Miller, speaking as a younger writer, conceded that there was reason to mistrust the machine-like precision of Ibsen's plots, but declared that Ibsen nevertheless had significance for him in "his remorselessness, his hard logic, the clean edges of his work."

Naturalism

Naturalism can be defined broadly or narrowly. In the preceding text I employed this rather ambiguous term as though it were generally interchangeable with "realism." This has, indeed, been the case on the European continent, as Europeans will say "Naturalismus" or "naturalisme" when we would say "realism."

As an intensive term, however, naturalism signifies not only a strict, often extreme, mode of realism, but a rather narrow dogma introduced into dramatic theory by Émile Zola in 1873, in his familiar and perhaps overrated preface to *Thérèse Raquin*, the unsuccessful play that he had fashioned out of his own naturalistic novel. Zola formulated a creed that was consonant with nineteenth-century idolatry of mechanistic science as the key to all truth. He especially reflected the advances made in physiology by Claude Bernard (1813-1878), the founder of experimental medicine, with whose researches, as recorded in *An Introduction to the Study of Experimental Medicine* (1865), Zola was extremely impressed.

Zola's program for the theatre called upon writers to concentrate on data arrived at objectively, and to adopt the hypothesis that man is primarily an animal whose emotions can be submitted to the same laboratory tests as "sugar and vitriol," to use Taine's expression. The strictly naturalistic view was mechanistic, physiological, and deterministic. The individual was to be exhibited as the product, puppet, and victim of the inexorable forces of heredity, instinct, and environment, for man was to be regarded as a wholly natural object subject to natural processes. Since the naturalists could consistently consider moral issues only as manifestations of the "laws" of physiology and psychology, they were more inimical to Victorian moralism than were Ibsen and Shaw, who were strong believers in the moral will.[1] Naturalists subordinated morality to the order of nature.

The strict application of these standards of naturalism to playwriting resulted in the presentation of environments and of more or less animal (that is, instinctive) behavior on the stage.

[1] That is, the naturalist would have done so, had he been consistent, had he been heeded, and had naturalism persisted.

Pictures of degradation, disease, and sexual license abounded in advanced theatrical circles after 1880. (As usual, there was a time lag in the theatre; naturalism had established itself in European fiction about two decades earlier.) Among plays reflecting the naturalist dogma are Gerhart Hauptmann's *Before Sunrise* (1889), *The Beaver Coat* (1893), and *Rose Bernd* (1903); Strindberg's *The Dance of Death* (1901); and Schnitzler's *Reigen* (1897), best known here by the title of the French motion picture made from it, *La Ronde*. Naturalism became a *cause célèbre*, and its progress was punctuated by conflicts with censorship.

Naturalists required of the actor the utmost authenticity in speech, appearance, and movement, even encouraging him to turn his back to the audience when the action called for it, thus giving the proscenium arch the character of a fourth wall. They also called for the utmost naturalness in playwriting, discouraging plot maneuvering even more than Ibsen did, and favoring the employment of dialect. They advocated dialect not for poetic effect, but for the sake of realism of the phonograph, supplementary to their ideal realism in scenery, which constituted a realism of the camera. Dialect in a play by Hauptmann or Galsworthy was, indeed, likely to be unlovely and jangling.

Zola's passion for naturalism in 1873 also made him a quixotic advocate of "naturalness." He seemed bent on liberating the drama from dramatic structure, although his *Thérèse Raquin*, a play of murder and revenge, was anything but uncontrived. He declared somewhat grandiosely, "The word *art* displeases me: it contains I do not know what ideas of necessary arrangements. . . . To make art, is it not to mistake something which is outside man and outside nature?" Zola was successful, perhaps, in helping to rid the stage of romantic "heroic drama" and its "paraphernalia of armor, secret doors, poisoned wines and the rest," which were to find a refuge ultimately in the Hollywood factories of historical romance. But Zola came up against the refractoriness of the dramatic medium, which requires that a story must be greatly condensed and arranged. And the natural opposition of the artist to a consistent naturalism was stated, or rather thundered, by Nietzsche in *Twilight of the Idols* when he deplored the results of nonselection, "a mass of daubs, at best a piece of mosaic," and protested that "nature is no model. . . . This lying in the dust before trivial facts is unworthy of the thorough artist." Zola's call for thoroughly "unarranged" drama was heeded only to a limited extent. The realistic plays of Ibsen and Strindberg and Shaw were certainly not "unarranged," and Chekhov's only seemed so. The realists' use of the materials of social reality was interpretative, whereas Zola's "scientific" program for naturalism demanded absolute objectivity and clinical detachment.

Naturalism, however, did not cause any changes in dramatic form that were not implicit in realism as practiced by courageous playwrights. If the naturalistic theatre encouraged the use of dialect on the stage, so did the poetic-nationalistic Irish movement. In demanding that the drama consist of "slice of life" scenes, Zola and his followers also discouraged plottiness and theatrical contrivance; but so did realists, such as Ibsen and Shaw, who opposed drama of intrigue without embracing a Naturalist program. Of the preference for naturalness erected (and somewhat distorted) into an article of naturalistic faith by Zolaism, the kindest thing to be said is that it was, on the negative side, a renunciation of easy and banal means of winning public interest; and, on the positive side, that it expressed one of the oldest ideals of art—namely, the Horatian one of the art of concealing art. Perhaps Randall Jarrell has expressed it best in contemporary terms when, in writing of Robert Frost's poetic power, but mentioning also Thomas Hardy's, he referred to "the tremendous strength . . . of things merely put down and left to speak for themselves." [2] But, as in the case of all theories of art, the worse practice of the theory prevailed far more frequently than the better.

For my argument, then, the term "naturalism" has no partic-

[2] *Poetry and the Age* (Vintage Books ed., 1955), p. 28.

ular meaning not already embodied in the term "realism." I would note only two historically important points: the first is that the naturalists led by Zola, most of whom had a flair for publicity, were particularly effective in championing dramatic realism and encouraging its extension. They supported the plays of Ibsen, Strindberg, and Tolstoy, and they were the first to rally to the support of Antoine's historic Théâtre Libre, although Antoine himself tried to disclaim exclusive adherence to naturalism. A second fact to bear in mind is that doctrinaire naturalists soon alienated the public with the grossness of their plays and the tawdriness of their stage productions. Naturalism was responsible to a considerable extent for the antirealistic reaction represented by Maeterlinck's "symbolist" plays and Rostand's flamboyantly romantic pieces before the nineteenth century came to a close. Deterministic views and fascination with raw animalism, however, received too much support from the social conflicts and wars of the twentieth century to permit them to wither away quietly. And it may also be argued that by minimizing the role of reason in human life, naturalism prepared the ground for the excesses of expressionists and surrealists.

Verse and Verse-Realism

On reflection it would appear that the verse-prose polarity had little validity during the formative period of modern realism and has even less today. We know that Ibsen deliberately abandoned verse dialogue after having written *Brand* and *Peer Gynt*, two of the greatest verse dramas composed after the death of Racine. They were completed in 1866 and 1867, respectively, and not until 1881, when he created *Ghosts,* did the "father of modern drama" write a prose work of comparable stature. Not until then did he compose comparably penetrating drama of ideas or drama of critical realism, too.

Ibsen, it is true, believed that the use of prose was essential to realistic drama, and other pioneers agreed with him. But his theory is confounded by his own practice. He was able to attain heights of realistic theatre "theatrically," and to write poetically both in prose and verse. He returned to verse drama with his last play, *When We Dead Awaken.* The feebleness of that work is due to weak playwriting, not to the use of verse. *When We Dead Awaken* was preceded by ten plays in prose, among which probably only *A Doll's House* would have lost force as realistic drama if it had been written in verse. Nor can one be certain of the necessity of making even that single exception when one considers how well T. S. Eliot's parlor conversation is conducted in verse during the first act of *The Cocktail Party.* Verse would have harmonized well enough with the dramatic intensities of *Ghosts* and *Hedda Gabler* and with the symbol-charged conflicts of *An Enemy of the People, The Wild Duck, Rosmersholm, The Master Builder, Little Eyolf,* and *John Gabriel Borkman.* Considerable expository and disquisitory dullness might have been spared us if the dialogue had been fined down and submitted to a governing verse rhythm.

The age in which Ibsen and his successors made their mark was distinctly an age of prose—of journalism and of the prose-epic or novel. The Romantic poetry of the nineteenth century tended to be too luxuriant for drama; it was certainly more descriptive and reflective than dramatic. The neo-Romantic poetry of the latter part of the century was principally escape poetry. It was either pseudomedieval, and thus decidedly more suitable for Rossetti-tinted blessed damozels than for unvarnished Noras and Hedda Gablers; or it was allusively private, "symbolist" poetry. In the modern period, besides, most writers for the stage have graduated from fields in which prose is the medium —fiction, journalism, law, sociology, or even science. Chekhov called literature his mistress and medicine his lawful wife. Even if we refuse to take Chekhov's statement at face value, it is still true that this master of the short story came to the theatre as a prose writer, as did Gogol, Turgenev, Tolstoy, Gorki, Shaw, Galsworthy, Maugham, Molnar, Pirandello, Saroyan, and many other playwrights.

Finally, it is probable that the impulse to write verse drama was lessened by the vogue of prose-poetry, which started when the boundaries between verse and poetry began to be blurred by Romantic writers such as Novalis, Poe, and De Quincey. Reasons for composing verse drama became less than compelling when playwrights could employ cadenced prose as evocative, imaginative, or atmospheric as Synge's, O'Casey's, and Chekhov's. So exquisite a poet as García Lorca turned from the writing of verse tragedies such as *Yerma* and *Blood Wedding* to prose drama for his last play, *The House of Bernarda Alba*. Even Eliot (who nevertheless cast his final vote for verse) was moved to express amazement at the power of prose drama: "There are great prose dramatists—such as Ibsen and Chekhov—who have at times done things of which I would not otherwise have supposed prose to be capable . . ." Eliot concluded that "no play should be written in verse for which prose is *dramatically* adequate." [1]

Nevertheless, the vogue of prose dialogue proved to be a pitfall for ordinary writers, who lacked the power to transcend the commonplace and who did not realize that even dramatic prose is already well above the level of the fumbling language of ordinary conversation. And notably, too, the rage for familiar characters and situations deprived the drama of that "fascination of the abomination," the stock in trade alike of gothic romanticism and popular melodrama, that had motivated both eloquence and magniloquence for more than three-quarters of a century before *Ghosts*.

A countermovement did arise in the 1890's with the atmospheric prose of Maeterlinck and the pyrotechnical verse of Rostand. But the trend, whether toward prose-poetry, of which O'Casey and Giraudoux became the masters in our time, or toward verse drama, for which Claudel, Hofmannsthal, Yeats, García Lorca, and Eliot maintained an uninterrupted apostolate,

[1] *Poetry and Drama* (London: Faber and Faber, 1951), p. 12.

has been associated with realism only intermittently. The prose-poets tended to disavow realism from the start, as did Maeter-linck and Synge, or to abandon it, as did Strindberg, Masefield, and O'Casey. It remains to be remarked only that, despite such defections, dramatic realists have continued to use prose-poetry; examples can be found in the work of such reputable contemporaries as Carl Zuckmayer, Charles Vildrac, Albert Camus, Paul Vincent Carroll, Clifford Odets, Tennessee Williams and Arthur Miller. And Eliot's terse fragment *Sweeney Agonistes,* portions of *The Cocktail Party* and *The Confidential Clerk,* Fry's *Venus Observed* (if it is not too tenuous for realism), and some scenes in *Winterset* suggest that verse is not essentially in conflict with dramatic realism. The "language of power" lends itself naturally to rhythmic utterance.

There still exists the danger of turgidity that was great in nineteenth-century verse-making, as Maxwell Anderson's lapses in several verse plays made evident. Yet how can we possibly ignore the fact that much of the greatest verse ever written— that of Homer, Sophocles, Dante, and Racine, for instance—was notably simple and direct, even when characterized by regularity of meter? Besides, there is a long "tradition of conversational language in poetry," as Eliot has reminded us, so that the "tone of common speech" can be applied to "the topics of common intercourse." [2] It was unnecessary for realists to forego the use of verse in order to further their cause, although it is perhaps only now, long after the period of struggle for realism, that we can realize the extent of the loss and conclude that it was not necessary. And the loss certainly need not have been entailed because of the resolve of the realists, as foreshadowed by Hugo's preface to *Cromwell,* to show the seamy side of life. If they had no beautiful world to exhibit, they could nevertheless have been the first to realize, with Hugo, that poetry is not dependent

[2] From *The Use of Poetry and the Use of Criticism* (London: Faber and Faber, 1933).

on beauty in its object; and verse, of course, is even less so. Again we are indebted to Eliot for a terse statement on a subject within his competence when he states that "the essential advantage for a poet is not to have a beautiful world with which to deal: it is to be able to see beneath both beauty and ugliness; to see the boredom, and the horror, and the glory." [3]

Nor is the loss of verse to realistic drama irrecoverable, even at this time, though I know only of unproduced verse plays (by the American poet Ettore Rella) which are realistic from beginning to end, as neither *The Cocktail Party* nor *Winterset* is. Not even the realists' concern with "this time, this place," their very necessary concern with environment, need be an impediment. Some excellent verse does not convey the sense of an action taking place at a particular time in a particular place, but some very good verse (Homer's, Chaucer's, Villon's, Dante's, Wordsworth's, and Frost's) does. There can only be agreement among poets today that in using verse they need not forego the advantages of prose. Finally, it must be conceded that in English literature, if perhaps still not in French literature, there are no great requirements of regularity and there is much freedom within the flexible boundaries of form.

It may be argued, with seeming logic, that if verse can be free enough to adopt "the tone of common speech" and to talk of "the topics of common intercourse" there is no need for versification at all. If we are asked whether prose won't do just as well, we are forced to concede that prose has often served well enough. And I refer to straightforward, "plain" prose, not to that "half-formed poetry" which is "prose-poetry" and which does not invariably possess the virtues that are attributed to it. In prose-poetry the writer may succumb to prolixity and thus graze the periphery instead of striking at the heart of the matter, for there are excesses native to emotion and imagination that must be controlled if art is to have an effect of finality. But if prose has served the drama well enough, we have not yet found the answer to the question of why verse is desirable. One answer,

[3] *Ibid.*, p. 106.

already proposed, is that good versification can discipline prose. It can also discipline prose-poetry, which sometimes needs the bit and the bridle even more. Also, poetry "is language in depth, language at its most intense; which makes it peculiarly fitted for drama, which is life at its most intense." [4] Verse, as Eliot and others have noted, can prove helpful in keeping the actor and the audience attuned to the harmonies of true poetry when they appear, as they should, in the climaxes.

Verse, even when it looks like "sliced-up prose," can also provide dramatic punctuation, causing the eye—and, what is far more important, the ear—to rest on the word that should be dramatically emphatic. In the play *Venus Observed,* in the lines

> I'd like it,
> Father, if Mrs. Dill would have an apple,

the word "father" is much more heavily pointed, seeming to say "Father, are you attending?" than it would be if the lines were typed or printed as prose.[5] And, as the same commentator, A. L. Pattison, points out, prominence can also be given to words by means of the assonances and alliterations that are native to verse. We may note particularly the significance of "stranger" and "unexpected," the words used by the celestial psychiatrist Sir Harcourt-Reilly in the lines

> But let me tell you, that to approach the stranger
> Is to invite the unexpected. . . .

in the first act of *The Cocktail Party.* We note "stranger" because it stands at the end of the first line, and "unexpected" because of the alliterative echo of "approach." If the emphasis had been different, the dramatic meaning would have been different. Nor is it certain that these two significant and poetic

[4] A. L. Pattison, "Which Is the Opposite of Prose?", *Drama* (Summer 1954), p. 30.
[5] *Ibid.,* p. 31.

lines would have come with the same force of order and music[6] had not verse, however prosaic, been used in the play.

Whether for the tragic sense or for the comic spirit, for the storm of passion or for the thrust of satire (for which versification can often sharpen the point), verse, we must conclude, could have been used to good purpose by dramatic realism. And there is no reason why it cannot be so used now or at some favorable time in the future.

[6] We may hear the musical effect of the *r* in "approach" and "stranger," of the *t*'s, and, the modulation of the vowels.

The Second Transition

FROM REALISM TO EXPRESSIONISM

The intelligible . . . lies at the periphery
of experience, the surd at its core; and
intelligence is but one centrifugal ray
darting from the slime to the stars. . . .
. . . the core is an irresponsible, ungoverned,
irrecoverable dream—GEORGE SANTAYANA,
The Life of Reason

Realism as Modern Classicism

REALISM, CRYSTALLIZED IN EUROPE BETWEEN 1875 AND 1890, RAP-idly became the classic form of modern drama and theatre there. From it stemmed developments ranging from naturalism to poetic realism. In reaction against it arose those other dramatic styles, comprising the *second phase* of modernism, that have borne such names as symbolism, expressionism, and surrealism, all indicative of their antirealistic nature. Moreover, as so often happens when a reaction sets in against something that exerts a strong hold, the very departures from realism have each incorporated one or more of its principles or elements. In one way or another, indeed, opponents of realistic art have tended to justify their endeavors, no matter how bizarre, on the grounds that only their way of writing or staging a play expresses reality. The one principle to which certain antirealists subscribed more or less generally, sometimes even extravagantly, is the same one that sparked the realistic movement—namely, the concept of theatre as a means of revealing "truth."

Even in 1890 it might have been apparent to a student of civilization that realism would retain its hold upon the Western theatre. Excesses of illusionist detail or of verisimilitude might disappear from the stage, it was clear, but the objective presentation of social circumstances and psychological tension would not. It is surely not difficult to understand why Ibsenism, unlike the romanticism envisioned by Hugo and realized later in the Wagnerian art-synthesis,[1] was bound to prevail in the modern theatre long after realistic playwriting and stagecraft had lost their novelty. The concern with facts was not likely to diminish after the time of Ibsen and Zola. The sociological interest could only be intensified in an age of social crises and conflicts. The generally positivist doctrine of the world after 1875 also lent support to the social problem play and the psychological drama. The creators of realistic theatre felt rooted in the modern world, whereas the proponents of the new modes of theatrical stylization beginning with the eighteen-nineties were apt to make a cult of their sense of alienation. With the exception of a few revolutionary Central European expressionists and epic realists after 1918, the antirealists tended to cultivate a private world. One may concede, of course, that expressionists, dadaists, and surrealists reflected the confusion and disintegration of society as many more placid playwrights and showmen did not. One might say, for instance, that after 1914 Cocteau was a better barometer of the social weather than Galsworthy, just as Ibsen had been better than Pinero after 1875. But for all that, theatrical estheticism was not a social force in the direct and constructive manner in which realism was a social force following the appearance of *A Doll's House* in 1879.

[1] Wagner's most completely realized "composite art works," the music-dramas *Tristan and Isolde* and *Die Meistersinger,* were completed in 1865 and 1868 respectively; his *Ring of the Nibelungs* tetralogy, in the years 1869 to 1876. Ibsen's *A Doll's House* appeared in 1879; *Ghosts,* in 1881. The first theatre consistently devoted to realistic stage production, André Antoine's Théâtre Libre, opened in 1887; its equivalent in Germany, Die Freie Bühne, in 1889.

The realists *felt at home* in the very world they intended to reform. They were confident that they could know virtually everything that needed to be known about man, society, and life, and they appeared to believe that all they needed—all that humanity ever needed—was the will to discover the truth and to put rational policies into operation. This was explicit doctrine in the work of Shaw. Doctrinaire naturalists, of course, were confident that they could unlock all mysteries with their little key of mechanistic science. Neither realists nor naturalists felt ineffectual. Nor did either their friends or their enemies consider them ineffectual.

Fierce battles were fought over Ibsenism. Advocates of critical realism took up arms as though they were serving the cause of enlightenment and the emancipation of the human race. And their Victorian opponents held their ground as stubbornly as if they were repelling the forces of hell; they thought of themselves as defenders of civilization rather than of an insignificant world of make-believe. Among critics, for example, the most obdurate of the American conservatives, William Winter, complained in *The Wallet of Time* (1913) that not only had the Ibsenites "altogether mistaken the province of the Theatre in choosing it as the fit medium for the expression of sociological views," but that these views "would disrupt society." Ibsen's plays were "intolerable," according to Winter, because "in the expressive phrase of Wordsworth, they 'murder to dissect.'" A "reformer who calls you to crawl with him into a sewer, merely to see and breathe its feculence, is a pest," Winter protested. He could only conclude that Ibsen had a "disordered brain" and suffered from "mental astigmatism."

A new Ibsen production or the opening of a new theatre dedicated to realism was likely to be considered an event of major importance, an event to which even governments and political parties were far from indifferent. The production of Hauptmann's *The Weavers* in 1892 resulted in the removal of the Kaiser's coat of arms from the Deutsches Theater, the fore-most theatre of Berlin, and the premiere was the occasion of a demonstration by the German Social Democratic Party, led by the veteran socialist August Bebel. Police were stationed around the Moscow Art Theatre in order to prevent a revolutionary outburst when Gorki's *The Lower Depths* opened in 1902. An outgrowth of the Irish nationalist movement after 1899, the Ab-bey Theatre of Dublin served as an outpost of the Irish in-telligentsia during the first quarter of our century. As late as 1925, O'Casey's realistic drama of the Easter Rebellion in *The Plough and the Stars* could still arouse political demonstrations. And censorship battles raged over realism everywhere. Ibsen was compelled to supply a tame ending, one in which Nora returned to her husband, before *A Doll's House* could get its first produc-tion in a German theatre. America first saw the play, under the title of *Thora,* in a bowdlerized version in which husband and wife were conventionally reconciled. We can learn much from the review of this production in the Louisville *Courier-Journal* of December 8, 1883.[2] The reviewer was satisfied with the play until the discussion scene of the last act, which Shaw later singled out for praise as the truly modern feature of the work. The act, this reviewer wrote, "begins dramatically, but ends turgidly."

The change in the dénouement, made by someone responsi-ble for the production in which the celebrated actress Helena Modjeska went on tour, is described as follows:

Thoroughly disillusioned as to his [Helmer's] character, she [Nora-Thora] withdraws, dons a street dress, and announces her intention of leaving her husband for ever. He expostu-lates, argues, and pleads in vain, but finally, through the medium of the children, some indefinite talk about "re-ligion," there is a reunion and a falling curtain on a happy family tableau.

The anonymous American critic's comment is instructive: he is obviously too intelligent to be convinced by this reconciliation

[2] Reprinted in *The American Theatre as Seen by Its Critics,* ed. Montrose J. Moses and John Mason Brown (Norton, 1934).

and too Victorian to be able to approve of Nora's leaving her home. "The principal inconsistence," he writes, "is at this point. . . . In the original drama, Thora carries out the logical situation by leaving her husband. Probably after all, the most consistent ending would be in her death."

There can be no doubt that the establishment of realism in the theatre involved moral and intellectual conflicts. The battle over realism was not a mere quarrel between rival groups of entertainers. It would be difficult to find a single problem of the age or a single idea associated with modern thought that did not enter the theatre. If the stage became so important in the opinion of the public and drew into its orbit intellectual leaders who encouraged the pioneering dramatic companies, the reason is that the theatre became, for better or worse, a sort of forum. Perhaps even Shaw did not express the essence of critical, "modern," realism as well as did Ludwig Lewisohn when he reminded us in *The Creative Life* that there are actions in life that require "assumptions into which are packed whole histories, mythologies, philosophies." An idea underlying an action could be "of far more startling import, of far more searing terror, than the individual action itself." Plays dealing with such ideas (Lewisohn called them "ideas of actions") were the extra-artistic justification of dramatic modernism. But such plays could also possess artistic justification: "plays in which the ideas of actions are brought to the bar of dramatic justice make the mere rattle of action seem as tame and senseless as the movements of little animals." One was not to be deluded by the practical showmen who found such plays "talky"; the plays in which "ideas of actions" are exhibited and judged were significant (and here the extra-artistic and artistic judgments blended, as they did in other intellectual endorsements of realistic drama) because "by these ideas we live and die." [3]

It is true that the realistic drama and the type of stage pro-

[3] Barrett H. Clark, *European Theories of the Drama* (Crown Publishers, 1947), p. 511. These claims for realism were made, it is

duction in which the fourth-wall convention is observed are not perfectly adapted to the forensic development of a subject and the making of direct appeals to the audience. The play structure is too confining; the style of stage production is too self-limiting. Both the play and the performance favor the objective representation of character and action. Nevertheless, representationalism did not make impossible the thrust of argument and the exemplary (or even case-history) exhibition of issues that related the stage to society; and critical realism actually favored the presentation of arguments and the examination of issues. It is not wrong to attribute an almost forensic form as well as forensic tone to realistic plays otherwise as different as John Galsworthy's *Justice* and Sidney Kingsley's *Dead End,* Shaw's *Major Barbara* and Miller's *All My Sons,* Henry Becque's *The Vultures* and Lillian Hellman's *The Little Foxes.* The action of *All My Sons,* for example, is drawn as tight as a noose around the offending character's throat while his petty *laisser-faire* philosophy is exposed. His story may be defined as a case history of antisocial individualism. The other plays (along with many others since the writing of *A Doll's House* and *Ghosts*) also move steadily toward their objectives of exposing a situation or indicting a social philosophy or a convention. Even so seemingly casual a work as *The Cherry Orchard* is a relentless demonstration of social fact. It is even more evident that such a play as *Death of a Salesman* constitutes forensic drama: it is both a modification and an extension of dramatic realism. The play is not only a case history of success worship and self-delusion in a materialistic society; it has many of the formal features of a demonstration —much debate, much retrospective exposition and analysis, and a final, pointed summation in the cemetery scene. What values a man shall live by is the question that is examined. For *Death of a Salesman* to become a dramatic demonstration pure and simple, only a more candid use of the stage as a platform would be re-

worth noting, in 1924, in the very midst of the swirl of nonrealistic art movements abroad and the continued resistance of Broadway to "talky plays."

quired. In this work, as in more conventionally realistic plays, the nuances of characterization and the tangled threads of human motivation constitute the dramatic texture. But it is an explicit issue or argument that gives these works their particular direction or flow of action. And in the drama, indeed, the *movement* is the *form* to an even greater degree than is the formal structure.

It is to be noted, of course, that the "classical" elements of realism are not solely those of an expository or argumentative character. We can speak with some accuracy of the presence of musical form in the work of Chekhov and Shaw; the former wrote social fugues, as it were, and the latter, comedies of ideas in sonata form or in the form of a theme and variations.[4] In each, the musical form is a model of lucidity; the movement proceeds with logic and clarity. There are also many distinguished works of dramatic realism which simply represent a situation instead of pressing an argument; Elmer Rice's *Street Scene* may serve as an example. Or a realistic play may be a "slice of life," and not necessarily a "naturalistic" one like *Street Scene*. Two familiar examples would be the 1955 Broadway dramatization of *The Diary of Anne Frank* and Carson McCullers' *The Member of the Wedding*. The dramatic structure, as in the last-mentioned play, may be fluid instead of forced, but the form will still be found to be more or less classically stable. Unless the playwright has botched his job, the work will have clear outlines, point-by-point development, instantly recognizable norms of character, and action set in a clearly indicated environment. It would seem that the realistic theatre has been preserved in our century not merely out of inertia, but as a result of the unwillingness of the age to abandon a mirror in which it sees reflections of whatever

[4] An example of the "theme and variations" type of play is Shaw's *Getting Married*. Edmund Wilson has written stimulatingly on the musical character of Shaw's plays in *The Triple Thinkers* (Harcourt, Brace, 1938).

sanity it still retains. The mirror may be somewhat cracked and flyblown, but there are recognizable images in it.

In criticism, whether it is as favorable to modern drama as Ludwig Lewisohn's *Modern Drama,* published in 1920, or as unfavorable as Joseph Wood Krutch's *"Modernism" in Modern Drama* (1953), dramatic realism has been considered to be the polar opposite of classicism. Usually, too, this contrast is so presented by contemporary critics as to suggest that the modern realistic theatre has lacked nobility or has failed to endow man with tragic stature.[5] Nevertheless, it is possible to contend, as I do here, that realism has the essential character of a modern classicism. Its world is one of objectivity, reason, order, and responsibility—the responsibility of the individual to his fellow man and the responsibility of the artist to his society.

I would not be so extravagant as to maintain that realistic drama since *A Doll's House,* or even the best work in that mode, is "classical" according to any definition dominant in the age of Pericles, Elizabeth I, or Louis XIV. Nor would I argue that there has been absolute accord between the humanistic views of those ages and the views expressed by Ibsen and his successors. But I would suggest that the existence of differences is not decisive, since there were also differences—and rather marked ones—between the classicism of Greece and that of Louis XIV's France. Finally, we must realize that the aspects of modern realism we have been most apt to consider unclassical—the clinical examination of men's motivations, the readiness to define as neurosis that which earlier ages explained as fate or will, all the belittlement of the individual that psychiatry and sociology have insinuated into dramatic art—are not intrinsic to dramatic form. There can be little doubt that the weakening of humanism was essentially a moral and not a dramaturgic manifestation, a matter of value judgments and not of realistic style and dramaturgy. Moreover, it is obvious that the realistic drama and humanism have agreed very well, since among the realistic writers will be

[5] *The Modern Temper,* by Joseph Wood Krutch (Harcourt, Brace, 1929).

found distinguished advocates of the worth and responsibility of the individual such as Ibsen, Tolstoy, Chekhov, Shaw, and O'Casey.

Above all, we must insist upon the difference between the idea of a realistic theatre and the vulgarized, pseudonaturalistic version of that idea—namely, the idea of a theatre as merely the show place for illusionism. When antirealists belabor illusionism, they are actually flogging a dead horse—and one that had never had much life in it anyway, so far as Ibsen, Strindberg, Chekhov, and Shaw were concerned. No one despised mere verisimilitude as much as they did, as Shaw's contempt for Pinero's pseudo-Ibsenism alone would indicate. To what, indeed, could present-day critics of illusionism subscribe with more enthusiasm than to Strindberg's complaint, in the foreword to his naturalistic masterpiece *Miss Julie*, that the theatre has been "an elementary school for the young, for the semi-educated, and for women who still have a primitive capacity for deceiving themselves and letting themselves be deceived." [6] Mere illusionism had no future, for it could never have become anything more than stage trickery. The melodramas of the late nineteenth century became veritable orgies of sensationalism of the *Ben Hur* variety; and, in time, they were quite naturally succeeded by the lavish motion-picture spectacles typified by Cecil B. De Mille's productions. The illusionism of David Belasco's spectacular stage productions in the early years of our century also made no contribution to realistic modernism. If illusionism were mistaken for realism, it could be maintained that realistic theatre art was the culmination of a long story of decline rather than of progress, a decline that started as soon as the European theatre began to discard the platform stage of Shakespeare and Lope de Vega.

Verisimilitude in playwriting, even in combination with middle-class moralism and democratic interest in the common man, did not make any significant contribution to a vital modern

[6] *Six Plays by Strindberg* (Doubleday Anchor Books, 1955), p. 61.

theatre. The middle-class drama of the late eighteenth century, Diderot's genre of *drame bourgeois*, easily sank into complacency and sentimentality. The result could be a moralizing play like George Lillo's eighteenth-century melodrama *The London Merchant*, to which employers are said to have sent their apprentices so that they might take its story to heart as a warning against wayward behavior. Even the more or less critical problem plays of the pre-Ibsen theatre, for example Émile Augier's *The Marriage of Olympia*, stood only at the foothills of modern drama. In that play, written as late as 1855, the author was primarily concerned with the fact that "women with a past" were worming themselves into good society. Classicism should not be confused with the defense of convention, but with the preservation of the values of civilization.

It was one of the failings of the pseudomodern Victorian playwrights, whether in England or France, that they treated respectable society as though its standards lay at the very heart of the principles of Western civilization, instead of being simply manifestations of its superficial materialism and complacency. Classicism in art is not the amber that preserves a period's commonplaceness, but instead its most meaningful human experience and its most perturbing dilemmas and discoveries—those of an Antigone or an Oedipus. The pre-Ibsenite writers of problem plays were not concerned with these realities any more than were their pseudo-Ibsenite successors after 1880, such as Sir Arthur Wing Pinero and Henry Arthur Jones in England. At best, playwrights of this breed were concerned with a morality that was barely, if at all, distinguishable from middle-class prepossessions or interests.

In commenting on Pinero's *The Second Mrs. Tanqueray*, once heralded in England and America as an extremely advanced, realistic work, Shaw pointed out how adroitly the author contrived to avoid the challenge of realistic inquiry and left Victorian convention intact by making a woman with a past fail in honorable wedlock. In order to do so, Pinero went out of his way to provide a transparently contrived circumstance: the second

Mrs. Tanqueray turns out to be the discarded mistress of a man who becomes her stepdaughter's fiancé. Pinero, then, used realistic detail as little more than a façade behind which to conceal the rigid dictate of Victorian moralism according to which a fallen woman must remain fallen. Victorian playgoers could assume that Pinero's contrivance was "reality," whereas Pinero had actually gone out of his way to spare his public any realistic analysis of the problem. The method is comparable to that used in producing the Hollywood motion picture in which every visual detail is so accurate as to cause the unwary spectator to assume that the film's premises are also accurate. Shaw, writing in 1895, correctly described Pinero's kind of playwriting (in *The Notorious Mrs. Ebbsmith*) as "the barest art of theatrical sensation." Shaw added that in this case Pinero had "no idea beyond that of doing something daring and bringing down the house by running away from the consequences."

Dramatic realism had classical qualities not because it came as an end phase of stage illusionism and *drame bourgeois,* but because it crystallized a responsible view of theatre. In all classical art the work stands in some fundamental relation to its age. This is as true of the farces of Aristophanes as of the tragedies of Sophocles, of the "low" and "high" comedies of Molière as of the tragedies of Racine. As Francis Fergusson says in *The Idea of a Theatre,* the classical stage is indeed an institution "formed at the center of the life and awareness of the community." But it does not follow that the classical writer feels invariably obliged to endorse the life of his times, since it may deteriorate as Athenian life deteriorated after the death of Pericles and during the career of Euripides. Nor is the playwright committed to the glorification of commonplaces or to the sedulous support of the values of the unimaginative, the smug, or the self-interested. The true classicist is devoted to ideal values, not to adulterated ones. Also, if the age grows in self-criticism, as the modern period has done, the spirit of an age may be more deeply expressed by playwrights who defy convention than by those who accept or simply ignore it.

The tragedians of Athens expressed the Periclean humanism of the democratic *polis* or city-state; Shakespeare, the individualistic and enterprising humanism of the Renaissance; Molière and Racine, the cult of reason and order that prevailed in the times of Louis XIV. Modern realism is an expression of modern liberal humanism, not merely in echoing modern ideas, but in representing those ideas concretely in characterization, environmental reality, and dramatic action.

There is also a sort of classicism in the suitability of means to ends and in the proper use of the theatrical medium. We cannot deny that the living actor is the true medium of theatre art, this despite the artistry evidenced in stage production or scenic design. If the actor's means are inadequate to the end of character creation, excellence in all other aspects of the production is of little value except in opera, where the musical rather than the dramatic element is the paramount consideration. Realism has not proved to be the dead end in acting it has been in scenery. It could not be surpassed, and therefore made obsolete, by the illusion-making motion-picture camera.

The very nature of some notable principles of antirealistic theatrical art, such as those of Appia and Copeau, made convincing performance in acting essential. ("Scenic illusion," declared Appia, "is the living presence of the actor." [7]) When Appia and Copeau fought naturalism by stripping the stage bare, molding the actor in light, and treating acting as mobile sculpture, they only made inner realism more necessary. By disengaging the actor from the décor they made him the center of attention. *More* reality, rather than less, was bound to be required of the performer on a so-called plastic or space stage. No longer in a naturalistic setting or related to the décor of a shallow stage like a figure in relief, the actor had to achieve some

[7] "Comment reformer notre mise en scène," *La Revue*, June 1, 1904. Translated in *Directing the Play*, ed. Toby Cole and Helen Krich Chinoy (Bobbs-Merrill, 1953), pp. 111-119.

roundedness of characterization if he was not to look like an animated dummy. On the non-naturalistic ramps and levels of "space" and "plastic" stages, the usual alternative to being a thoroughly realized human being was to be a dancer-actor of choreographic theatre in the Tairov style, a phantasmagoric figure in an expressionist nightmare, or an actor-athlete performing acrobatic feats in Meyerhold's theatrical experiments.

William McCollom was surely correct in his statement, which is applicable to all normal productions outside a circus and away from an erector-set construction on stage, that "in acting regarded as sculpture . . . the continuity is determined not so much by the laws of composition as by the mind of the character-actor." [8] The search for psychological realism has had to go on, if only because the actor has to play a part convincingly even when the production is a stylized one. Brecht understood this fact, as shown by his not abolishing *all* realism in acting in his epic-theatre productions even while proposing degrees of alienation, or disengagement, from the character the actor is playing. The succinct statement of William McCollom is appropriate here as a warning to fanatical stylizers:

> The actor's art should be, in the best sense, naturalistic, the director's should not. The director must give expression to symbolic, abstract, and plastic values, but for the actor such values are secondary. . . . *The actor must be subjective, the director objective.*[9]

The actor must certainly create a life for the character he is playing, for otherwise he will merely articulate the lines written for him by the playwright. This is not enough, since even Shakespeare did not put into words all the thoughts and feelings that many characters must express on the stage. Also, what will the

[8] "Reflections on the Art of Acting," *National Theatre Conference Bulletin* (March 1950), pp. 31-42.
[9] *Ibid.*

actor do with himself between speeches when he must remain on the stage? McCollom once asked a professor of English what he thought Juliet was doing while the Nurse rambled on about her aches and pains instead of giving Juliet the news she had been waiting for. "Since Juliet was not speaking at this point in the play, the professor had no idea what she was thinking about." The actress, of course, would have to know; and as Shakespeare does not tell her in dialogue, she has to create an inner life for herself.

Nor is it always sufficient for the actor to project the emotional and mental life of his own part; it is often necessary for him to enter into the life of some other character in the play as well, so that he knows—and lets the audience know that he knows—what the other is feeling and thinking. He needs a *realistic imagination* and a realistic capacity for empathy. If he learns to make himself at home in his own character's skin, he may also learn how to look beneath the surface of other characters. Nina Gourfinkel, writing about Stanislavsky, reminds us that

> psychological depth of acting came to Stanislavski by way of Ibsen, Hauptmann, and Tchekov, who offer little opportunity for external characterization. Here interpretation "must be based on the inner life of the characters and pruned of all pseudo-scenic elements." [10]

By "pseudo-scenic elements" it is assumed that Stanislavsky meant posture, various physical indices of a character, and make-up. Stanislavsky came to minimize their importance, so that in playing Lövborg in *Hedda Gabler* he dispensed with strongly distinguishing features such as he had used earlier in playing Dr. Stockmann in *An Enemy of the People*. For Stockmann he had invented characteristic features such as shortsightedness, hesitating speech, and a tripping way of walking. Of Stanislavsky's Lövborg a critic is said to have remarked, "His make-up seemed

[10] Nina Gourfinkel, "L'Acteur selon Stanislavski," in *World Theatre*, Vol. LV, No. 1 (1955), pp. 15-16.

to come from inside." [11] Contrast Brecht's statements: "The actor on the stage will not identify completely with the character. . . . He is not Lear, Harpagon, Schweik—he shows them." [12]

Involved in these problems of acting, above all, is the *centrality of man* that constitutes the ultimate classicism of the theatre's great periods. It is granted that dramatic realism has given priority to men of average rather than exceptional stature. However, was the individual treated more fully by the postrealistic schools of dramatists if we except such self-elected neoromanticists as Rostand and D'Annunzio? The contrary was generally true. In comparison to rival modes of theatre, dramatic realism gave man a distinct habitation and relatedness to his milieu: a set of coordinates, so to speak, by which he could be located in time and space. Realism gave him the recognizable features of a functioning human being. It endowed him with "existence," if not "essence," whereas in antirealistic drama he is likely to have essence without existence. [13] In extreme instances man has become a shriek and a gesture in an expressionist storm, an interchangeable part of an abstraction or a social machine, or a protean character in a Pirandellian universe, whereas in the realistic theatre he has been, at worst, only a dullard. As elevated by romanticists, he has been in danger of being elevated out of the modern world. Symbolist playwrights have treated him as a sensorium in a fairyland or as a shadow in a landscape of nuances, if not, indeed, in a forest of symbols. (It is remarkable how unsymbolic are the human characters of the great classic drama of Athens, England, and France, how securely they belong to an objective world from which the playwright did not appear to be particularly alienated.) The differences between the realistic and stylized antirealistic modes of

[11] *Ibid.*
[12] *Ibid.*, p. 17.
[13] Compare *The Weavers*, for instance, with Andreyev's symbolist drama *King Hunger;* the latter deals with hunger, whereas the former deals with hungry men.

PIONEER SYMBOLISM *The ghost scenes (Scene 1, above, and 4, below) of the first act of* Hamlet *were conceived thus by Gordon Craig. The first scene uses vertical masses as a characteristic expression of Craig's symbolist idea of theatre; the second illustrates, in addition, the use of the screens and curtains upon which Craig relied for simplification of the stage picture. Despite Craig's scant success in putting his ideas to work, the theatre was stimulated by his general principles. He reduced the presentation of environment to a few significant details endowed with poetic or symbolic value—a pillar, a door, a block of masonry, and so on. Although his sketches did not require any fundamental violation of the fourth-wall convention, he did "spiritualize away" the realists' kind of environment. The symbolists, as Gorelik says, showed "how the soul of environment is separated from its body . . . by using a part as a symbol of the whole."*

Craig did not confine his symbolist ministrations to poetic drama; he also designed Ibsen's Rosmersholm, *for example, in 1906. Peter Brook (writing in the British periodical* Drama, Winter 1954) *conceded that "the ideas of Craig are not applicable to much of the world's theatre" —an important admission on the part of the most imaginative contemporary British director. Brook also declared that Craig overestimated the power of the spotlight and was mistaken in regarding it as a painter's brush capable of producing endless variations: "The beams of a lamp are straight, unbending and tinted only by the tones of gelatine that hang in front of them. In range and subtlety, in shade and colour they can never equal the painter's brush." It is especially true that Craig expected too much dramatic statement from scenery alone.*

FORMALISM—A STAGE FOR ACTION *Louis Jouvet designed the stripped permanent stage—un* tréteau nu—*shown in this model for Jacques Copeau's small Parisian playhouse the Théâtre du Vieux-Colombier, founded in 1913 and modified in 1922.*

On Copeau's functional stage the action could take place more or less "presentationally," for, in contrast to a picture-frame stage, there was no proscenium to frame a deep setting; much of the action could transpire on the prominent apron, or forestage. An effective design of movement could be achieved by the actors, as in a celebrated production of Twelfth Night in which the action occurred on four levels—the main stage, the balcony, the doors at either wing of the stage, and the area below the apron where the dungeon scene was played. In every kind of production, the scenic simplicity favored by Copeau provided much scope for movement and enabled the stage director to achieve a fluidity of action conformable to the pattern of the individual play. This was the case even if the story was as realistic in substance as The Brothers Karamazov, adapted for the stage by Jacques Copeau himself in collaboration with Jean Croué. "For," as Waldo Frank declared, "drama is eternally concerned with the planes, colors, metabolic changes of human action."

FORMALIST STAGE WITH DÉCOR *Copeau's permanent setting is shown here in use at the Théâtre du Vieux-Colombier. Although the stage is supplied with illusionistic details, the formal and theatrical character of the* mise en scène *is quite apparent. Since the stage was shallow, décor, mostly made up of screens and frames, provided a semiformal background for the actor, whose primacy in stage production was constantly affirmed by Copeau. (The actors were expected to create "scenic volume" by their performance; the picture formed by the physical scenery was regarded by Copeau as secondary to the ensemble of their movements even when the stage was supplied with décor.) An effect of formalism was further secured by the use of simple arches, which appeared in various combinations and constituted a pattern. An alcove or inner stage appeared at the back, and the gallery or balcony stage above it was disclosed in some scenes. Moreover, the steps leading from the stage related the playing areas to the auditorium. A peephole stage was an utter impossibility at the Vieux-Colombier. Adaptations of Copeau's kind of stage came into vogue, so that Jules Romains could justifiably associate the art-theatre movement after 1913 with "the multiplication of the Vieux-Colombier."*

treatment have been apparent in stage production, too. Gordon Craig's towering curtains and screens dwarf the individual into insignificance. Symbolist designs express abstract beauty and produce the magic of moods. They serve the actor as a man far less effectively than the actor as a figure. It is not surprising that Craig should have entertained the notion of displacing the live performer with a super-marionette completely subservient to the will of the stage director, for Craig was primarily interested in *design,* and not in the refractory human personality. "Art arrives only by design" was one of his favorite slogans.[14] "Composition" took precedence on the antirealistic stage; and the ultra-esthetic movements characteristically exalted the virtuoso scene designer and stage director.

Stanislavsky's cardinal principle was the development of the actor as a character in the production. In Stanislavsky's view the director's main function was to enable the actor to *live* the character. "Growing" the character, partly by external observation but largely by evoking his own sensory memory and his memory of emotions felt by himself, was and remains the main work of the Stanislavskian actor. And Stanislavskian principles are properly described as "inner realism," for they are an outgrowth of the realistic movement in the theatre. As noted previously, the individual was the central fact of theatre for Stanislavsky after he had passed his early phase of external realism.

Gordon Craig and Max Reinhardt and other leaders of theatrical estheticism inaugurated a counter-movement in which the actor-individual was more or less subordinated to evocative arrangements on the stage. Gordon Craig never saw the fulfillment of his dream of employing the super-marionette. Although he surely did not think that the marionette could replace the actor completely, his longing for a more tractable instrument than the human performer is understandable in the light of his passion for design. Craig's dream was an ambitious one: the *régisseur-*

[14] *On the Art of the Theatre* (Chicago: Browne's Bookstore, 1911), p. 55.

autocrat would rule every aspect of the stage production. It was with this aim in mind that he wrote in 1911, "To make any work of art, it is clear we may only work in those materials with which we can calculate. Man is not one of these materials."

Craig's hope of making use of an *Über-Marionette* was indeed nearly fulfilled, but in a way that could only have distressed his ultrarefined sensibility, when the autocrat-director Meyerhold went through a phase of extreme constructivism during the early years of the Soviet regime. And it must be said that a tendency to mechanize the actor had been present in Meyerhold's work even before the Russian Revolution. The starring actress Komisarjevskaya, in parting company with Meyerhold in 1907, warned him in a letter that he was moving along "the road which leads to the puppet show." [15] After 1918, Meyerhold even attempted to turn the actor into an acrobat. His theatre, as Josef Gregor wrote in Dickinson's *Theatre in a Changing Europe,* "was a theatre peopled with puppets with angular mechanical motions and driven from outside themselves."

And this passion for mechanization, which was also embodied in extreme forms of expressionist staging, was widespread after World War I in Central Europe as well as Soviet Russia. The vogue of machine worship was strong in Italy, too, where mechanistic stylization was dubbed "futurism" because mechanical art was regarded as the inevitable art of the future. Futurism in Italy had its beginnings in the first decade of the century as a cult in painting. It entrenched itself briefly upon the stage under the leadership of the poet F. T. Marinetti, the director Enrico Prampolini, and others. The Futurist Manifesto of 1909 had read in part: "we feel the need of delivering ourselves from old sensibilities, in order to create definitely the new plastic art inspired by the machine."

[15] Anna Irene Miller, *The Independent Theatre in Europe* (New York: Long and Smith, 1927), p. 365.

Antirealism and realism wove tangled skeins in the practice of the constructivists after 1918. The skeletal structure or construction, an outgrowth of Appian strivings for a plastic stage, was adopted in Russia before World War I for the purely esthetic purpose of achieving abstract effects of beauty and universality. With the postwar cult of the machine age and the glorification of a so-called dynamic world, the esthetic construction became an apparatus for developing a muscular theatre and affirming a strenuously materialistic society in symbols of industrial construction. Huntly Carter, reporting from Russia in *The New Spirit in the Russian Theatre,* endeavored to explain the new justification for constructivism.[16] He came close to saying that the post-1918 practitioners of constructivism were trying to serve two apparently incompatible ideals at the same time—those of abstractionism and environmentalism. Dramatic action tended toward abstraction on the ramps and scaffolds, yet the illusion of environment was conveyed by the representative constructions. Carter was unequivocal in declaring that "the constructive form was conceived of in relation to the structure of environmental form," and that constructivism had brought "the ideas of the builder, the architect, the engineer, the mechanic into the theatre" and showed the public "a new conception of the surroundings of social life." Meyerhold's early method of construction "rested, like that of an engineer, on excessive simplification, condensation and conservation." It is hardly surprising that the acting style in productions based on such engineering principles should present the actor as a "tool." Characteristically, Carter's generally enthusiastic description of Meyerhold's acting system included such phrases as "the actor as a social tool," "the influence of Taylorism," "behaviourism, which attempts to cut out mind and to introduce muscular perception and speech," and "Pavlov's reflexology, a theory of reflex action." It is nevertheless quite evident that this mechanical or scientific realism had noth-

[16] London: Brentano, Ltd., 1929; pp. 66-87.

ing in common with the humanistic realism that had modernized the theatre after 1880.

Symbolism and the Illusion of Unreality

No sooner had realism won its war against vestigial romanticism and the pseudo realism of the mid-nineteenth century than it was challenged by a rising school of symbolist playwriting, led by Maurice Maeterlinck, and by symbolist theatrical artists who formulated programs and founded little art-theatres. The first of these, the Théâtre d'Art, was established in Paris in 1890 by the poet Paul Fort. This neo-romantic (or, rather, symbolist) enterprise was significantly dedicated "to the sense of the mysterious." Before long the sturdy, realistic Ibsen dramas were being elbowed in the theatrical world by such "mood" plays as Maeterlinck's *The Blind* and *Pelléas and Mélisande,* by such religious miracle plays as Paul Claudel's *The Tidings Brought to Mary* and Karl Vollmöller's religious spectacle *The Miracle,* and such symbol-threaded poetic pieces as Hauptmann's *The Sunken Bell.*

Indefinite, irrational feelings and visions, allegedly more real than observed phenomena and issues rationally discussed, became the special province of the art theatres. The drama, according to the symbolist program, was to forego topicality and deal with the unalterable verities. The symbolists were bent upon universalizing the theatre, and they succeeded, although often enough in a void. Universalization by means more musical than dramatic led, on one hand, to the tone-poem type of dramatic composition favored by Maeterlinck, and, on the other, to the use of light as a visual equivalent of music. The Swiss designer Adolphe Appia, who has been designated the father of symbolist lighting, had worked in Wagner's famous opera house at Bayreuth, and his first essay on scenic design, published in 1895, dealt with the *mise en scène* in Wagnerian drama.[17] Like Wagner, Appia thought of opera as a superior drama constituting a synthesis of the arts; and the achievement of such a synthesis was the object of the *avant-garde* stage directors in whose view the stage productions of the realists were crude and incomplete. The new poet-playwrights and visionaries of stage production generally refrained from trying to duplicate the gigantic proportions of Wagnerian music-drama, but they were Wagnerian artists in their mysticism and reliance on verbal mood music. Had not Wagner declared that "Music is the soul of drama"?

Symbolist theatre became fashionable in the 1890's. The movement brought great visual beauty to the stage. Many artists, led by Craig, moreover, labored for the greater glory of a theatre in which visions of universal import, not workaday problems, would be exhibited. The movement brought the poet back into the field of playwriting after his exile by realism. Maeterlinck, Rostand, Hofmannsthal, Claudel, Yeats, and others functioned primarily as poets when they wrote plays, although some symbolists also had a flair for theatre. That the results were in some ways highly gratifying cannot be denied. Nearly everything that has been impressive in American stage design, for example, stems from the introduction of symbolist design for which Robert Edmond Jones was chiefly responsible. In summarizing his views, Jones wrote that "a good scene design should not be a picture but an image," and that he expected the setting to be "an expectancy, a foreboding, a tension." [18] Jones, Lee Simonson, and their successors, as well as their distinguished European colleagues, made of scenery a visual participant, an element that spoke to the eyes often more tellingly than the text of the play spoke to the ear. They were instrumental in causing the setting

[17] *La Mise en scène du drame Wagnerien* (*The Staging of Wagner's Music-Dramas*), Paris, 1895; this study was followed by *Die Musik und die Inszenierung* (*Music and the Stage Setting*), Munich, 1899.

[18] *The Dramatic Imagination* (Duell, Sloan, and Pearce, 1941), p. 25.

to function as an interpretative organ of the stage production. And the working principle behind this accomplishment was invariably *simplification;* art in the theatre, Jones declared, should be "not descriptive, but evocative," and he set at the head of his chapter of advice to young stage designers a sentence by Michelangelo: "Beauty is the purgation of superfluities."

Beauty, of course, was also both the catchword and the consuming passion of the playwrights who came under symbolist influence. John Millington Synge, the greatest of these in the English-speaking world, did not fulfill Yeats's ethereal dreams of an art theatre for Ireland. Instead he gave Dublin's Abbey Theatre more substantial drama in *Riders to the Sea* and other plays than Yeats was able to whip up in his pre-1914 period out of "a little mist, some fairies, and a psaltery," as an unkind critic of Yeats wrote in the Boston *Evening Transcript.* Nevertheless, the exquisite sensibility and language of Synge's folk plays derive from his adherence to the symbolist program in the theatre. He echoed that program in the 1907 preface to the *Playboy of the Western World* when he protested against Ibsen's and Zola's way of "dealing with the reality of life in joyless and pallid words," as a result of which, he claimed, "the intellectual modern drama has failed." He even employed symbolist, almost "decadent," terms in justifying laughter. In the preface to his hilarious farce *The Tinker's Wedding,* he wrote that "Baudelaire calls laughter the greatest sign of the Satanic element in man"—a reference hardly calculated to endear the play to the Irish public, which found it outrageously anticlerical. Perhaps the most appealing element in O'Neill's early realistic plays, especially those dealing with the sea, is their brooding atmospheric quality. And in our own times, Tennessee Williams has brought to the theatre a symbolist sensibility.

Nevertheless, it is difficult not to arrive at the conclusion that the symbolist achievement in playwriting fell short of expectations. Only in the one-act play did the results prove entirely rewarding. The short flight of poetic perception, the brief excursion rather than the exploration of an action or argument, was the symbolist playwrights' main contribution to the modern drama which they set out to transfigure. Except for a rarity like *The Playboy of the Western World,* which is leavened by a folk humor that owes nothing to symbolism, the masterpieces of the movement are short pieces such as Maeterlinck's *The Intruder* and Synge's *Riders to the Sea.* The best of these plays is probably the latter, and the persuasiveness and power of the work derive not so much from the symbolism of the sea as from the reality of ordinary existence conveyed by the play. Synge's justly celebrated poetic dialogue, too, is derived from the dialect of the Aran Islanders, among whom he lived for a time. The dialogue of *Riders to the Sea* is the dramatically shaped speech of real people, so that here again Synge unintentionally gained a victory for realism.

Yeats, who was the sponsor of Synge as well as of Ireland's Abbey Theatre, dreamed of establishing a symbolist theatre, but got instead a realistic one. And if the drama produced by Irish playwrights was poetic, it was essentially realistic peasant drama. It was poetic because the natural speech of the Irish peasantry abounded in imagery and cadence. Yeats himself managed to create impressive poetic theatre in a series of remarkable short plays, such as *A Full Moon in March* and *Purgatory.* But they were written after 1917 when the symbolist movement had receded in Europe and the possibility of giving the Irish national theatre a new antirealistic direction had vanished.

Extreme symbolism in playwriting resulted in a negation, rather than in a new form, of drama whenever the play became static and stopped dead in its tracks or moved in a fog of chiaroscuro impenetrable by any clear dramatic meaning, as was the case in Maeterlinck's *The Seven Princesses* and in his moody passage to nowhere, *The Death of Tintagiles.* Such misty endeavors were usually associated with an ambition to express the inexpressible—an aspiration to which the classic answer remains Samuel Johnson's comment on the mystic Jacob Boehme, "if what Jacob has to say is ineffable, Jacob should not say it." Carried to their logical extreme in the theatre, symbolist principles would have undermined dramatic art, since a play must embody specific action capable of active materialization—that is, of realization on the stage.

The cult of the mysterious and the mystical reached such extremes that the following satirical description by Rémy de Gourmont of the exemplary drama of the "soul state" is hardly exaggerated:

> Hidden in mist somewhere there is an island, and on that island there is a castle, and in that castle there is a great room lit by a little lamp. And in that room people are waiting. Waiting for what? They don't know! They're waiting for somebody to knock at their door, waiting for their lamp to go out, waiting for Fear and Death. They talk. Yes, they speak words that shatter the silence of the moment. And then they listen again, leaving their sentences unfinished, their gestures uncompleted. They are listening. They are waiting. Will she come perhaps, or won't she? Yes, she will come; she always comes. But it is late, and she will not come perhaps until the morrow. The people collected under that little lamp in that great room have, nevertheless, begun to smile; they still have hope. Then there is a knock—a *knock,* and that is all there is: And it is Life Complete, All of Life.[19]

And that is drama complete, all of drama, drama equally remote from pre-Ibsen drama of "action" and modern "drama of ideas"!

The effect, we may add, was not substantially different when the drama was active and dealt with something as specific as social conflict. The subject could be generalized or symbolized away by the idealizing faculty if the playwright happened to be a poetic playwright—say, an Émile Verhaeren, the celebrated

[19] Rémy de Gourmont, *Le Livre des masques.*—Quoted in a slightly different translation in S. J. I. Lawson's translation of *Belphégor* by Julien Benda (New York, 1929), p. 47.

Flemish rhapsode in the Whitman tradition who wrote *Les Aubes* in 1898, or Andreyev, who wrote *King Hunger* in 1907. Poetry or some rhetorical substitute could always be used to abet the process of erosion by generalization and liquification by symbolization. "Poetic drama" became synonymous in the public mind with attenuated drama, and little has happened in recent decades to eradicate that impression. By comparison with the events of history, symbolic literary pieces such as the Nobel Prize winner Lagerkvist's *The Man Without a Soul,* Philip Barry's *Liberty Jones,* and Fry's *A Sleep of Prisoners* were indubitably feeble.

As for moderate symbolist or neo-romantic developments in playwriting, as well as moderately symbolic stage settings, it must be noted that they did not actually transform the theatre. Fantasies such as Maeterlinck's *Blue Bird,* Sutton Vane's *Outward Bound,* and Sir James Barrie's *Dear Brutus* and *Mary Rose* present themselves to us as "real" stories. In these and similar plays we are expected, indeed, to be absorbed or stimulated by the very contrast between the imagined action and its matter-of-fact presentation. Realistic *structure* remained intact in many neo-romantic and symbolist plays, even in those which were written in verse; only the texture of the writing was affected by moderate antirealism. This is equally apparent in Rostand's *Cyrano de Bergerac,* Maxwell Anderson's *Elizabeth the Queen* and *Winterset,* and Christopher Fry's *The Lady's Not for Burning.* The one departure from conventional realistic dramaturgy in many poetic pieces is a reversion to the use of soliloquy.

The realists' idea of theatre as the art of producing an illusion of social and psychological reality and the symbolists' ideal of theatre as the art of producing the illusion of spiritual reality were not actually in conflict, although they sometimes appeared to be. The realists used illusion for one kind of truth, the symbolists, for another. Where the former demanded reality from the theatre, the latter demanded magic. And magic is, of course, entirely dependent upon illusion.

Illusion *per se* was well served by some of the innovations of the Appia-Craig school, so that it became possible to justify the scenic revolution of the symbolist scene designers on grounds entirely agreeable to realists. For one thing, both symbolists and realists opposed the use of the old makeshift and artificial-looking scenery. And if Craig and other advocates of the art theatre wanted a unified, thoroughly supervised stage production, so did the painstaking Stanislavsky and other pioneers of realistic theatre. An able spokesman for the more or less symbolist art theatre was Hiram Kelly Moderwell. In his book *The Theatre of Today*, published in 1914, he called attention to the symbolists' concept of *Inszenierung* not as the mere designing of scenery, but as the complete process of putting a play upon the stage by a single ruling spirit, the super-director or *régisseur*, who was then becoming the autocrat of the theatre. The symbolist school expected the *régisseur* to endow the stage production with a "soul"—that is, with a spiritual and universal meaning. Moderwell also set forth the great improvements in the creation of verisimilitude that had been accomplished by the new plastic staging, improvements that could serve the realists just as well as they were serving the symbolists:

> A landscape in modern *inscenierung* is not a paper and canvas copy of leaves and grass and shrubbery, but the picture of that landscape, the leaves forming a dark mass, the road a cleft of white in the greenery, and the shrubbery a mass of dark at the side. The background is a real solid, not a flimsy panel; it is a real distance, not a flapping sky curtain. . . . Light and shade are not painted on canvas, but are the living consequences of a real light.[20]

Even the mood-inducing lighting effects advocated by Appia promoted illusion. They brought the spectator into intimate relation with the stage action or stage picture; the expressive shadows of Appian lighting could cast a spell on the spectator or draw him emotionally into the scene. The natural light that prevailed in the open-air Greek and Elizabethan theatres must

[20] Pages 65-66.

have had the very opposite (and thus nonillusionistic) effect of "distancing" and "cooling off" the drama on the stage. Irving Pichel was surely right in reminding us that

> light in these ancient theatres—the light of the sun—did not reinforce the "mood" of the play or scene, but mitigated it. Oedipus, his eyes streaming blood; or the wholesale slaughters of Elizabethan tragedies, must have seemed happily less terrible to an audience seated in the sun.[21]

Symbolist playwrights, in the main, merely blurred or softened the outlines of realistic dramaturgy with their mood-drenched style of writing, their mysterious pauses and repetitions, their portentous indefiniteness. The fourth-wall convention, indeed, had an advantage for the devoted symbolist, who preferred indistinct effects to distinct ones. By separating the actor from the audience, the fourth-wall convention "distanced" the dramatic performance; and the romanticism of the symbolists disposed them to favor some means of distancing experience and of keeping reality veiled and at arm's length. The theory of "esthetic distance," propounded for contemporary American theatre practice by John Dolman,[22] is, in a sense, a symbolist ideal,

[21] "Lighting," *Theatre Arts* (March 1934), p. 616.
[22] *The Art of Play Production* (Harper, 1928), pp. 35-62. Dolman referred to the theory developed in Ethel Puffer's book *The Psychology of Beauty* (published in 1905, while the symbolist movement was still in vogue) that "complete aesthetic pleasure is to be found only in perfect repose," and that such repose appeared "only in a perfect balance of emphatic responses, a balance equivalent to neutralization." This view accorded very well, of course, with Maeterlinck's ideal of static drama. Nothing, however, was more remote from the aims of such aggressive realists as Ibsen, Strindberg, and Shaw than a "balance of emphatic responses." Bertram Jessup, in an article entitled "The Play as Esthetic Object" (*Educational Theatre Journal*, October 1952) supplied an admirably lucid description of the theory of esthetic distance, also referred to as "psychic distance," in saying "that a work of art fails as a work when it engages the spectator's real-life interests, practical or theoretical, so intimately that he gets worked up about them." However, Ibsen, Strindberg, and Shaw, as well as many later realists, wanted the spectator to get "worked

but the pathos of distance or remoteness that appears, for instance, in Gordon Craig's settings, is a romantic manifestation independent of the psychology of audience reaction that Dolman had in mind.

A new use was found for the fourth-wall convention by the symbolists; it helped them to create a different kind of illusion than that favored by the realists—namely, the *illusion of unreality*. This illusion reflected the belief that we live in a mysterious, "poetic" universe rather than in a concrete world of facts. At the same time, however, the illusion of reality also acquired a new, practical justification. It was often felt to be a necessity by those who wrote and staged fantasies, fables, miracle plays, and symbolic dramas or allegories. The playwright who composed a fantasy such as *The Sunken Bell* or *The Blue Bird* actually needed more, rather than less, illusion of reality than the author of a thoroughly credible play such as *A Doll's House* or *Uncle Vanya*. The new stagecraft, therefore, had to be just as facile in making the unreal seem real as in making the real seem unreal.

The symbolist movement, it is true, offered one radical dramaturgic concept—namely, the idea of "static drama." But it was a sterile concept, except in the field of the short one-act play, and thus could not generate a new dramatic form. We can observe this best in Maeterlinck's famous one-act plays *The Intruder, Interior,* and *The Blind.* The absence of marked action in these works was explained by Maeterlinck as a profounder sort of

---

up." As a matter of fact, so did a number of expressionists (such as Toller and Hans von Chlumberg, when they wrote anti-war plays after World War I), the epic realists Erwin Piscator and Bertolt Brecht, and the postwar "theatricalist" producer-directors Meyerhold, Tairov, and Nikolai Okhlopkov, the latter a pioneer in central staging. It is worth observing, indeed, that even symbolist playwrights did not consider themselves absolutely committed to esthetic detachment. "Repose" was surely not an objective in such passionate dramas of revolt as Émile Verhaeren's *Les Aubes* (translated as *The Dawn*) and Leonid Andreyev's *King Hunger.*

realism, evocative of "a deeper, more human, more universal life." When he decried action-filled dramas as superficial and inharmonious with modern probings into life, Maeterlinck was actually fighting the same battle against melodrama that had been fought by the realists and, especially, their extremist wing, the naturalists. His "static drama" was not genuinely "new" drama. It was naturalistic playwriting with its teeth drawn.

A sentence that is not usually quoted precedes the famous passage in Maeterlinck's manifesto of 1896, "The Tragical in Daily Life," which begins with his belief that "an old man seated in his armchair . . . giving unconscious ear to all the eternal laws that reign about his house" lives the ideal life for treatment in modern drama.[23] The neglected sentence is: "I admire Othello, but he does not appear to me to live the august life of a Hamlet, who has time to live, inasmuch as he does not act" (p. 105). But the sentence in Maeterlinck's essay containing the key to the symbolist *mystique* is the rhetorical question (p. 99): "Must we indeed roar like the Atrides before the Eternal God will reveal himself in our life?"

Only for purposes of classification, nevertheless, are we obliged to place Maeterlinck in absolute opposition to Ibsen. Maeterlinck perceived no gulf between himself and the master of realism. Like Henry James, Maeterlinck noted a good deal of symbolism and obscurity—an ambiguity or subtlety that used to be called "Northern mist"—in Ibsen's work. He admired this quality, whereas other critics at that time complained that Ibsen was too obscure. Maeterlinck's manifesto concludes with four complimentary paragraphs about *The Wild Duck*. Ibsen, referred to as "the old master," is said to have "freed certain powers of the soul that have never yet been free." Maeterlinck was also impressed with *The Master Builder* and was especially pleased to be able to quote its hero, Solness, who tells his Nordic Lorelei,

[23] Maurice Maeterlinck, *Le Tragique quotidien*, 1896: Translated as "The Tragical in Daily Life," in *The Treasure of the Humble*, New York and London, 1907. Reproduced in part in Barrett H. Clark's *European Theories of the Drama* (New York, Crown Publishers, 1947), pp. 412-413.

'Look you, Hilda, look you! There is sorcery in you, too, as there is in me. It is this sorcery that imposes action on the powers of the beyond. And we *have* to yield to it. Whether we want to or not, we must." According to Maeterlinck, Hilda and Solness are, therefore, "the first characters in drama who feel, for instance, that they are living in the atmosphere of the soul." And for Maeterlinck to say that he found "soul" in a play was, of course, the highest praise.

The temptation to call Chekhov a symbolist was strong among friends of the symbolist movement. Hiram Moderwell, writing in 1914, claimed him for the symbolists by relating Chekhovian playwriting to static drama. Chekhov's plays "are almost completely static" and are written for the sake of character: "For whole acts there may be no sign of plot-action. Acting occurs only when the author needs it for the purpose of producing a change in character." The plays "have no movement, they do not seem to be 'getting anywhere,'" and to appreciate them "you must be content to sit back in your seat with a soul at rest," in "the mood in which one sits for hours before a wood fire, learning to know a friend from remarks dropped at long intervals in the silence." The critic was pleased to add that the dramas of Chekhov's friend Gorki were also "static," especially *The Lower Depths*.[24] Since the original publication of Moderwell's views, hardly any support has been given them. Chekhov himself would have rejected them, for his rejection of symbolist art in general is clear enough in *The Sea-Gull*. Chekhov parodies symbolist writing in the play within the play written by the character Konstantin, the young artist. Chekhov's reflector-character, Doctor Dorn, says of Konstantin's work, "He creates impressions, never more than that, but on mere impressions you don't go far." And Konstantin himself admits, before tearing up all his manuscripts and shooting himself, that "I still move in a chaos of images and dreams." At the beginning of the play he had declared,

[24] *The Theatre of Today* (1914), pp. 190-193.

THE "ELIZABETHAN" PLATFORM STAGE *This scene, from the Shakespearewrights' 1955 production of* The Merchant of Venice *in New York, illustrates the use of a platform and an architectural background of abstract character in contemporary productions. The scene photographed here presented Portia's residence more than it represented it. Nor could one have determined without hearing the dialogue whether the scene was an interior or an exterior view. For a more or less interior view, as here, the scene was indeed illusionistically adequate, although too abstract for realism. For an exterior scene, the stage, which remained unaltered throughout the production, was distinctly nonillusionistic or formal. (The steps leading from the low platform to the floor of the auditorium might have suggested a descent to a Venetian canal, but such an illusionistic effect in an exterior scene would have been subjective, since nothing in the stage business of the production involved the use of canals.)*

In the 1950's the Shakespearewrights distinguished themselves by the excellence of their economical and vigorous off-Broadway productions. By that time, however, so-called "Elizabethan staging" already had a long history. William Poel's experiments began about sixty years earlier with his staging of Measure for Measure *in 1893, for which he converted the Royalty Theatre of London into a near-replica of the Fortune Theatre of Elizabethan times. The next year Poel founded the Elizabethan Stage Society, which gave Elizabethan productions from 1895 to 1905. (See Robert Speaight's* William Poel and the Elizabethan Revival, *London, 1954.)*

A critical analysis of Elizabethan staging has long been overdue. A Shakespearean production, of course, needs a great deal more than a platform in order to deserve a certificate of merit. For one thing, the actors must be able to make the characters come to life and to speak Shakespeare's music. Furthermore, the absence of all décor is not necessarily a virtue. And it is a question indeed whether the platform may not be treated more imaginatively—perhaps with more creative use of levels—than an antiquarian interest or simple convenience requires. Photograph: Zinn-Arthur. Courtesy of the Shakespearewrights.

THE CONSTRUCTIVIST PLATFORM *This exemplary constructivist setting for Tairov's Kamerny Theatre was designed by Alexandra Exter in 1926. A "vertical construction," distinctly theatrical and rhythmic, it is particularly adapted for dance movement with angular stylization. In Tairov's theatricalism, dramatic art was largely conceived in terms of rhythm, and this involved the actor in movements from level to level. Painted scenery and furniture were displaced at the Kamerny by sculptural volumes by 1916, and were later replaced by constructivist scaffolds and ramps. The stage was "liberated" from humdrum realism by being broken up into angles and multiple levels. For Stanislavskian psychological acting Tairov strove to substitute athletic performances aiming at expressive movement and "rhythmic harmony." After 1918, the Kamerny Theatre began to veer from estheticism to social utilitarianism. But the shift of interest, expedient and indeed compulsory under Soviet rule, did not greatly disagree at first with the Kamerny Theatre's original penchant for broadly generalized external action as contrasted with "inner realism" or psychological art developed by Stanislavsky.*

"We must have new forms. New forms we must have, and if we can't get them we'd better have nothing at all." It is doubtful that Chekhov the realist agreed with him, and Chekhov made his ultimately self-critical hero retract this statement in the last act of the play.[25] Yet Chekhov was a very *flexible* realist.

Much symbolist writing for the theatre sounded as if the authors and their creations were talking around a subject or were trying to attach themselves to an experience constantly undergoing deliquescence. The symbolist plays of Maeterlinck, Hofmannsthal, Hauptmann, the young Yeats (from 1892 to 1917), and Alexander Blok variously provide substitutions of fancy, mood, sentiment, and lyric poetry for the substantial characters and well-marked conflicts of realistic drama. Writing of Ibsen in 1893, Henry James could declare, ". . . I feel in him, to the pitch of almost intolerable boredom, the presence and the insistence of life." No such confession could have been wrung from James by the plays of the symbolists. Their elusive and allusive style fingered life through veils. Ronald Peacock, in *The Poet in the Theatre*,[26] refers to Ibsen's "extraordinary sense of precipitated crisis," and adds that Ibsen's situations "seem to have been shaped under the compulsion of an acute emotional response to the utmost concentration of conflict and tension." In the work of only one notable symbolist dramatist, Andreyev, could this compulsion be found. And in Andreyev, the compulsion nearly always borders on hysteria.

In the field of writing, symbolism was intrinsically a program for poets rather than playwrights. When Mallarmé wrote in an early poem, *Les Fenêtres*, "ici-bas est maître"—that is, "the world below is master"—he indicated the direction of the literary movement of which he himself became the leader. Symbolism was essentially an in-going style, whereas the drama is essentially an out-going art.

Compromises were bound to be made in practice, of course; the alternative would have been for the symbolist theatre to re-

[25] The lines quoted are from Stark Young's translation.
[26] New York, Harcourt, Brace & Co., 1945, p. 79.

main a coterie theatre. Practical playwrights like James M. Barrie and Maeterlinck (in his latter days) became merchandisers of fantasy, mysticism, and saccharine. Symbolism proved to be quite profitable once the cult of beauty and spirituality had been translated into show business. It is surely not an irrelevancy to remark here that the antirealistic theatre proved to be no more invulnerable to commercialization than the realistic theatre. And it must be added that an encounter with the anodynes of Maeterlinck and Barrie was not likely to prove stimulating for someone accustomed to the iconoclasm and remorseless analysis of Ibsen or Shaw. It was not difficult to agree with George Jean Nathan's cross remark in the *American Mercury* that "Symbolism is the child of poetic courage and intellectual cowardice." [27]

Subjectivist Disintegration and Epic Reintegration

If symbolism, in the main, merely softened and attenuated realistic dramatic art, expressionism actually caused its disintegration. For expressionism followed a view of life and art that required the destruction of the external shape of reality. And once the expressionist movement was in full swing in the theatre, other antirealistic styles multiplied, each adding a new corrosive factor or principle (that is, some special idea of theatre), since every new school was convinced that the theatre should be remodeled according to its own standards. For the expressionist, the stage was to be a means of projecting the disintegration of modern man and twentieth-century society. For the futurist and the constructivist, the stage was to express the marvelously dynamic nature of the machine. For the surrealist, the stage was to effect a release of the free fantasy of the unconscious which realism in art rigorously restrained.

[27] *American Mercury Reader* (Garden City, N.Y., 1946), p. 355.

The proponents of the new schools discarded realistic dramaturgy as old-fashioned and unsuitable to their requirements. And at the same time each school claimed that it expressed "reality" better than the others. The expressionist claimed that dramatic action patterned after discontinuous dream formation, as in Strindberg's *The Dream Play,* came closest to the truth about life. The expressionist was also ostensibly making some comment on modern man and the machine age in placing more or less twisted and fragmentary characters on the stage. Society, as described by German expressionists, was often indeed little better than a nightmare. Scenic visualization is needed to supplement the text of such rarely staged plays as Georg Kaiser's *From Morn to Midnight* and *Man and the Masses* if we are to grasp their total effect. Fortunately, one good scenic record of the expressionists' social picture is still available: Fritz Lang's memorable film *Metropolis,* made in Germany in 1926.

The surrealists went even further than the expressionists: they rejected familiar reality, with its orderliness and tidy logic, as a delusion. The façade of reality, according to the surrealists, had to be wrecked if the true life of the unconscious were to become manifest in art. And in order to destroy that façade, it was necessary, of course, to destroy the realistic form of drama. Once the façade was removed, irrational occurrences, such as those in Jean Cocteau's *Orpheus* and E. E. Cummings' *him,* would evoke, if not indeed represent, the anxieties, obsessions, and primitive wishes that constitute the true reality that lies behind the surface of everyday behavior.[28]

Inconsistencies, tricks, enigmas, startling juxtapositions, sophisticated anachronism such as Eurydice's receiving letters delivered by a mailman, and, above all, fantasies, such as Orpheus' passage to Death through a mirror—all these fabrications that may well puzzle an audience seem not only permissi-

[28] We must not, however, always take a solemn view of such dramatic exercises; they are sparked by sheer theatrical exuberance and license, as well as, I believe, by the aggressive bohemianism and the nihilistic spirit of dadaism.

ble but desirable to those who agree with Cocteau and the surrealists that fundamental reality is, as D. H. Lawrence would
have called it, a "fantasia of the unconscious." These devices seem
especially appropriate if it is believed, with Jung and his disciples, that the unconscious contains in the forms of symbols the
archetypal emotions of the human race. Thus Wallace Fowlie
defines Cocteau's treatment of the myth of Orpheus and Eurydice as "a meditation of death." [29] And if we yield ourselves entirely to the fantastic occurrences in Cocteau's *Orpheus*, it is
possible that our sense of death may be powerfully, if irra-
tionally, evoked. We may end with a sense of reality unrelated
to reason—a sense that realism, with its concentration on moral
and social issues and objective data, does not evoke. For Cocteau's disintegrative fantasy parallels the disintegration following
death itself, or the sense of disintegration inherent in our common fear of death. We may apply to our possible experience[30] of
more or less surrealistic work the words of André Breton in his
famous manifesto of surrealism: "What is admirable in the fantastic is that it becomes real."

Finally, it is obvious that the modernistic mechanists,
whether "futurists" or "constructivists," were also convinced that
they served reality. When their plays and stage productions made
automata of the characters and turned acting into acrobatics or
puppeteering, they were calling attention to the partial mechanization of their age and the total mechanization that they predicated for the future. Speed, power, and force epitomized their
idea of theatre.[31]

The emphasis on social reality, however, became most pro-

[29] *The Age of Surrealism* (Denver, 1950), p. 128.
[30] I say "possible experience" because neither the playwright nor
the director can be certain that the playgoer will have the experience he is supposed to have in response to the play, whereas the
realist can be certain that his points will be well understood if
he has acquitted himself with competence.
[31] *Proclama sul teatro futurista*, by F. T. Marinetti (1915).

nounced and effective when the director Erwin Piscator and the poet Bertolt Brecht began in the 1920's to develop the modes of playwriting and stage production now known as "epic realism." In the view of the epic realists, drama and the theatre had to undergo a marked expansion of action and setting. Perhaps no one has stated the case for scenic extension of realism more lucidly than the Group Theatre's scene designer Mordecai Gorelik.[32] He maintained that the modern designer

> faces more and more often the problem of how to show two or more scenes simultaneously taking place. One stage is no longer enough on which to present the many facets of a modern dramatic situation: where formerly dramatists wrote plays in three leisurely acts, modern authors pile scene on scene. . . . For the designer the task becomes that of finding half-a-dozen stages where only one was before.

The wheel, then, now turned full circle, back to the multiple stage of the Middle Ages. Reinhardt had returned to this convention early in our century in staging Hofmannsthal's *The Great World Theatre* on separate little stages or "mansions," set in a row. But a quarter of a century later, in 1934, when the vogue of Hofmannsthal's neo-romantic religiosity had been dispersed by the great storm of the economic depression and the fascism of the 1930's, the theatre was urged by Mr. Gorelik to pass out of its introverted period, "to leave dramatic unity for dramatic simultaneity," not for the sake of poetry, but of realism. Henceforth the stage must be able to accommodate not the reality of the individual bourgeois parlor, with its private interests and problems, but the reality of society, with its collective, multifaceted situations and issues. It is significant that in 1934 this highly gifted designer was speaking the language of stylization or theatrical convention without which the modern form of theatre known as "epic" would be formally indistinguishable from the theatre of nineteenth-century realism. In designing *Men*

[32] "The Conquest of Stage Space," *Theatre Arts,* (March 1934), pp. 213-218.

in White, Sidney Kingsley's Pulitzer Prize-winning drama, Gorelik demonstrated how the principle of multiplicity or simultaneity could be successfully followed. He referred to the "conventionalization" of his setting for *Men in White.* Most of it was permanent, although many different scenes were needed in the production. Gorelik called the setting "a formalized structure which does not represent a hospital, but is, rather, suggested by one," and explained that "within this abstract framework, successive scenes in different parts of the hospital are indicated by means of properties."

In neither his designs nor explanations, however, did Gorelik at that time take the direction which would have brought him into the "epic" school. Instead, he noted how his solution of the problem of space (his "mechanical contrivance for obtaining a stage space," as he called it) was accepted by all types of playgoers: "To the layman this type of setting, which ten years ago would have seemed peculiar, is now 'realism.'" He reflected that "the average conception of what is artistically 'real' depends on the prevailing culture and temper of the times."

Epic theatre, however, is candidly theatrical and, one might even say, joyously so. The epic realists, too, required the theatre and the drama to leave the tight little world of private life to which Ibsen's realism was confined. For the theatre to deal effectively with modern realities, plays would have to become "epic" or extensively narrative again, as they had been in the Romantic and Elizabethan theatres. The drama could be thoroughly episodic, as were Brecht's *Mother Courage* and *The Caucasian Circle of Chalk,* but could nevertheless be unified by the demonstration of some point about men's involvement in an issue that is fundamentally social. Neither the play nor the stage production would be required to maintain any consistent illusion of actuality. On the contrary, such illusion was to be destroyed by fragmentation of scenes and settings, by the interruption of action, and by a deliberate severing of suspense. For the aim of epic theatre was to present a demonstration of some aspect of social reality, and an exposition of how things work takes a mechanism apart instead of simply photographing the machine once all the parts are in place.

The demonstration might deal with the past in order to provide instruction, as does Brecht's *Galileo;* with the recent past, like Piscator's satirical World War I epic *The Good Soldier Schweik,* or Paul Green's rueful satire on the Wilsonian era, *Johnny Johnson;* or with the present, like *The Private Life of the Master Race,* a semidocumentary drama written by Brecht during World War II that reviewed the rise and collapse of Nazism. The play might be pure fiction, like Brecht's *The Caucasian Circle of Chalk* and *The Good Woman of Setzuan;* the latter is, indeed, a fable set in China which calls for Chinese gods to appear in the first and last episodes without offering any rationalistic explanation for their presence. Or the play might be entirely documentary, as were the "living newspapers" developed during the economic depression of the 1930's—plays appropriately entitled *Power* and *One-third of a Nation* and dealing respectively with the development and ownership of electric power and the problem of abolishing slums in accordance with President Roosevelt's statement that one-third of the nation was ill housed. Whatever the specific treatment of a subject, the shape of the epic drama —a web of episodes, with narratives and lyrical interruptions, choral chants and hortatory lectures—was radically different from that of the realistic drama; and the epic productions, even when abounding in realistic detail, did not employ strictly realistic acting, but stylized the performances to various degrees.

A demonstration of the working of social forces cannot rest upon the inwardness of private sensation and the meticulous creation of characters who draw attention to their private selves rather than to the factors operative in the world around them. And the stage, when adapted to the requirements of the demonstration, cannot use the static settings of the realistic theatre. Moving or revolving platforms, treadmills carrying pieces of scenery, charts, cartoons, and projected films were pressed into service by epic stage directors. The stage was made dynamic. It was treated as a constantly operating machine, practical because it provided visual aids to learning. The "stage-as-machine" concept, treated in other instances as a theatrical toy for playful effects, as in one modernist staging of Aristophanes' comedy *Lysistrata*, was used by Piscator, for example, in staging Robert Penn Warren's *All the King's Men,* which had first been written as a play before being turned into a novel. This play was not only epic in its dimensions (it dealt with a political figure whose career involved an entire state and affected an entire nation), but it was compounded in the epic manner of various elements; it had scenes of narration, commentary, and analysis as well as of episodic action. In producing this drama, Piscator employed a constantly (and to the critic Brooks Atkinson, annoyingly) revolving stage structure that looked like a machine with a high rectangular frame. Some scenes were also placed on the platform in front of this "machine," and a neutral area near the wings was occupied by the narrator-character, who analyzed the action or otherwise commented on it.

Perhaps nothing, however, exemplifies the essential theatricality of epic realism so much as the type of acting Brecht has endeavored to develop and on which he has written in some detail. The subject of epic acting requires too much space to be discussed here, but a few points may be noted. For example, Brecht came to rely a great deal on gesture. In an article written for a special issue of *World Theatre,* he declared (in addition to claiming for epic acting "naturalness," "humor," and "earthiness"), that "all emotion must become visible and be developed into gesture," and that the emotion "must free itself, *so that it may be treated in the grand manner."* [33] Brecht also recommended a study of the Chinese theatre, because Chinese acting has been "masterly in the treatment of gesture." It is obvious that he believes that it will never do for the actor *not* to stylize his

[33] *World Theatre,* Vol. IV, No. 1 (1955). The italics are mine.

performance. And it is by stressing theatricalization of the action that Brecht gets the effect he especially wants—the *Verfremdung*, or alienation[34] he believes necessary to his kind of theatre.

Whether factual or imaginative in subject matter as well as treatment, epic theatre represents a revolutionary twentieth-century departure from the essentially settled, individually oriented, emotion-based middle-class world of the realistic drama of the nineteenth century. That drama tended to present the individual as an end in himself; epic realism, however, may be in some jeopardy whenever the sympathy of the playwright (or the actor) creates rounded and moving characterization. Brecht was disturbed, for example, when his Zurich audience identified itself with the "Niobe-heroine" of his *Mother Courage;* therefore he made alterations in the text with the object of reducing the emotional charge of the play. The camp-following mother, who loses all her children, was not to be allowed to interpose her suffering humanity between the public and the author's intention to demonstrate "das rein merkantile Wesen des Kriegs," the "purely commercial nature of war." [35] Brecht has rejected the value of emotional identification and catharsis on the grounds that a play should leave audiences in possession of their critical faculties so that they may learn something conducive to social realism. He has been a strenuous opponent of illusionistic stage production and Stanislavskian acting, which is individualistic "inner realism" based upon the actor's thorough identification with the character he plays. Brecht, calling for *Verfremdung* instead, requires the actor to stand outside the part so that his performance may become a more or less detached comment on the character. Epic theatre is both antirealistic and anti-Aristotelian; and this cool, rationalistic school of neorealism has actually jolted the foundations of Western drama more drastically, because much more effectively, than any of the primarily subjectivistic deviations from realism. After the vogue of subjectivity, epic

[34] See "The Alienation Effect" in *Actors on Acting,* ed. Toby Cole and Helen Krich Chinoy, pp. 281-285.
[35] Brecht's *Versuche 20/21* (Frankfurt am Main, 1949).

objectivity introduced a mode of reintegration into dramatic art; but this reintegration was nothing less than revolutionary when consistently accomplished.

The Expressionist Assault on the Theatre

We may conclude, then, that once expressionists began to violate the realistic form in dramaturgy and stage production (first Strindberg in his late plays, then his followers before and after World War I), it was possible for the character of drama and theatre to be reshaped endlessly. And in each phase of that reshaping, as I have briefly indicated, there were involved concepts of dramatic art or ideas of theatre art that had been developed in reaction to realistic dramaturgy and stagecraft.

To some degree, nearly every school of theatre that departed radically from realism can be described as tending to be more or less expressionistic, and the term "expressionism" has therefore been used rather loosely at times to differentiate from realism all the antirealistic modern styles. There is one advantage in so using the term: it covers a concept of theatre as the comprehensive dramatic *expression*, rather than the more or less literal *representation*, of a subject. Nevertheless, "expressionism" is a confusing term when employed so broadly. Not only have the definitions and claims of its exponents been contradictory, but my generalization has thus far made bedfellows of incompatible schools. The epic realism of Piscator and Brecht, for example, is objective art, whereas expressionism is predominantly subjective; the epic realist considers himself to be an opponent of both naturalism and expressionism.

"Expressionism" is least confusing as a term when used to describe a single, more or less distinct, style of playwriting and theatrical production. It is the general style which, beginning in some of the work of Strindberg at the turn of the century (notably *The Dream Play* and *The Ghost Sonata*) became a theatrical movement in the years from just before to just after World War I. Strindberg struck the keynote of the expressionist theory of theatre when he wrote, in his preface to *The Dream Play* (1902) that in this play, as in his earlier trilogy *To Damascus*,

> Anything may happen; everything is possible and probable. Time and space do not exist. On an insignificant background of reality, Imagination designs and embroiders novel patterns; a medley of memories, experiences, free fantasies, absurdities, and improvisations.

He rightly called this play a *dream play* because, as he declared, "The author has tried to imitate the disconnected but seemingly logical form of the dream." His successors in expressionist experimentation made a veritable cult of morbid introspection and emotionally disturbed pictures of external reality.

Schizophrenic, oedipal, and murder fantasies especially abounded in the Central European literary world that produced explosive pieces such as Walter Hasenclever's *The Son* and Paul Kornfeld's *The Seduction* even before the traumatic experience of World War I.[36] The world of Ibsenism and the world of extreme expressionistic (not to say surrealistic) stylization had nothing in common; or one might say that the world of the former could be found shattered to shards in the nightmare world of the latter. "The intelligent man known to history flourishes within a dullard and holds a lunatic in leash." So says Santayana in *The Life of Reason*. In ultraexpressionistic theatre, the intelli-

---

[36] A few dates should prove helpful here: Strindberg's two most influential expressionistic plays, *The Dream Play* and *The Ghost Sonata*, were published in 1902 and 1907 respectively. The expressionistic drama reached its peak in Europe between 1912 and 1925; it was paralleled in fiction by the work of Kafka and Joyce. The minor vogue of expressionism in the American theatre occurred between 1920, the date of O'Neill's *The Emperor Jones*, and 1924, the date of George S. Kaufman and Marc Connelly's *Beggar on Horseback*.

gent man was never found without the lunatic, and sometimes could not be distinguished from him.

Oskar Kokoschka, one of the early Central European expressionists who was a playwright as well as a painter, plainly declared in a manifesto that "we must harken closely to our inner voice. . . . All that is required of us is to release control. . . . All laws are left behind. One's soul is a reverberation of the universe." [37] Another leader of the movement, Lothar Schreyer, called it "the spiritual movement of a time that places inner experience above external life." Often some social or spiritual problem dealt with in a play was presented in a character's dream. Interest in psychoanalysis gave special support to the dream-technique in the theatre after 1912. But it is a generally subjective orientation rather than dream formation *per se* that is most characteristic of expressionism. And expressionism did, of course, differ in degree and in the manner in which it was used in plays and stage productions. It could permeate a play entirely, so that everything about it was fantastic and expressively distorted, as in *The Dream Play* and *The Ghost Sonata*, or it could share the play, more or less, with the realistic style, as in O'Casey's *The Silver Tassie*. Expressionism could be intensive in some scenes and mild in others. In O'Neill's *The Hairy Ape*, for instance, the Fifth Avenue scene, in which Yank's frustration and disorientation reach a climax, is unmistakably expressionistic. The style of some other scenes (such as Scene 2, on the promenade deck, and Scene 7, in an "I.W.W. local") is not particularly distinguishable from naturalism. Expressionism, moreover, could be either a means towards an end, as when it was employed to underscore some plot situation or some character's state of mind; or it could be an end in itself, as when the entire play and the production were intended to exhibit a chaotic or nihilistic view of reality, as in the previously mentioned Strindberg plays.

[37] Edith Hoffman, *Kokoschka: Life and Work* (London: Faber and Faber, 1947), p. 286.

Whether expressionism was employed partially or completely in playwriting and play production, this much is clear: dramatic form and styles of acting and stage production were more drastically altered by expressionism than by any other style. In the twentieth-century theatre, expressionism introduced the most distinctive modifications of dramatic form and exemplified the most intensive use of free dramatic presentation short of surrealist "free-association" methods. In expressionism could be found the boldest assertion of the artist as the creator of a world independent of objective appearance and the expression of his defiance of a society more inexorable than that of the philistine-Victorian bourgeoisie—namely, the machine-age world whose destructiveness was the theme of such fanciful plays as *Gas* and *R.U.R.*

The expressionist playwright dispensed with the "middle-class" clutter to be found in men's minds and showed only the springs of passion. He did not hesitate to present depersonalized characters, individuals transformed into stark symbols or allegorical types deprived of a personal name—figures called merely Man, Woman, The Unknown, and so on. And the individual was likely to be placed in a truncated scene usually deprived of the padding of "manners" and small talk customary in cup-and-saucer living-room scenes. Only the *dramatic moment* was allowed to matter. This moment was given to the spectator without the familiar preparatory detail of nineteenth-century realism; frequently, it was hurled at him like a missile. In some plays the individual was submerged in the automatism of a milling and shrieking chorus, as in the mob scenes of Kaiser's *Gas,* Toller's *Man and the Masses,* and O'Neill's *The Hairy Ape* (in the firemen's forecastle of Scenes 1 and 4). The expressionist, giving the reins to his own fancy and intensifying his characters' subjective states, felt free to distort all manifestations of character and environment and to shuttle back and forth in time and space. For his purposes the imagination was entirely free to violate the rules of logic and art.

The physical transformations of characters and settings

called for in expressionist dramas offered almost operatic opportunities for the exercise of imagination by the scene designer and the stage electrician. Georg Kaiser calls for the sudden transformation of a snow-laden tree into a skeleton in *From Morn to Midnight*. In Strindberg's *Dream Play* there are such stage directions as the one that reads, rather blithely, "The background is lit up by the burning castle and reveals a wall of human faces, questioning, grieving, despairing. As the castle breaks into flames, the bud on the roof opens into a gigantic chrysanthemum." It is not this sort of Wagnerianism, however, that represents an essential change in form. Fundamental change is to be found in the expressionist treatment of the dramatic action and characterization—that is, in a characteristic fragmentation and distortion of their substance. The distortion, besides, could be motivated either by a character's state of mind (the play being shown through his disturbed sensorium), or by the author's intention to reveal his own disturbed frame of mind or make a figurative appraisal of man and the world. Most of the scenes in *From Morn to Midnight* and *The Emperor Jones* are "subjective" in the sense that the fantastic action and environment are dramatically related to the state of mind of an absconding cashier and an escaping Negro dictator respectively. In other plays, such as *The Dream Play* and *The Ghost Sonata*, the entire work is the phantasmagoria of the author-poet. In still other plays, there is a continual interchange between the real and the unreal that defies analysis, while in some dramas, such as the rather elementary *Beggar on Horseback*, there is a clear distinction between real action and the main character's dream.

Among the changes wrought by expressionism in the structure and the texture of the drama, those that affected dialogue were especially notable. Dialogue was subjected to weird abbreviations and distortions, so that it became frequently violent, telegraphic, and enigmatic. This was particularly true of the work of the German expressionists between 1912 and 1925.

Examples of such dialogue from Ernst Toller's play about the postwar uprising, *Man and the Masses* (1919), read as follows in Louis Untermeyer's translation:

CHORUS
>Someone tell the doorman:
>Five hundred
>gay
>young girls
>Wanted here.
>Meanwhile . . .
>
>We donate.
>We dance!
>Help
>The unfortunate.
>
>Schools.
>Barracks.
>War.
>Always.

THE GUARDS: To the wall with him.
NAMELESS ONE: Guns loaded?
THE GUARDS: Loaded.
THE PRISONER (*against the wall*): Life! Life!

Even a moderately expressionist play such as *The Hairy Ape,* produced in 1922, employs this kind of telegraphese, as in the chorus of stokers in the first scene, which reads:

>Gif me a drink dere, you!
>'Ave a wet!
>Salute
>Gesundheit!
>Skoal!
>Drunk as a lord, God stiffen you!
>Luck!

—and so on for 28 consecutive speeches. The action, especially in the Fifth Avenue scene, becomes increasingly frantic as well as unreal, as in the following episode in which Yank, the burly half-animal and half-human stoker, confronts the well-dressed men and women who have come out of church:

> YANK: . . . I'm steel and steam and smoke and de rest of it. It moves—speed—twenty-five stories up—and me at de top and bottom—movin'! Youse simps don't move. You're only dolls I winds up to see 'em spin . . . [*But as they seem neither to see nor hear him, he flies into a fury . . . He turns in a rage on the* Men, *bumping viciously into them but not jarring them the least bit. Rather it is he who recoils after each collision . . .*]

It would be possible to cite many situations and sequences of dialogue much more fantastic than any of O'Neill's. Such German dramatists as Hasenclever, Kaiser, Von Unruh, and Toller were particularly fertile between 1912 and 1925 in evoking violent states of mind, and German stage directors such as Leopold Jessner and Jürgen Fehling were past masters in the art of staging plays with expressive speed, exaggeration and distortion. And it is to be noted that much support for this type of theatre came from a general spread of expressionist views of art, especially in painting. Oskar Kokoschka, considered one of the most gifted of expressionist painters, was also the author of several inchoate plays—*Sphinx* and *Straw Man, The Hope of Women,* and *The Burning Bush*—during the period of 1909-1913 when he also exhibited some of his most daring paintings in Vienna. At the climax of expressionist fervor in Germany, the playwright Kasimir Edschmidt could boast, rather naively but not inaccurately, that "the expressionist believes in a reality which he himself creates against all other reality." [38] A major revolution in the theatre was implied in this statement; if one had taken the expressionists' claims at face value, it could have been assumed that the age of realism was, indeed, over.

[38] Thomas L. Dickinson, *The Theatre in a Changing Europe* (Holt, 1937), p. 23.

Ironically, however, it was expressionism, not realism, that became outmoded. Even in Central Europe the movement was virtually dead by 1925, while the realistic theatre which expressionism was supposed to have extinguished continued to press strong claims. Nor were these claims fundamentally challenged by any great successes in nonrealistic playwriting when the expressionists' efforts were supplemented by those of surrealists in France. Stage production, once greatly enriched by symbolist art, was further enriched (when not utterly disintegrated, of course) by expressionism and by such other experiments in stylization as surrealism and constructivism. But one by one the extremist antirealistic kinds of theatre went out of fashion—perhaps for the reason that they had come *into* fashion. (I believe it was Joyce who said once, "Futurism has no future.") The various revolts against realism in the theatre were fizzling out by 1930.

Nevertheless, one cannot rule out expressionism, both in the general sense of antirealistic dramaturgy and in the specific sense of an extravagantly subjective style, as the *second* radical phase of dramatic modernism.

Although theatrical fashions have come and gone, something indeed remained from each change in dramatic form and style of production. There remained not merely a collection of plays written more or less under the influence of some literary or theatrical program, but also a variety of theatrical practices. The ramps used so freely during the expressionist 1920's are in common use today. Skeletal settings will be found nowadays in productions of realistic plays like Elmer Rice's *Two on an Island,* allegorical ones like Robert Anderson's *All Summer Long,* and semi-expressionistic, semirealistic ones like *Death of a Salesman.* And it is almost everywhere evident that naturalistic clutter of detail on the stage has been displaced by tasteful selectivity, even in dominantly realistic productions. This "selective realism" can be called "imaginative realism" when it is at its freest, as in Elia Kazan's staging of Tennessee Williams' *Cat on a Hot Tin Roof* in 1955. No other term would do justice to room partitions and house walls suggested by wire-like verticals, imaginary doors that have to be "opened" and "closed" with conventional rehearsal movements, and a platform built out beyond the footlight area into the front rows of the theatre. And the imagination was further aroused—or taxed—when Mr. Kazan's actors, standing on this quasi-Elizabethan platform, looked intently into space as though gazing into a mirror hanging on the fourth wall and addressed their thoughts, *treated as both soliloquy and colloquy* at the same time, to characters standing behind them.

In various ways, then, playwriting and stage production were retheatricalized by the various schools of stylization that germinated after 1890. In scenic art, there were even instances of a return to painted scenery; with some modifications, indeed, so that the old perspective wing-and-drop settings have not returned, except in period revivals such as the Theatre Guild production of Molière's *The School for Husbands* in the 1930's. Changes in the training of actors and in styles of performances have also reflected various degrees of retheatricalization. If extreme deviations have become uncommon, modifications of realism continue to appear. Jacques Copeau, a leading figure of the reformation of the postnaturalistic theatre as early as 1913, summed up the minimal modifications in scenery about a quarter of a century later for the 1935 edition of the *Encyclopédie Française:* "Our designers . . . aim at impressions rather than descriptions. . . . They single out a part in order to indicate the whole; a tree instead of a forest, a pillar instead of a temple." [39] As for the art of acting, the most generally held view amounts to perhaps a little more than the statement from Vakhtangov, Stanislavsky's most talented if by no means submissive pupil, that "the actor's inner experience must be conveyed to the auditorium with the help of theatrical means." [40] Vakhtangov made this declaration in 1922; by then, indeed, there was no longer

[39] *Directing the Play,* ed. Toby Cole and Helen Krich Chinoy (Bobbs-Merrill Co., 1952), p. 149.
[40] *Ibid.,* p. 160.

any unmodified realism in the theatre without special reason.

The modern stage, however, has not reached any noticeable equilibrium: conflicts and confusions have abounded, an almost continuous state of crisis has existed in the theatre, and the search for new forms of dramatic art has gone on both with and without fanfare. At the midcentury, all theatrical movements with an antirealistic program, except epic theatre, appear to have exhausted themselves. But the impulse to retheatricalize the art that militant nineteenth-century realism had detheatricalized has continued to make itself felt.

A Note on Romanticism and Symbolism

It is well known, of course, that a particularly strong current of antirealistic modern theatre can be subsumed under the loose heading of "romanticism," just as it can be subsumed under the loose name of "poetic drama." Romanticism was revived in the theatre after 1890 (the revival has been labeled "neo-romanticism"), and the first masterpiece in this mode, *Cyrano de Bergerac*, has been one of the favorite plays of the modern stage. Romanticism has indeed continued to yield attractive and popular plays throughout the century: familiar examples in English are Maxwell Anderson's Elizabethan verse plays *Elizabeth the Queen, Mary of Scotland,* and *Anne of the Thousand Days* and Christopher Fry's verse play *The Lady's Not for Burning.* Neo-romanticism, however, did not by itself introduce any change of dramatic form that cannot be described as a reversion from Ibsen's realistic dramaturgy to the loose Elizabethan dramaturgy of the theatre of Schiller, Goethe, and Hugo. There has been, therefore, no need to discuss neo-romanticism in this essay.

127

Some confusion results, however, from the fact that the spirit of symbolist drama and stage production was undeniably romantic. Even in treating familiar scenes of life, symbolist dramatic art sought to evoke mystery and wonder and the pathos of romantic isolation. The romantic drama, however, is *explicit*, whereas the symbolist drama is suggestive. The former has the clear outlines of a well-defined action, whereas the latter has an elusive, penumbral content. Romantic drama is insistent—as insistent on the plot and the point of honor as *Hernani*—even when mysterious; symbolist drama is ambiguous—as ambiguous as Maeterlinck's *Interior*—even when its content is simple. The language of a contemporary romantic play such as *The Lady's Not for Burning* may indeed bear the implications of poetry and the innuendo of wit, but there can be no doubt that the author has spoken out and has permitted his characters to speak out even more explicitly than their situation warrants. The neo-romantic poet will undoubtedly employ metaphor in his verse or poetic prose, but in symbolist playwriting the play itself may actually become metaphor. Maeterlinck's *The Blind*, Andreyev's *The Black Maskers*, and Yeats' *A Full Moon in March* are examples of metaphorical drama. Inevitably, too, the symbolist movement was propitious to the return of allegory; thus, different degrees of allegorical abstractness have appeared in such plays as Hugo von Hofmannsthal's *Jedermann* (*Everyman*), Andreyev's *The Life of Man,* and Philip Barry's *Here Come the Clowns.* The treatment of environment is, as usual in the theatre, another test. Briefly, the romanticist *glamorizes* the environment or uses it for effects of horror, but, unlike the symbolist, he does not abstract it into a symbol of the soul of the play or the state of mind of a character.

Symbolism, then, produced more radical, as well as more modern, departures from realistic drama than did neo-romanticism. And symbolist scene design, as well as stage production, was also more radical than neo-romantic art. Vivid and glamorous settings for a bakeshop or a battlefield are the standard requirement for *Cyrano de Bergerac.* A symbolist design by Gordon

Craig is, by contrast, *abstract*. Craig exhorted the readers of his early essay *On the Art of the Theatre*: "Do not first look at Nature, but look in the play of the poet." But this was a very moderate statement for Craig and his disciples. They were more inclined to say "Look into the soul of the play." When Robert Edmond Jones designed the Arthur Hopkins production of *Macbeth* in 1921, he relied mainly on three arches set against a dark background. At one point, they hung over the stage and looked like three baleful masks glaring down at Macbeth. At another point in the play, the arches, which otherwise suggested the interior of a Scottish castle-fortress, were crazily tilted as a symbol of the upheaval in the soul of the characters and in the world they have unbalanced with murder and usurpation of power. And at the close of the tragedy the arches toppled over, signifying that Macbeth's destined end had come. Here, obviously, Jones, functioning as an ultra-symbolist designer in this celebrated production, had no intention of providing an objective environment. Here "setting" became "symbol."

After the appearance of symbolist theatre in the 1890's, it became customary for the various antirealistic movements to take liberties with environment that even the romanticists of the "storm and stress" period had not taken; a climax in the arbitrary fragmentation and phantasmagoric reassembling of environmental detail was reached by the expressionists. Henceforth no school of stylization failed to substitute some degree of abstraction for pictorial realism—not excluding the school of epic realism which gave great ideological importance to environmentalism.

It was the symbolist movement, not neo-romanticism, moreover, that made *metaphor* a cornerstone of antirealistic dramaturgy. Expressionist drama and theatre were distinctly metaphorical; and even the epic realists, who had no use for symbolist and expressionist subjectivity, have tended to present their dramatic action as a partly symbolic epitome of a social situation or a problem in social action. Brecht's parables *The Caucasian Circle of Chalk* and *The Good Woman of Setzuan* and the Piscator version of *An American Tragedy* illustrate the important role of metaphor. In epic-styled stage productions, besides, symbolic scenic elements have appeared frequently, although without the veils of Maeterlinckian soul-fetishism.

Because symbols have been employed not only by symbolist playwrights, but even by the classic realist (in such plays as *The Wild Duck, Rosmersholm, The Master Builder, John Gabriel Borkman, The Sea-Gull, The Cherry Orchard, Golden Boy,* and *All My Sons*), it is ill-advised indeed to lump all kinds of symbolization together. Mordecai Gorelik's statement that metaphors are to be judged qualitatively is highly important. There is a significant difference "between a symbol which is packed with observation and experience, and one which is large and 'simple' only because it is pretentious and lacking in observation and experience." [1]

[1] *New Theatres for Old* (New York: Samuel French, 1940), p. 263.

3

Theatricalism and Crisis

*Let it be remembered by all who care for
the art of the theatre: the play is a show,
but only in the sense that it is not real
life but a performance enacted on the stage
before an audience.*—ALEXANDER BAKSHY,
The Theatre Unbound

AN ACCOMMODATION BETWEEN THE REALISTIC AND ANTIREALISTIC modes of theatre has long been apparent in playwriting and play production. Often it has been made as a matter of routine practice, and sometimes it has been the unique achievement of talented artists. Not only do we now accept the *coexistence* of different kinds of drama and stage production, but we observe with equanimity the erosion of distinctions once strongly insisted upon by the proponents of various theatrical movements.

The distinctions have lost their sharpness both in playwriting and in critical jargon. Indeed, the labels "symbolism," "surrealism," and "expressionism" no longer possess much significance for most contemporary plays and performances. This is true of even those plays in which it is possible to detect symbolism (for example, Williams' *Summer and Smoke*) or surrealism (Saroyan's *Sweeney in the Trees*), or expressionism (*Death of a Salesman*). It would be as difficult as it would be useless to find exact labels

133

for such plays as Saroyan's *My Heart's in the Highlands* and *The Time of Your Life*, Giraudoux' *The Madwoman of Chaillot*, and the Anouilh-Fry comedy *Ring 'Round the Moon*. So, with commendable discretion, the authors are apt to be content with calling such dramas "poetic plays," "fantasies," or "improvisations." The Anouilh-Fry piece was subtitled a "charade," and Anouilh called his *Thieves' Carnival* (*Le Bal des voleurs*, 1932) a *comédie-ballet*.

William Saroyan was certainly most thorough, if not necessarily most perceptive, in describing a mode of free dramatic creativity when he described his *Sweeney in the Trees* as "a play, a dream, a poem, a travesty, a fable, a symphony, a parable, a comedy, a tragedy, a farce, a vaudeville, a song and dance, a statement on money, a report on life, an essay on art and religion, a theatrical entertainment, a circus, anything you like, whatever you please." [1] With few emendations one could apply some of these descriptions to Giraudoux' *Intermezzo* and *The Madwoman of Chaillot*, Wilder's *The Skin of Our Teeth*, and other pieces by Saroyan, such as *My Heart's in the Highlands* and *The Time of Your Life*. Nor are we greatly disturbed when these works are, as Wolcott Gibbs said of *The Time of Your Life*, "occasionally balanced on the thin edge of absurdity." We do not require of such plays the unimpeachable consistency of a drama by Ibsen or Sophocles.

There have also been with us for many decades those more or less unified plays in which contrasting, perhaps theoretically incompatible, modes of drama coexist or intermingle. Even in sociological drama, such as Paul Osborn's dramatization of the Marquand novel *Point of No Return*, the main character's past and present may interweave quite freely. An early example of presenting the same situation both objectively and subjectively was provided by Gerhart Hauptmann in *The Assumption of Hannele* (*Hanneles Himmelfahrt*, 1893). The playwright combined an appallingly naturalistic picture of a child's death in the workhouse with the fairy-tale world of her delirium. The demarcation

[1] *The Beautiful People, Sweeney in the Trees*, and *Across the Board on Tomorrow Morning* (Harcourt, Brace, 1941), p. 106.

between objective reality and fantasy was clearly maintained while the coexistence of the two dramatic modes was justified by the fact that the dying girl's delirium is as "true" as any other element in the play.

Symbolic figures and objects were used in the realistic drama almost from the beginning of the modern theatre, so that it was almost routine procedure for Arthur Miller to use a stunted backyard tree to symbolize the family catastrophe of *All My Sons* in 1947. We may cite *The Wild Duck* and *The Sea-Gull* as early examples of such "natural" use of symbols. The symbolism of the sea gull is particularly striking in its application to Chekhov's heroine, Nina, who is seduced by the middle-aged novelist Trigorin. Trigorin himself implants awareness of the symbol in the playgoer's mind as well as Nina's. The sight of a dead gull shot down near the lake by the frustrated young man Konstantin gives Trigorin an idea for a story about a country girl like Nina who has lived in freedom until one day a man sees her and, being momentarily unoccupied, "destroys her like the sea-gull there." David Magarshack aptly describes the symbolism as "a poetic way of expressing the very common fact of life, namely, the destruction of beauty by people who do not see it and are not aware of the terrible crime they commit." [2] Konstantin kills the bird because he wants to frighten Nina with a threat of suicide, and Nina's lover Trigorin wantonly seduces her because of middle-aged vanity. Magarshack's "the very common fact of life" is the key phrase here: the realist's symbol originates in objective fact and is definite, whereas the symbolists' symbol is by its very nature indeterminate.

Today we do not hesitate to mingle realistic and symbolic styles. A noteworthy recent example was the 1948 Broadway production of *Death of a Salesman,* with its skeletal setting against a background of apartment houses towering over Willy Loman's one-family home. The contrast was clearly designed to serve as a symbol of the "little man's precariously sustained

[2] *Chekhov the Dramatist* (New York: Auverne Publishers, 1952.)

individualism," and there were other details of poetic treatment that were worth noticing—the sudden lyrical transfiguration of the setting when leaves in rich profusion were projected on a screen, for instance, and the strongly contrasting use of the starkly neutral forestage for Willy's burial at the end.

Another notable example was the 1952 New York production of *Desire Under the Elms*, staged by Harold Clurman and designed by Mordecai Gorelik. Neither Clurman nor Gorelik had previously made consistent use of antirealistic stylization; they had been associated with Broadway's most developed realistic producing enterprise, the Group Theatre, during the 1930's. Nevertheless, they did not hesitate to stage O'Neill's farm tragedy in a formally designed setting, essentially a screen with platforms, framed by a cut-out drop of two elms forming an arch. Remembering that Mr. Gorelik was the designer of such plays as Odets' *Awake and Sing!* and *Golden Boy*, we can follow his comments on his scenic treatment of *Desire under the Elms* with special interest:

> The designer has chosen as his dominant theme the idea of "under the elms," as expressed by the silhouette of a house under the silhouettes of two great trees. While the design has a superficial air of naturalism, it is in fact basically theatricalist in style. The silhouette of the house is established by means of a roof-line and chimney, plus the eaves and porch; its interior is influenced by cubism in the relationship of the rooms and by constructivism in the partly curved cross-sectioning of the floors. In general, the "house" is merely an elaborate screen enclosing a lower and an upper ledge. . . .
>
> The trees are a cut-out drop, treated as a semi-silhouette. The drop is bordered [drawn on top from the "tree" right to the "tree" left of the "house"] by a curved line which emphasizes its frank theatricalism.[3]

Productions such as these show a pragmatic fusion of realistic and theatrical elements according to the requirements of a

[3] John Gassner, *Producing the Play* (New York: The Dryden Press, 1953), pp. 353-354.

play, or according to the stage director's and designer's inter-
pretation. It is obvious from their handling of *Desire Under the
Elms* that Clurman and Gorelik did not consider O'Neill's play
significant as either sociology or genre painting, agreeing in this
respect with the author himself, who had always disavowed naturalism in spite of his penchant for naturalistic situations. It was
the fateful love and hatred, the tragic absolutes, that they found
valuable in *Desire Under the Elms* and that they elected to
represent in the formalistically designed stage setting. No mystique of art enters into the practices described here. Practical artists arrive at craft-judgments; they make decisions based on their
analysis of the play and then proceed to carry them out, hoping
for the best results. Called upon to subscribe to any single principle of creation, they would be likely to agree with Anatole
France's declaration, "There are no other rules than usage, taste,
and passions, our virtues and our vices, all our weaknesses, all
our forces." [4]

One may wonder, indeed, why there has been (since 1940,
let us say) any quarrel over stylization in dramatic art.
Conflict between realism and theatricalization has become
largely theoretical, if not indeed illusory. If realists still look
askance at tub-thumping for theatricalized drama, it is only because they suspect that there is charlatanry, cultural decadence,
or escapism in the opposite camp. They cling to some degree of
literalness or actualism out of a resolve to defend the theatre as
an instrument of the modern rationalistic and scientific mind or
liberal spirit. They can point, as a justification of their wariness,
to the theological or traditionalist character of the revival of
poetic drama in England under T. S. Eliot, the cultivation of a
theatre for the élite by Yeats in Dublin, and the *snobisme,* the
social ambiguity, and the preciosity of other departures from
realism. When the realist encounters work as bizarre as

[4] *French Folly in Maxims,* ed. Henry Pène Du Bois (New York,
1894), p. 111.

BRITISH FORMALISM   A *formalistic, modified constructivist, so-called podium setting was used by Terence Gray for his Cambridge Festival Theatre production of* Antigone. *This theatre, which opened in 1926 and closed in 1933, was the most advanced stage organization in England. It was resolutely antirealistic under the directorship of Gray, who dismissed realistic stage production as "the old game of illusion and glamour and all the rest of nineteenth century hocus pocus and bamboozle." (See Norman Marshall's* The Other Theatre, *London, 1948.) The stage, in Gray's view, should be "a raised platform designed to give the greatest mutual relations of the actors playing their parts in each play, and accordingly for each play there should be a specially designed raised platform, the levels and angles of which fulfil a function in emphasising the dramatic platform" (p. 54). Gray's productions required expert lighting, and his associate Hedley Briggs became England's most important lighting specialist.*

PICTORIAL THEATRICALISM   *The picturesque theatricalism cultivated for simplicity is exemplified by the "Jesus at the Tomb of Lazarus" scene from* Le Mystère de la passion des Théophiliens, *an adaptation of medieval drama by Gustave Cohen, first produced at Rouen, then at Brussels, and then at Paris in 1950. There was a cultivated naiveté in the toylike scenery, partly constructed (in the foreground) and partly painted on a drop in the background. In such theatricalist stage productions it was, naturally, not essential to avoid painted scenery; the theatrical character of the performances actually invited the use of painted scenery in combination with constructions.*

AMATEUR THEATRICALISM *The "animated house" was used in Fordham University Theatre's playful production of William Saroyan's* Sam Ego's House, *designed and directed in 1953 by William Riva for arena-stage presentation. Here theatricalism was obviously given full sway.* Courtesy of Edgar Kloten of the Fordham University Theatre. Photograph: Du Rona.

POETIC EXPRESSION AND SYMBOLISM *The Group Theatre production of William Saroyan's* My Heart's in the Highlands *used non-realistic scenery which some observers loosely called surrealistic. Robert Lewis, who staged the play in 1939, wrote in John Gassner's* Producing the Play *(p. 297): "In addition to the usual work on the psychological meaning and development of the performance, it was necessary . . . to find the poetic expression of that content. . . . For example, at one point the old man with the trumpet plays a song for the villagers and they give him food. The feeling I had about this moment was: the people are nourished by art. The image that came to my mind was:* a plant flowering as it is watered." *Mr. Lewis built up a picture with his actors, as seen in the photograph. This, together with the associated color, stage movement, lighting, and music, constitutes what Mr. Lewis calls "theatre poetry," a translation of Cocteau's* poésie de théâtre. Photo: Alfred Valente. Courtesy of The Group Theatre.

Picasso's surrealistic *Desire Trapped by the Tail,* as formalized and rigidly conventionalized as Yeats's *Half-Moon in March,* as involved and introverted as Cummings' *him* and Saroyan's *Jim Dandy,* or, for that matter, as mystifyingly moralistic as Eliot's *The Family Reunion,* he is tempted to damn a good deal of antirealistic stylization as perversity and pretension.

Crisis in the Contemporary Theatre

There has been a general crisis in the theatre, both in America and abroad, that has been more or less distinct from economic and political difficulties. The problem is essentially one of inner disharmony. There has been too much dismal division in the theatre between the humdrum and the showy, between the commonplaceness of realism and the arid "artiness" of antirealism.

The conflicting claims of realism and theatre have seldom been creatively solved in the theatre of recent years. It has been rare for an acting company to work with freshness and a secure sense of style on both the realistic and nonrealistic levels of artistry. By and large, the theatre has been divided between commercial-professional sterility and noncommercial or commercial-experimental futility; and surely an important reason is that theatricalism has been so often misused or used only frivolously, as a rule, when used well. One may, in truth, conclude that the solution of the esthetic crisis depends on our knowing when and how to combine the resources of realistic and theatricalist artistry. And unfortunately the theatre's usual muddle and opportunism are not conducive to the *knowing* of anything. Normally, the commercial theatre just feels its way and hopes for the best, and the academic and community theatres "think out" a production and then are forced to content themselves with inescapable compromises.

We know what realistic technique is in the fields of playwriting, acting, directing, scenic design, lighting, and costuming.

But do we actually know today what we want from the realism of art? It would be patently absurd to assert that *Hamlet* and *The Trojan Women* are deficient in realism because Shakespeare, writing for his platform stage, and Euripides, writing for the hillside theatre of Dionysus, did not employ realistic techniques of the kind developed in the late nineteenth century. They never heard of the fourth-wall convention, which could not at any rate have been maintained on the Elizabethan and Attic stages, but it would be ridiculous not to number these and other poet-playwrights among the theatre's great realists.

We must realize, then, that realism cannot be created by technique alone. Realism was not merely a technique in the work of Strindberg, Shaw, or Chekhov. The idea of realistic theatre has been badly shaken, has been often and seriously called in question, because the "idea" has been confused with technique. Indeed, in many instances, only the technique has been left to realism, while the essence has been allowed to evaporate. This has been the case, no doubt, for reasons that range from indifference to cowardice, from complacency to honest uncertainty. In most latter-day plays and productions, for example, enviroment, although featured in the settings and omnipresent in the small talk of the characters, has borne no relation to the spine of the drama: we are offered realistic form without realistic substance. Such realism, as I have stressed before, is not at all essential to dramatic art and is certainly not indispensable to modern theatre.

Conversely, we must realize, as some of the best artists of the modern theatre have done, that the cause of a true realism has been well served by some degree of stylization. An actual theatricalization of the substance and meaning of the play may reveal more, rather than less, to the playgoer. Numerous writers of problem plays from Dumas *fils* grinding out *La Question d'argent* (*A Question of Money*) on behalf of business honesty in 1857 to, shall we say, Howard Lindsay and Russel Crouse writing *The Prescott Proposals* on behalf of amity at the United Nations in

1953, have dealt with facts, or have pretended to deal with them. But more, rather than less, so did Toller, Georg Kaiser, O'Casey and Jean Giraudoux make vivid and strong use of the life of their times in such nonrealistic pieces as *Man and the Masses, From Morn to Midnight, The Silver Tassie,* and *The Madwoman of Chaillot.* Surely, too, among stage directors, Jessner and Piscator in Germany, Meyerhold and Tairov in Russia, and Elia Kazan in America have sometimes achieved more, rather than less, relatedness when they have resorted to theatricalist stylization.

Why, then, is our theatre not consistently following the dual course of enriching realism with imagination and enriching theatricalism with realism in such degree that the clamor for "new forms" will at last end after some sixty or seventy years? No other period of theatrical history has had so many and so varied stylistic experiments, and none has professed so thorough a devotion to the idea of freedom in theatrical art, as the period from the publication of Hugo's preface to *Cromwell* to the present. Why have the realistic drama and theatre, without radical modifications, remained dominant in spite of the exertions of extremely talented would-be stylizers, theatricalizers, and ultramodernizers? Why has not any particular "modernist" mode—that is, nonrealistic mode—supplanted the "modern"—that is, realistic—one?

Perhaps the most comprehensive answer is that the nonrealistic modes of theatre, often so fascinating in transmutations from symbolism to surrealism, failed to crystallize into an adequate and reliable dramatic form. Realistic dramatic art, whatever its limitations, has been to modern theatre what Shakespearean dramaturgy was to the Elizabethan period and Sophoclean dramaturgy to the Periclean Age. That is the meaning of my previously elaborated argument that realism has been a modern kind of classicism. The nonrealistic modes of theatre fall more or less under the one category of *theatricalism.* But theatricalism has not yet acquired any classical configurations because it has not found a consistent form. The idea of theatricalist art has been with us throughout the century, but its various formal and stylistic manifestations have been tentative, elusive, or fractured—as many an expressionist play, for example, has been fractured. Of theatricalism it may be said that "The One remains, the many change and pass." Its "idea" persists and is, in my opinion, essentially sound, but its forms have been transitory.

Theatricalism: *Pro* and *Con*

Perhaps we shall understand the situation better if we attempt to understand the general character of theatricalism. The fundamental premise of realism is the Aristotelian one that drama is an imitation of an action; realists held, therefore, that the most desirable theatre is that in which imitation is the closest. The fundamental premise of theatricalism is that theatre is not imitation in the narrow sense, which Aristotle himself never could have held, since the Greek drama upon which he based conclusions in his *Poetics* was not realistically imitative.[5] For the theatricalist, the object of action and of all other "imitative" elements is not imitation but *creativeness*, and a special kind

[5] S. H. Butcher, in *Aristotle's Theory of Poetry and Fine Art* (4th ed., Dover Publications, 1951), argues well that "imitation" is a *creative act:* "It is the expression of the concrete thing under an image which answers to its true idea." To reproduce the universal "in a simple and sensuous form is not to reflect a reality already familiar through sense perceptions" (p. 154). It is "rivalry of nature." Certainly esthetic semblance could not have meant slavish imitation for Aristotle, who wrote that the author "ought to prefer probable impossibilities to possible improbabilities" (p. 128). Nevertheless, Aristotle was apparently inclined to place reliance on "imitation" somewhat in our ordinary sense of the term. Art, for Aristotle, involves sensuous perception rather than symbolization. "A work of art," Butcher declares (p. 124), "is a likeness ($\delta\mu o\iota\omega\mu\alpha$), and not a symbolic representation of it." Symbolists and other antirealists, then, could draw even less comfort from Aristotle than literal realists.

of creativeness at that. The realists would agree, of course, as to the value of creativeness. But the theatricalist goes one step further, and that step is the truly decisive one for the theory and practice of pure theatricalism. He maintains that there is never any sense in pretending that one is not in the theatre; that no amount of make-believe is reality itself; that in short, theatre is the medium of dramatic art, and effectiveness in art consists in *using* the medium rather than concealing it. In the theatricalist view, concealment of the medium is tantamount to the nullification of art. Therefore, the theatricalist feels that plays should be written and staged in such a manner that there will be no pretense that what is happening on the stage is real. The object of writing and performing for the medium is to create theatre— theatrical actions, characterizations, and images—and nothing else. The object of going to a "show" is nothing else than seeing or experiencing a show, not reality. The appropriate reply to theatricalist extremism is no doubt this: The realists have maintained that the theatrical medium should be made as unobtrusive as possible in order to establish the illusion of reality. The anti-theatricalist can argue that it is surely unnecessary to expose all the strings of a piano in order to play the instrument, and that only infants would need to see the inside wiring in order to be convinced that the instrument is being played.

Even in so distinguished a play as *The Skin of Our Teeth* the intrusion of self-conscious theatricality somewhat blunts the edge of comedy and causes the essential action to mark time. Now and then the play's "playfulness" becomes altogether too arch. But one can go further in criticizing Wilder's theatricality and maintain that the intrusion of "theatre" weakens the power of the play, especially in the last act, which occurs immediately after a world-devastating war. If the human race has survived only by the skin of its teeth, one is tempted to ask, what is the author so cheerful about? In the first and second acts, the audience could be reminded that man has been the same throughout history in his aspirations and contradictions. The humor attendant upon the theatrical blending of life in suburban New Jersey with life during the Ice Age, or the linking of the legend of Noah with an Atlantic City convention, was in accord with the author's comment on the human race. But in the third act, which deals with contemporary disaster, the theatricalism is not only inappropriate because it is played in the wrong key and is perhaps insufficiently climactic for a dramatic masterpiece, but it is evasive as well. The author has apparently nothing to say that he hasn't already told us twice. So he repeats himself again, quotes the right authors, who give us the right schoolbook assurances in a pageant-like procession of the show's backstage personnel; and he reminds us for the third time that *The Skin of Our Teeth* is just a show. Ibsen and Shaw would have scorned to beg off so lightly. Ibsen would have reserved the full power of his meaning for the showdown—what Shaw would have called the element of "discussion" in the play. And if Shaw and Ibsen had had no answer, they would have said so, as Shaw did so eloquently in *Too True To Be Good,* thus turning the very sense of failure into an affirmative passion.

Nevertheless, *The Skin of Our Teeth* is perhaps the best out-and-out theatricalist work of the American theatre.[6] The dangers of theatricalist exploitation of theatre are more striking in such exercises in the construction of the play-within-a-play as Maxwell Anderson's *Joan of Lorraine* and Pirandello's *Tonight We Improvise.* To perceive these dangers we need only compare the first-mentioned with *Saint Joan,* in which Shaw refrains from turning theatricalist somersaults until the epilogue.[7] We could also compare *Tonight We Improvise* with Pirandello's *Six Characters in Search of an Author,* in which the intensity of life routs the artifice of theatre; the reverse is true in *Tonight We Impro-*

[6] Except for Cummings' too esoteric, dadaist-surrealist play *him,* which for all its muddle has a quality of imagination and power of expression absent in many better-built plays.
[7] And even in this fantasy Shaw speaks his mind manfully through the action and Joan's words instead of coyly playing at play-making.

vise, in which the author's theatricality tends to destroy the life of the play.

In stage production, of course, theatricalization has prevailed from time immemorial. The range of theatricalism has been endless. Its manifestations as vaudeville, burlesque, clowning, juggling, and miming have been inexhaustibly delightful. True satire and pathos have come within the orbit of the candidly theatrical artistry for which Max Pallenberg in Germany, Jean-Louis Barrault in France, Beatrice Lillie in England, and Chaplin in America have become celebrated. Also, some theatricalist performers have specialized in more restrained, "serious" modes, as have Cornelia Otis Skinner and Angna Enters and the superbly dramatic Ruth Draper. Others have relied upon the dance, as have Martha Graham and Paul Draper and many others who have performed in a variety of distinctive styles; still others are vocal and instrumental musicians. To rule these and many other virtuosi out of even the most serious discussion of dramatic art is to rule the theatre out of it.

There is no self-consciousness, however, in the theatricality of such performers. In some *avant-garde* endeavors, on the contrary, there appears a disconcerting self-consciousness about theatricality. In one otherwise absorbing off-Broadway production, Genet's *The Maids,* the stage-action consisted of two servant girls pretending that they were mistress and maid respectively. Although both characters were nearly hysterical with snarling and shouting at each other, the director apparently saw fit to remind the public that it was in the theatre by allowing the production's stage manager and an actress waiting for her cues to be visible at one side of the stage. In a Theatre Union production of Brecht's *Mother* in the 1930's, much of the lighting equipment was exposed to the full view of the audience. Although justified by epic-theatre principles and by the anti-illusionist alienation-effect objective, this theatricalist reminder was, from a common-sense view, superfluous. The choral marching and chanting of the actors in this production were also sufficient to inform the audience that the greasepaint of theatre had been laid on with a trowel. In a New York ANTA production of Brecht's *Galileo,* the chief actor, Charles Laughton, stripped to the waist and then costumed himself publicly. The present writer was not alone in considering this expedient neither necessary nor edifying.

Unredundant theatricalist productions are also encountered, of course; these are usually the ones in which the theatricalism is naturally motivated, easily and gaily justified. An example is the delightful Gaston Baty production in 1938 of *Le Chapeau de paille d'Italie* which the present writer saw revived at the Comédie Française in 1950. Labiche's extravagant comedy was appropriately staged as a sort of comic ballet, as an interminable wedding march, and an irrepressible romp across the stage. There could be no question here of awkwardly calling attention to the theatricality of the play and the production.[8]

A theatre freed from all pretense of reproducing reality has been the modern theatricalist ideal. To some theatricalists, even the symbolists of the Craig-Appia school have been vain tricksters. They hold that dramatic action is not an experience offered as a slice of real or imaginary life, but *histrionic reality.* Performance should be openly *histrionic.* In the pure theatricalist style, as explained by its most ardent propagandist, Alexander Bakshy, the performance will be solely "a happening in that real world which is the gathering of actors and spectators come together, the first to practice, and the second to watch, the act of undisguised and glorying make-believe." Love and hatred will be "stage love" and "stage hatred" (the opposite of the love and hatred of Stanislavsky-trained actors), and character will be "stage character." As for the play itself, Bakshy explains:

[8] Tastefulness, of course, cannot be assured by any "production idea" alone. It is possible to overproduce this type of play and to be overstrenuous in directing it, as was Orson Welles, according to some opinions, in staging the play for the Federal Theatre under the title of *Horse Eats Hat.*

The staginess of the play will mean an exhibition of life in terms of the theatre. . . . Nor will the playwright . . . be bound by considerations of realistic, psychological, or some supernatural truth. His aim will be dramatic truth, and in bodying it forth on the stage, he will be free to treat his material—the elements of human character and action—in any fashion he may choose so long as his convention is made intelligible, is theatrical in its nature, and lays no claim to be anything but a method of presentation.[9]

And the ideal stage of theatricalism will, of course, be "a stage and nothing but a stage . . . serving as a pedestal on which the plastic structure of the dramatic show is raised by the actors." It must be a stage freed from the proscenium arch, no longer a picture-frame stage or a peephole stage, but a platform frankly intended for the actor's use. Scenery on such a stage is not pictorial except insofar as the actor's action and dialogue require environmental details; and even these can be theatricalized by the production.

The relation of the spectator to such a theatrical production can be open and independent, says Bakshy, as the spectator knows that he is not supposed to lose himself in an illusion or to succumb to some spell. He is enabled to retain his freedom as an observer; he is treated as the detached critical spectator for whom the show is being put on rather than as a victim of an illusionist's trickery. (The specialist in "illusionism" may be a naturalist who is intent on conjuring up a real environment for the spectator, or a symbolist who tries to make the spectator lose himself in an imaginary world and in a mystical experience.) So much for the generalized aim of the theatricalists!

It must be observed, however, that the theatricalist idea of theatre has been carried out in actual productions in various ways and to various degrees. The question of whether it is, has been, or could be a satisfactory alternative to critical realism in

[9] Alexander Bakshy, *The Theatre Unbound* (London: Cecil Palmer, 1923), p. 18. The essay from which I quote was first published in 1921.

the modern theatre can be answered only in relation to kinds and degrees of achievement. Concerning this question, the following summary conclusions are offered as a basis for further investigation and assessment.

1. Theatricalism ruled the stage in classical times, in the age of Shakespeare, and in the age of Molière, although illusionistic scenic elements provided the illusion of place and although actors surely provided more or less convincing characterizations instead of merely declaiming poetry and prose.[10] In our century, however, theatricalism has commanded the stage consistently and successfully only in the music hall, in vaudeville, and in musical comedies and plays. Theatricalism is indeed the only style that has ever been possible for these forms of entertainment, as well as for opera. Even as realistic a play as Elmer Rice's *Street Scene* had to become a thoroughly theatrical "show," rather than a social document, when turned into a "music-drama" with a score by Kurt Weill.

In so far as theatricalist stylization has improved the composition and staging of musical shows, giving us an *Oklahoma!* instead of *The Student Prince,* the results should satisfy everyone. And insofar as a critical spirit, first brought into modern theatre by Ibsen and his fellow iconoclasts, has found expression in such musical pieces as *The Three-Penny Opera* and *Finian's Rainbow,* theatricalism has proved itself capable of expressing the modern age rather than merely entertaining it. But, obviously, there is nothing remarkable in the success of theatricalism in the musical theatre, which realism has never dominated and cannot be expected to dominate. Obviously, too, plays written for the nonrealistic theatres of the past lend themselves rather well to especially stylized staging. Hence, to deter-

---

[10] The infiltration of scenic illusionism into the premodern, pre-realistic theatres is vividly recounted by Lee Simonson in *The Stage Is Set* (Harcourt, Brace, 1932); see especially Part II, significantly entitled "Myths of Lost Purity."

mine the possibilities of theatricalism for the modern stage we must examine its effectiveness in areas other than musical entertainments and classic revivals.

2. Some degree of theatricalism has been an element in all efforts to depart from realistic playwriting and staging since 1890. Thus, the symbolists, who have been designated earlier as illusionists, theatricalized their presentations to the degree that they transformed experience into symbolic atmosphere or reverie. And the expressionists, who also supported an illusionism of sorts in making their picture of the world conform to the subjective state of some character (or of the author), theatricalized phenomena by "expressively" distorting them. These modernists were not pure or absolute theatricalists. Their motives were essentially extratheatrical. But they did liberate the stage and the drama from humdrum imitations of the humdrum, and they did provide theatricalized pictures and expressions of the individual and the world.

If the symbolists who followed Maeterlinck or Craig failed to establish symbolist drama as *the* modern form of drama and a symbolist style of staging as *the* modern style of theatre, one reason is that it is against the nature of the theatre to exist in a mist and to thrive on vagueness. Drama and theatre are among the most definite of all the arts. It is also against the nature of the drama and theatre to be stationary and meditative. Maeterlinck himself discovered this, and therefore abandoned his theory of static drama. Then, left without a form of drama to support his symbolist idea of theatre, he partially abandoned the idea itself. Writing to the late Barrett H. Clark, he said: "You must not attach too great importance to the expression "Static"; it was an invention, a theory of my youth, worth what most literary theories are worth—that is, almost nothing." [11] And if the expression-

---

[11] Barrett H. Clark, *A Study of Modern Drama* (Appleton-Century, 1938), p. 163. In this letter, indeed, Maeterlinck goes much further; he declares: "Whether a play be static or dynamic, *symbolistic* or *realistic,* is of little consequence." Strange words from the bellwether, program-maker and patron saint of dramatic symbolism. But, then, they were written about 1925, after the virtual

ist playwrights and stage directors failed to establish expressionism as *the* twentieth-century style, one compelling reason is that
although the theatre can take note of a disturbed area of experience, it cannot thrive in it.

Expressionism could *supplement* realism but could not take
its place in the modern theatre. Indeed, expressionism still serves
this supplementary purpose in certain plays, *Death of a Salesman* being a good example. We may well ask ourselves, however, whether *Death of a Salesman* would have been so tre-
mendously effective if it had been thoroughly expressionistic.

Theatricalism, finally, has been freely employed by Piscator,
Brecht, and other epic realists. But they have theatricalized
playwriting and stage production for other than purely theatricalist purposes. They have destroyed the fourth-wall convention in order to demonstrate ideas and ideologies.

3. We have also had in twentieth-century theatre a type of
theatricalist endeavor that has not been associated with some
other, specialized, program and technique such as expressionism
or epic realism. This kind of theatre represents a disposition to
favor the concept of theatre as *an end in itself;* and we may
therefore call it simply "pure theatricalism." To suggest its range
we may refer to four key figures who had formulated their general theories and put them into practice more or less independ-
ently by 1914. These men are Alexander Tairov, Vsevolod Meyerhold, Eugene Vakhtangov, and Jacques Copeau; their work is
now well known to students of theatrical history.

Tairov founded his Kamerny ("chamber") Theatre in Moscow in 1914 to express his opposition to Stanislavsky's realistic
methods at the Moscow Art Theatre. Tairov's objective was to
retheatricalize the stage by favoring such nonrealistic plays as
Oscar Wilde's *Salome,* which became one of the outstanding

---

disappearance of specifically symbolist drama—more than a quarter of a century after the writing of *The Intruder, Interior,* and
The Blind, Maeterlinck's three exemplary "static" dramas.

early productions of the Kamerny Theatre. Tairov favored abstract rather than realistic scenic design, and he developed stylized gestures and movements for his actors almost as though he were a ballet-master. As Norris Houghton has declared, "Stanislavski had told his actor to forget that he was on the stage; Tairov told his actor always to remember that he was on the stage." [12] Tairov's approach was one of sophisticated cosmopolitanism and estheticism. When he found it necessary to discard this attitude after the Russian Revolution of 1917, he moderated his absolute or autonomous theatricality and presented plays with realistic subject matter that lent themselves to moderate stylization. He succeeded especially with Eugene O'Neill's plays *All God's Chillun Got Wings* and *Desire Under the Elms.* Tairov's career was, however, especially noteworthy for his efforts to use the related art of the dance as a means of making the theatre theatrical.

Meyerhold left Stanislavsky before World War I in search of a satisfactory nonrealistic convention or style. His quest led him from one experiment to another, ensured him a brilliant career for about two decades, and ended when political reverses lost him his position in 1937; he disappeared sometime after, presumably in one of the Communist purges. Although he came to be considered a spokesman for social revolution after the fall of the Russian monarchy in 1917, his primary interests in the theatre were artistic. Norris Houghton declared, without entertaining derogatory intentions, that "this champion of proletarian art" was "paradoxically enough, a complete aristocrat." [13]

Meyerhold carried his pursuit of new dramatic modes to its most sensational point by developing constructivistic scenery (that is, scenery consisting of ramps, steps, and slides that assured dynamic stage action but established environment only incidentally, if at all) and by evolving a dynamic style of acting that was free from Stanislavskian subjectivity or emotional depth. But "constructivism" was only one phase of the career of

[12] *Moscow Rehearsals* (Harcourt, Brace, 1936), p. 110.
[13] *Ibid.*, p. 96.

a creative director who strove to theatricalize the theatre throughout his career. The audience at a typical Meyerhold performance was never allowed to forget that it was in the theatre. By consciously associating itself with the actors in a game of make-believe, often satiric, the public was expected to participate in the making of theatre instead of submitting passively to the illusion created by the realistic convention. By eliminating the proscenium and removing the front curtain, as well as by flooding the auditorium with light, Meyerhold banished the picture-frame stage from his theatres and bridged the space between the actors and the spectators. (See pp. 192-198.)

A third leader of theatricalist stylization, Eugene Vakhtangov (1883-1922), Stanislavsky's favorite and regrettably short-lived protégé, never completely broke off relations with the Moscow Art Theatre. In comparison with Tairov and Meyerhold, he was a moderate. Declaring that "feeling is the same in theatre and life, but the means and methods of presenting them are different," he endeavored to reconcile the theatrical aims of Stanislavsky and Meyerhold; that is, he tried to reconcile the search for *reality* with the search for *form,* the humanist's interest in realism with the esthete's interest in art for art's sake. Vakhtangov, too, disregarded the fourth-wall convention. He actually ridiculed it in his celebrated 1921 production of *Princess Turandot* when he had the stagehands, who had been shifting scenery in sight of the audience, perform ballets burlesquing the romantic action of Carlo Gozzi's eighteenth-century play. He also had the actors, wearing evening dress, line up on the stage at the beginning of the performance and introduce themselves, after which they costumed themselves in full view of the audience. But Vakhtangov strove for spontaneity and naturalness in acting, and wanted the actor to be thoroughly human, not a robot. He objected, for instance, to Meyerhold's sacrificing of individuality in characterization, and to the assumption that it was impossible to have both emotional truth *and* theatrical reality. But unlike the Stanislav-

"LIVING NEWSPAPER" THEATRICALISM This scene from the "living newspaper" Power, produced by the Federal Theatre in New York in 1937, directed by Brett Warren and with settings by Howard Bay, presents a Supreme Court hearing of the arguments on TVA. The judges of the Court were represented by nine masks to which the characters addressed themselves without evoking any recognition or response. Nonillusionistic, theatricalized staging was properly employed for this documentary, "epic" form of drama, which blended journalism and presentational theatre. Hallie Flanagan Davis, director of the Federal Theatre, described this type of drama in her noteworthy history of this theatre (Arena, New York, 1940, p. 70) as "factual and formal, musical and acrobatic, abstract and concrete, visual and aural, psychological, economic, and social." She noted that the form was "as American as Walt Disney, the March of Dimes, and the Congressional Record," yet also derivative in some of its features from Aristophanes, the commedia dell' arte, Mei Lan Fang pantomime, and contemporary "epic" and "agit-prop" types of theatre.

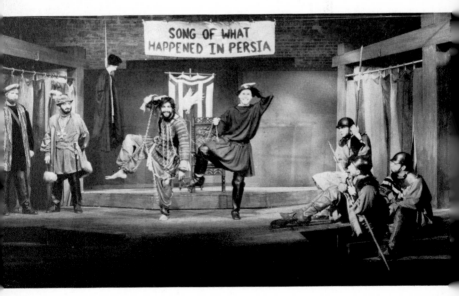

PAGEANT-STYLE THEATRICALISM   *In the banquet scene of Max Reinhardt's open-air production of Hugo von Hofmannsthal's* Everyman *(Jedermann), given annually since 1920, the portals of the Salzburg Cathedral were utilized as a background. One allegorical character actually came out of the cathedral, so that the stage platform and the cathedral were dramatically related, as were other architectural elements in the cathedral square.*

EPIC THEATRICALISM   *In Bertolt Brecht's* The Caucasian Circle of Chalk, *as staged by Robert Schneideman for Northwestern University Theatre, Evanston, Illinois, in 1955, one may note the alienation effect achieved by functional, nonillusionistic scenery, built to reveal the solid brick of the theatre itself; the use of changeable signs and slogans; the participation in the action of a narrator and musicians; exploitation of contrasts; and an attempt at illustrative, cabaret-style gesture in the presentation of a ballad in place of the realistic pantomime used elsewhere in the production. (Settings by Lawrence Goodman, costumes by Ida Mae Goe.)* Photograph: W. B. Nickerson, Evanston, Ill.

skian realistic actor, Vakhtangov's actor was expected to perform two things at one time—both the role in the play and his critical or detached view of that role. Brecht wants the same duality.

Finally, we must refer, though with regretful brevity, to the work of Jacques Copeau, the leader of theatricalism in the West, who was most notably active between 1913 and 1924. Copeau became known chiefly for his Théâtre du Vieux Colombier, founded in 1913 in a small Parisian playhouse, where he built probably the first modern stage for *presentational* (as opposed to *representational*, or peephole) productions. Later he won much admiration as well for the school of acting he established after World War I. But he was perhaps most important to the theatre because of his influence on the brilliant French directors Charles Dullin and Louis Jouvet. Copeau, too, may be described as a reformer rather than a revolutionist in theatrical art. Like Vakhtangov, he emphasized characterization, individuality, and emotional truth even while stressing the histrionic nature of performance and giving primacy to the stage as a platform rather than an environment for pretended living. Much indeed has been made of Copeau's use of a bare platform stage (*un tréteau nu*) consisting of a permanent architectural setting backed by a few screens that could be changed for different plays to suggest different backgrounds. Verisimilitude in scenery had little value for Copeau, who disdained surface realism. Such realism, he protested, "seeks to make us believe in a pasteboard universe."

Copeau and his successors encouraged the development by Obey, Giraudoux, Anouilh, and others of a style of playwriting that made use of theatricality regardless of the intellectual substance, or even the topicality, of the work. The plays written in this style—such as Giraudoux' *Electra* and *The Madwoman of Chaillot*—are presented as constructions, so to speak. The author is thoroughly conscious of creating something for theatrical exhibition. Even in writing *Electra*, his tragedy on the subject of revenge, Giraudoux did not hesitate to employ theatrical devices and to have characters overleap the fourth wall by addressing the audience at length. After we have discarded the fiction that happenings on the stage have an extratheatrical reality, we can indeed let the actors talk to the audience.

Copeau made himself the leader of those who set themselves the objective of *rethéâtrisaler le théâtre*. But he had no use for dazzling stage effects and sheer directorial virtuosity. He encouraged a large measure of humanization in a period and in a country in which artifice was much favored. Because of the nature of retheatricalized playwriting, nevertheless, many French playwrights of the post-realistic school overcultivated artifice; as their contemporary Jean-Jacques Bernard, himself a dramatist of distinction, declared, "in their work, as in that of Giraudoux himself, you find deeply human touches alongside others which are merely exercises in what I might call intellectual tight-rope walking." [14]

It will be observed that each leader of the theatricalist movement made a clear-cut attempt to destroy the realists' "illusion of reality." If the results have been bewildering as well as gratifying, the reason is that theatricalism, like every other method, has suffered from misapplication. Theatricalism offers especially strong seductions to stage directors to display their virtuosity. The process of seduction starts, indeed, the moment they decide to violate the fourth-wall convention.

Those of us who are striving to develop the contemporary theatre should be aware of our danger: We are all parvenus in theatricalism, we who have rediscovered it for ourselves after it

[14] "Art and Artifice," *Drama* (London) (Winter 1952), p. 16. This "tight-rope walking," apparent also in the work of Italian writers such as Pirandello and Ugo Betti, becomes somewhat coy in Giraudoux' *Intermezzo* and *Electra*. It will be found even in so intensely serious and timely a work as his mordant play *La Guerre de Troie n'aura pas lieu* (1935), which contained two unnecessarily fantastic, somewhat sophomorically "literary" scenes omitted by the director Harold Clurman from his production of the play under the title of *Tiger at the Gates*. See the translation by Christopher Fry published by Oxford University Press (New York, 1955).

had been in vogue for some twenty-five centuries before Ibsen. We have embraced it self-consciously, while the clowns and other direct entertainers have been doing their job unostentatiously right under our uplifted noses. So it happens that we must give a little restraining consideration to some of our most ingenious practices and use them with discretion. By all means let us, for example, blow away the imaginary fourth wall for some purposes. Our candid histrionic art may even create a certain charm and establish a certain rapport between actors and audience, both of which results are desirable. Provided, however, that we do not get too much charm and too little else when we aim at more than a simple entertainment, and that we do not get too much "audience participation," which has been known to turn the theatre into a vaudeville show or a kindergarten! Audience participation can be overdone, as, for instance, when the actors go romping through the aisles, nearly barking the shins of the unwary aisle-sitters.

It is also somewhat disconcerting to find that the man sitting in back or in front of you is an actor when he starts yelling "Strike!" or "Hurray!" from his seat. The present writer, who has perhaps too tidy a bourgeois soul, likes to know where he stands in relation to the other people in the auditorium and therefore doesn't want to be startled out of his normal status as a spectator among spectators. But, then, it is usually the object of audience-participation devices to startle sedate persons out of their status of detached observers and make them "participate." The trouble is that there is an amazing number of happenings in which the normal auditor doesn't want to participate, and he may object to being pushed into something he very much wants to stay out of. If the production is "leftist," the playgoer is, of course, expected to feel like a "common man" and a member of the "masses" (that horrible cliché for human beings!). But playgoers do not feel like common men at all; they feel uncommon so long as they are in the theatre. There is nothing more irritatingly "sophisticated" than indicating to the audience that it is now going to participate in a game of make-believe with the actors. Playing at theatre while in the theatre can become preposterous, and that is one of the risks run when the theatricalist idea of theatre is pursued too strenuously.[15]

An illustration of pretentious make-believe is the use of imaginary props, as when the actor turns the nonexistent knobs of nonexistent doors. The habit of using such props persists incongruously even in "hard-boiled" stage direction, as in Kazan's production of Williams' naturalistic drama *Cat on a Hot Tin Roof*. The practice is more natural in the staging of "stylized" plays such as *Our Town* and *The Skin of Our Teeth*. Thornton Wilder built an entire one-act play for amateur production around the rehearsal technique of using imaginary properties, and little-theatre groups have been happy with *The Happy Journey from Camden to Trenton* ever since.

In England, the abolition of properties was one of the aims of the brilliant but unsuccessful theatrician Terence Gray when he headed the experimental Festival Theatre at Cambridge from

[15] Before continuing the account of theatricalist follies, it is only fair to remark that there are mitigating circumstances. These were ably formulated for the present author by Professor Barnard Hewitt of the University of Illinois in a letter, from which I quote with his permission: "I find that I share your irritation, or dissatisfaction, with the self-conscious theatricalism of much modern drama and theatre, but it occurs to me that some playwrights deliberately call attention to the theatricality of their drama not out of coyness or whimsicality, but with serious dramatic purpose. This is certainly true of Brecht. . . . Moreover, until theatricality becomes the expected form of drama and theatre, audiences will continue to be shocked to a degree no matter how unself-conscious the playwright manages to be. And I suppose the playwright cannot be altogether unself-conscious so long as theatricality is not the usual thing." I suppose one should add that the results inevitably differ even in the work of the same author; Pirandello is brilliantly successful with his theatricalist method in *Six Characters in Search of an Author* and *Henry IV*, but awkward and tiresome with the theatricalist flummery of some of his other plays. I myself have found his *Tonight We Improvise* particularly irritating after several readings.

1926 to 1933. Gray's views on "props" stressed the need for stylized performance:

> To hand a man a purse, to open and read a document on
> the stage, such things must be small when performed with the
> real objects in the actors' hands. The expressiveness of the
> action is confined to the dimensions of the object handled.
> Only by discarding the actual article can the gestures of
> giving or of reading be rendered really significant.

Norman Marshall, who reports at great length on Gray's experiments,[16] admits that this method was effective in large gestures
like crowning a king (the present writer himself doubts this),
but otherwise ineffective. Marshall declares that "the result became distractingly like a game of dumb crambo, and far too
much of the attention of the audience was spent in guessing
what props were indicated by the various gestures of the
actors." [17] Gray was also one of the theatricalists who directed
their actors to make their entrances and exits through the audience.

Marshall's account of the career of Gray is indeed the best
summary of the antirealistic adventure at its extremes in the
English-speaking world. Marshall, who had worked with Gray at
Cambridge, concluded that "seven years of ceaseless experiment
had in the end practically no effect upon the English theatre."
Nor was the blame to be laid entirely at the door of British
philistinism. Gray's work "was degenerating into mere freakish-
ness and eccentricity." His interest in directing was so all-
consuming and his production style so extreme that "he failed to
encourage a single author to write a play for production according to the methods practised at the Festival." Even Shakespeare's
work was little more than grist for the director's mill when Gray
put Sir Toby Belch and Sir Andrew Aguecheek on roller skates
and dressed Rosalind in a Boy Scout uniform. When Portia
started her "quality of mercy" speech in Gray's production of

[16] *The Other Theatre* (London: John Lehman, 1947), pp. 53-71.
[17] *Ibid.*, p. 61.

The Merchant of Venice, the court lapsed into attitudes of complete boredom and "the judge whiled away the time by playing with a yo-yo," then fashionable in England. Portia, moreover, spoke as perfunctorily as if she had delivered this speech "for the thousandth time." In one scene Shylock was shown fishing in a canal, and in the last scene, having been deprived of his wealth, he passed across the stage playing a barrel organ. Like more recent virtuoso directors, Gray was also so determined to make the theatre theatrical that he removed the "wings" from the stage so that the audience might see the actors waiting at the side to make their entrances, the electrician at his switchboard, the stagehands, the stacked scenery, and the stage manager holding the promptbook.

Ultimately, it was the "idea" of a production that dominated the Festival Theatre, and Gray therefore tended to favor poor actors who would take direction, although from time to time he had such promising young performers as Robert Morley, Maurice Evans, Margaret Rawlings, and Jessica Tandy in his Cambridge company. But the final word on his seven-year-long dedication to "production ideas" was no doubt said by Norman Marshall. The major weakness of Gray's "method of production, like all forms of expressionism [i.e., extreme stylization] in the theatre, was that it oversimplified the play. Subtlety ceased to exist and the attention of the audience was concentrated entirely on the broadest outlines of character and situation."

Marshall was reminded of what Kenneth Macgowan and Robert Edmond Jones wrote of Jessner in their book *Continental Stagecraft,* after having watched his work in the early 1920's: "He appeared to worship the obvious, to believe that the theatre is a place of ABC impressions and reactions . . . He flung out symbols right and left, but they were symbols of the primer. He directed in words of one syllable." Their last sentence may not have been entirely fair to Jessner, but their general criticism has been applicable to other theatricalist directors, not excluding the exponents of epic theatre. It is even applicable to the frequently brilliant playwriting of Bertolt Brecht, as it is a danger inherent in his theories of acting and production. Brecht has been rightly wary of professional productions of his work without "epic-trained" actors and without supervision by himself. The fiasco of the premiere of his *Mother Courage* at the Devon Arts Festival in 1955 justified his worst fears.[18]

"ABC impressions and reactions," unfortunately, have often been the final product of much intellectual maneuvering and stylization, for all ideas are simple enough as ideas; they become complicated only when they have to be applied in a human context. All external stylization becomes obvious and is easily exhausted. Only human nature is complex and affords an interest not easily exhausted by (and for) those who have imagination enough to penetrate surfaces.

It is ironical, alas, that the effort to achieve significant antirealistic stylization, particularly in the English-speaking countries, should have been made so often on the amateur or semiprofessional level, where the actors are so obviously unprepared for it. It is not surprising that back in 1927 so wise a mentor as Stark Young reminded the *avant-garde* that "the reason most of our extremely stylized productions seem so poor and misled is because the actors lack the needed style; and they miss this style because they do not command the simple, straight acting from which the style departs." [19] In working a little with actors at a university, the present writer found it necessary to invent the slogan "Out of reality, into reality": Out of the reality of themselves, into the reality of the characters they were to create on the stage, which, in turn, must be a theatrical reality for both the actor and the audience.

Even the mastery of simple mimicry is not to be overlooked. "A mimetic gift in the actor," said Stark Young, "corresponds to a good ear in the musician. . . . The imitation of others is an instinct born deep in us, and is the source of the actor's art."

[18] See *London Observer,* July 3, 1955.
[19] *The Theater* (New York: George H. Doran, 1927).

And Mr. Young added that the gift for mimicry in the actor is like a gift for likeness in a painter. "Such a knack will not make his drawing fine, but it will give him a kind of solid reality which he can begin with and which he can alter and force to his own ends." [20] When the incompetent actor "stylizes," he lets us see the style rather than the man, the effort rather than the achievement, the silhouette rather than the substance of the part. The nonprofessional companies and directors, however, have not been alone in giving us warning examples.

It is especially easy to turn theatricality to commercial advantage and yet win admiration for artistry from all but a few exceptionally tough-fibered critics. The career of the inventive and eclectic Max Reinhardt, whose memory deserves our respect for some achievements, could have served as a warning that the theatre is not necessarily best served by the specialists in theatricality. A widely experienced and practical man of the stage who had started out as a character actor for the naturalist Otto Brahm, Reinhardt was adept at turning all methods of staging to his advantage. He declared, it is true, that "there is no one form of the theatre that is the only true artistic form." Nevertheless, the passion to exploit the stage as a medium, to make good his contagious slogan that "the theatre belongs to the theatre," trapped even this astute *régisseur* and entrepeneur, whose followers in Central Europe appear to have been legion. Ever the virtuoso director who could commercialize Craig and turn symbolist dreams into world-astounding theatricality, Reinhardt achieved exciting, if not altogether satisfactory, effects at his Grosses Schauspielhaus, a reconstructed circus in Berlin. There he staged mass scenes on a large forestage that extended tongue-like into the audience, much as did the Elizabethan platform stage or a three-quarter arena stage. Reinhardt also planted actors in the audience (a device used many years later in the production of the strike drama *Waiting for Lefty* in 1935) when he

[20] *Ibid.*, pp. 57-71.

staged Romain Rolland's *Danton*. The object was, of course, to make the spectator a participant, as it were, in the historical events.

Theatricalism as employed in these and similar productions could be described as vulgarized illusionism; the vulgarization was acutely noted by the Berlin critic Herbert Ihering in discussing Reinhardt's 1910 production of *Oedipus Rex*, a turgid version of his less spectacular treatment of the same work in 1906. On a ramp or broad stairway leading to a palace front erected on the stage, the director had placed hundreds of extras who represented the Theban populace. The theatricalist "effect" was intensified, moreover, by having the players make their entrances and exits through the audience. Ihering remarked dryly that "When Reinhardt's chorus let loose, several housemaids fainted." [21] And what greater illusionism, actually as repellent to the critical realistic intellect of an Ibsen, Shaw, or Chekhov as to a haughty classicist, than Reinhardt's 1911-1912 staging of *The Miracle*. For that production, the interior of the playhouse was rebuilt as a cathedral, and the playgoers sat in it as make-believe communicants while religious processions went up and down the aisles. It is surely unnecessary to cite further evidence that the theatricalist theatre has indulged freely in illusionism and has cheapened it, too, in the time-honored manner of show business, whether the showman be an art-loving European or a Broadway philistine with faint claims to "culture."

Formalism

Absolute theatricalism was visually engrossing. It became too abstract, however, and developed theatrical form as an absolute experience far more expressive as pantomime than as discourse; and the drama is, after all, discourse. (Let us, indeed, avoid the genetic fallacy of assuming that because the theatre

[21] Mordecai Gorelik, *New Theatres for Old*, p. 219.

started as pantomime several thousand years ago, nonverbal drama is the best drama.) In extreme theatricalism there was too much form without content, just as in a good deal of humdrum realism there has been too much content without form.

Moderate theatricalism, which did not theatricalize humanity out of the theatre, has survived to prove artistically reliable. It influenced the revival of old plays written for the prerealistic stage without encouraging the destruction of the masterpiece in order to make a stage director's holiday. The concept of theatricalist art even encouraged the rise of some very agreeable and provocative playwriting, especially in France. It became apparent, as indicated previously, that it is unnecessary to banish *all* illusionism from the theatre in order to retheatricalize it. It is indeed almost impossible for the stage to avoid conveying some degree of illusion, unless the work is extravagantly playful and not intended to be taken seriously at all.

The effort to use the theatre theatrically but without doctrinaire rigor has continued as a matter of course; nor has the effort been confined to the pragmatic professional undertakings of show business in Paris, London, or New York. In our southeastern states since World War II there has been much work in a relatively new form of pageant-drama that is called "symphonic drama" by Paul Green, a pioneer in the form. Designed as a national or regional celebration revolving around some historical event, symphonic drama has a ritual pattern of sung, danced, and spoken scenes in varying combinations. Such productions as *The Lost Colony* and *The Common Glory* by Paul Green and *Horn in the West* and *Unto These Hills* by Kermit Hunter have exhibited forthright theatricalist stylization. The staging has been characterized by concentration on expressive spectacle and broad performance. Projecting or *presenting,* rather than representing, a story of the American land has been the objective in each production. Any effort to preserve the fourth-wall convention on open-air stages would have been quixotic and disastrous. However, the productions have not been so strongly stylized as to suggest an attempt to create abstract and coterie art.

At the other extreme in the American theatre is the arena-theatre movement that developed after 1940. This development, contrary to Reinhardt's example and the suggestion of bigness in the term "arena," has not favored large-scale production. In the usually very small theatres especially built or modified for arena staging or central staging, the fourth wall of the realistic stage is utterly abolished. The playing area is in the center and is completely surrounded or surrounded on three sides (in so-called "three-quarter-arena" style) by the audience. There can be no imaginary fourth wall in central staging because three real walls are lacking. The arena theatres, usually consisting of two or three tiers of seats, create an atmosphere of extreme intimacy; and the proponents of central staging have, indeed, tended to make "intimacy" their sole esthetic stock in trade.

Actually, arena theatres came into vogue because off-Broadway groups wanted to effect economies in scenery and backstage crew requirements. Intimacy is a deceptive concept and one that must be balanced, now and then, by the need for maintaining esthetic distance. For the spectator, one of the disturbing features of an unsuccessful Greenwich Village Circle-in-the-Square production was having a large, energetic, and deafening chorus of Mississippi Valley townspeople virtually in his lap.

Although this chapter is not the appropriate place for a discussion of the possibilities and limitations of the arena techniques now in use,[22] three points should be made here. First, since arena performances of nonmusical drama have been generally realistic rather than presentational or especially stylized, a blithe inconsistency is being maintained. If logic rather than habit (the habits of directors, players, and playgoers) dictated practice, perform-

[22] A detailed treatment of all aspects of central staging will be found in the present author's *Producing the Play*, 1953 ed., pp. 528-600, and a briefer description combined with provocative criticism is contained in *Principles of Theatre Art* by H. D. Albright, William Halstead, and Lee Mitchell (Houghton Mifflin, 1955), pp. 222-228.

ances on a centrally located stage would be at least as presentational as those that were given in the Elizabethan and Greek
theatres. Without possessing a single real wall, the arena theatre
nonetheless creates the illusion of environment by means of the
furniture, the properties, and the dialogue of the characters. The
second point to be noted is that arena staging, as a rule, is
theatricalist theatre at the start (that is, when the performance
begins) and *realistic* theatre at the end, after the audience has
become accustomed to the convention of having the actors in its
collective lap and after the illusion of reality has established its
hold on the playgoer. As on the proscenium stage, the actors
remain psychologically in their own world and keep out of the
audience's world by studiously ignoring the spectator; they speak
naturally, and they use stage properties naturalistically.

It would seem, indeed, that the theatricalism of arena staging is accidental rather than the result of planning, and that the
best effects may have been fortuitous. An esthetics of arena theatre does not yet exist, and it is not likely to be desired by the
partisans of arena staging so long as they want to produce every
kind of play. In arena theatre, then, we have occasionally engrossing and usually acceptable illustrations of the fusion of
realism and theatricalism by accommodation. In this respect
American arena staging (even by ambitiously experimental
groups) illustrates the characteristic pragmatism and eclecticism of show business, which, as noted previously, has mediated
between realistic and antirealistic modes of theatre more or less
haphazardly rather than by design.

Even moderate theatricalism, however, involves fundamental
modifications of procedure in playwriting and stage production
that must be thought out instead of being haphazardly hit upon.
Many attempts at theatrical realization of a play are weak and
unsuccessful because the authors and producers fail to realize
that they have made a commitment to a new style or form
of theatre. They operate too negatively. They take liberties with

the convention of realism, but do not discover for themselves any other convention that is vital and meaningful. The result, then, is haphazardness in writing and staging.

The principal choice in our century has lain between a great deal of vivacious theatricalism, particularly in musical comedy,[23] and formalism. And an intermediate, elegant theatricality should also be noted, although it has no distinctive form. It has been found everywhere on the commercial stage, but has been especially prevalent in England, where it appears in productions of both old and new plays. Whether applied to Farquhar's *The Beaux' Stratagem* or Fry's *Venus Observed, Antony and Cleopatra* or *Caesar and Cleopatra,* "elegant theatricality" is more distinguished by glossiness, glitter, and grace of movement than by incisiveness of meaning and vigor of experience. Laurence Olivier's revolving-stage production of *Caesar and Cleopatra* in the 1950's, for example, was eye-filling rather than mind-filling. The acting in this elegant style of production has no roughness, no crudity, but it also conveys no sense of the grain of the play or of the main characters. The stage production is likely to resolve itself into a succession of group pictures and passages of elocution. In Shakespearean productions, usually approved by academicians as well as by "the carriage trade," songs and dances, along with fetching costumes and attractive scenery, enrich even if they rarely enliven, the proceedings. The New York Theatre Guild's production of *As You Like It,* starring Katharine Hepburn, was duly applauded by the *Shakespeare Quarterly* despite the fact that, as a result of the stringing together of songs, there was more Rudolf Friml than Shakespeare in the proceedings. In

[23] Like opera and music-drama, musical comedies are so intrinsically theatricalist in character that there is little need to discuss them here. It is worth noting only that on Broadway the development of musical comedy has been in two opposite directions—toward the realistic character-drama and the problem play, as in Rodgers and Hammerstein musicals such as *South Pacific* and *The King and I,* and toward the use of the formalistic, nonverbal element of ballet, as in Agnes de Mille's *tour de force* at the end of the first act of *Oklahoma!*

productions intended to be "cultural," there is usually a suggestion of ritual in the presentation. The tone is one of gravity,
though it is not infrequently mixed with polite humor; and there
is considerable ceremoniousness in the actors' graceful movement
and good diction, as well as in the settings, the costuming, the
sedate musical accompaniment, and the conventional choreography. This type of patrician theatricalism reached the peak of
elaborateness in the Old Vic's *Midsummer Night's Dream* production of 1953-1954, which simply oozed culture while it
thrummed Mendelssohn.

Formalistic theatre is less likely to be exploited commer-
cially than this mode of theatrical elegance and cultivated ceremonialism. It is also less likely to be the vehicle of star actors,
although it has tended to become the indulgence of star
directors. It is usually characterized by a purity of esthetic aim
such as we associate with Copeau and Yeats, both of whom
retreated from the market place. They had noble aims, these and
other dreamers of stylized, more or less ritualistic, art: The spirit
of man would be liberated by the very process of setting bounds
—the bounds of art—to the imitation of an action and the
imitation of conversation. Man would be magnified to the degree
that action was purified of all but symbolic content, that characterization was refined into typicality, that speech was subjected
to the jeweled yoke of formal utterance. Life on the stage would
recover its antique grandeur to the degree that action was made
ritualistic, characterization sculptural, and language ceremonial.
That was the ideal of formalism virtually from the beginning of
the antinaturalistic reaction of the 1890's. Although it appears
to be an impossible ideal, it proved realizable enough when
formalism was blended with romanticism, as in the work of
Émile Verhaeren, Paul Claudel, and Yeats; and also, later on,
when it was mingled with realism, as in the work of Wilder,
Eliot, Williams, and Brecht.

In order to avoid confusion, it is perhaps also necessary to note that "formalism" has been used in communist propaganda as a loosely defined charge, wantonly applied against "decadent bourgeois culture." Politically, however, formalism is meaningless. *If* the word has any semantic value at all, it is that of signifying conspicuously formal play structure and artificially devised—hence "formal"—characterization, action, and speech. An exponent of Russian formalism, Shklovsky, once declared that "a work of art is the sum total of all the stylistic devices employed in it." He also expressed the extremist view when he wrote that art is always "free of life." [24] In England during the 1930's, Auden, Isherwood, Spender, and others wrote formalist drama from the "left" side of the political fence, and Eliot and others from the "right." [25] Tairov was able to move from a pre-Soviet estheticism to a post-Soviet "social-mindedness," and yet use formalistic elements in his stage productions both before and after 1918. And if Yeats's love of formalism inclined him toward a private type of theatre, there can be no doubt that it has also been possible. to employ formalism in mass productions of all kinds, whether religious, patriotic, fascist, or communistic. In 1918 Meyerhold staged an early Bolshevik outdoor mass-spectacle of revolution, *Mystery-Bouffe,* by the "futurist" poet Mayakovsky, along with another "formalistic" drama of revolution, Émile Verhaeren's *The Dawn.*

One may conclude that although formalism *could* have political manifestations, the limitations or dangers of the formalist theatre are not intrinsically political. One may legitimately criticize, instead, the pretentiousness of private appeal or the ostentatiousness of public appeal, the stiffness of action and speech, and the depersonalization of character that appeared in many experiments. Usually, moreover, the formalistic style of making

[24] Victor Erlich, *Russian Formalism-History-Doctrine,* with a Preface by René Wellek (The Hague, 1955).
[25] I refer to "antifascist" or "anti-imperialistic" work such as Auden's *The Dance of Death,* Spender's *The Trial of a Judge,* or Auden and Isherwood's *The Ascent of F6,* on the one hand, and Eliot's *Murder in the Cathedral* and *The Family Reunion,* on the other.

theatre was most deleterious to multi-dimensional acting. Automatism has been the greatest danger, regardless of the political position represented by the play and production. Stiffness and an effect of remoteness have been particularly evident when dramatic treatments have kept the actors from functioning in active communication with each other. "Players who give a clear-cut impression that they are in active communication with each other . . . are likely to seem most real." [26] Characters seem to be isolated or boxed off even in such literary plays as Yeats's *A Full Moon in March* and Eliot's *Murder in the Cathedral* and *Family Reunion,* in which the speakers are notably articulate.

It was probably inevitable that theatricalist and formalist experiments should have also favored the use of masks as in the classic theatre and in primitive rituals. Perhaps the most noteworthy incorporation of the mask as a psychological necessity in the drama was in *The Great God Brown,* in which one character assumed the mask of another to signify an exchange of character. O'Neill, it would seem, renounced the use of masks in his later work rather reluctantly; he included requests for an equivalent fixity of expression and exchange of facial appearance in his stage directions for *Mourning Becomes Electra.* But the first completely nonpsychological and formalistic use of masks in theatrical production appeared at least a decade and a half before *The Great God Brown* when Gordon Craig made some designs in 1911 for Yeats's production of *The Hour Glass* and *On Baile's Strand* at the Abbey Theatre. A formal masking of characters was a feature of productions of such work as Yeats's latter-day one-act plays inspired by the Japanese Noh plays, the Federal Theatre's "living newspaper" *Power,* and the Berliner Ensemble production of Brecht's *The Caucasian Circle of Chalk* that was seen in Paris in the summer of 1955. The motivation varied and will undoubtedly continue to vary: the mask helped

[26] Albright, Halstead, and Mitchell, *Principles of Theatre Art,* p. 120.

to depersonalize characters for one purpose or another. In *Power*, for instance, the motivation was plainly satirical, the nine masks representing the "nine old men," the justices of the U.S. Supreme Court, whom President Franklin D. Roosevelt had denounced for obstructing New Deal legislation. The mask emphasized the ritualistic character of some of Yeats's plays. And, in general, it could distance, elevate, and dignify dramatic experience, freeing it from the temporality and flux of realistic theatre. Craig sensed this, when he designed the mask for the Blind Man in Yeats's *On Baile's Strand*. "The advantage of a mask over a face," he wrote, "is that it is always repeating unerringly the poetic fancy." The theatre must learn the lesson of "durability" from Egyptian art and return to the ancient practice of covering the actor's face "in order that his expression—the visualized expression of the poetic spirit—shall be everlasting." [27]

Formalism is the result of a search for esthetic conventions that will be serviceable to the theatre in general and to the individual dramatist in particular. It is little short of remarkable how deliberately, almost desperately, those who expected a freely inspired or spontaneous art to emerge from theatricalism (which its advocate Alexander Bakshy called "the theatre unbound") turned to the pursuit of convention. Reinhardt, the gifted popularizer, knew which way the wind was blowing when he produced pantomime drama, staged plays against the formal background of a baroque screen in a palace ballroom, used the sets of individual stages which are called "mansions" in the simultaneous staging of one religious production, and presented Hofmannsthal's *Jedermann* (out of our medieval *Everyman*) on a platform in front of the baroque portals of the Salzburg Cathedral. Copeau's permanent architectural stage in Paris and attempts by others to abolish the proscenium arch from the stage reflected the search for formalistic theatre, as did the experiments of Meyerhold and Tairov; Barrault's later development of a mining technique continued the quest for formalistic art; and in playwriting, the search for new "forms" has been continuous.

[27] Janet Leeper, *Edward Gordon Craig: Designs for the Theatre* (Harmondsworth, England: King Penguin Books, 1948), p. 46.

The plays Yeats wrote after 1917 in the style of the Japanese Noh play provide examples of special conventionalization. In *A Full Moon in March*, the Swineherd who is the hero of the piece wears a mask over the upper part of his face, and the heroine, the Queen, is veiled. An inner curtain is drawn when he is to be beheaded at the Queen's order, while an Attendant recites a poem about a legendary beheading of a lover by an Irish queen. Next, the Queen appears, holding the severed head of the Swineherd, and her hands and costume are symbolically red. She begins to mimic the actions of singing, whereupon the Attendant actually sings the words for her while she dances out her feelings to the accompaniment of drum taps. Next, when the Head is supposedly singing, the Second Attendant sings the Head's words, while, as the stage direction reads, *"The Queen in her dance moves away from the head, alluring and refusing."* In the midst of the dance, when the Queen is supposed to laugh, the First Attendant laughs for her. The Second Attendant says: "She is laughing. How can she laugh,/Loving the dead." And the First Attendant replies, "She is crazy. That is why she is laughing," and the stage direction reads *"Laughs again as Queen."* The Queen, then, making no sound, takes up the Head, places her lips against its lips, and dances more and more rapidly. Finally, she sinks slowly down, and the Attendants close the play formally, singing a commentary to the effect that the virginally cruel lack "Their desecration and the lover's night."

A Full Moon in March is an extreme example of formalistic playwriting, but many other twentieth-century plays contain formalistic elements. The high point of T. S. Eliot's *The Cocktail Party* is the second act, in which Dr. Reilly, the psychiatrist-guardian, and his associates, Julia and Alex, assume a religious function. They perform a sort of ritual, reminiscent of the Mass, with their cocktail glasses. Reilly says, "And now we are ready for the libation." Alex calls for "the words for the building of the hearth," referring to the Chamberlaynes, who have been sent home by Dr. Reilly to repair their marriage; and Reilly pronounces a brief prayer for this couple while the "guardians" raise their glasses. Then Alex, referring to the heroine, Celia Copplestone, who is starting her journey toward eventual martyrdom, calls for "the words for those who go on a journey." And the three supernatural "guardians" start the chant "Protector of travellers / Bless the road," the formalism of which is partly established by the parallelism of the lines, as in Julia's stanza:

> Protect her from the Voices
> Protect her from the Visions
> Protect her in the tumult
> Protect her in the silence.

A third simple example is provided by the Spanish poet-playwright Federico García Lorca. In his tragedy of love, *Blood Wedding*, the climax comes when the heroine's lover, who has abducted her from her wedding, fights a fatal duel in a forest with the bridegroom. The most theatrically striking feature of the first scene of the third act is the apparition of the Moon and Death as allegorical figures. Moreover, their speeches are completely formal. The Moon, for example, says:

> Let me in! I come freezing
> down to walls and windows!
> Open roofs, open breasts
> Where I may warm myself!
> I'm cold! [28]

Colors are used formalistically by García Lorca in the costuming and décor of his fantastic play *The Love of Don Perlimpín and Belisa in His Garden*. Masks have been favored in some nonrealistic plays; they are indispensable to the dramatic meaning of O'Neill's *The Great God Brown*. (Masks, it will be remembered, were required in all plays written for the highly formal classic theatre of Athens.) Choruses, another formalistic feature of classic drama, reappear in dramatic modernism. The chorus of Canterbury women is the main structural element in

[28] Translation by Richard L. O'Connell and James Graham-Luján, *Three Tragedies of Lorca* (New Directions, 1947).

Murder in the Cathedral, and choruses play an important part in Giraudoux' *Electra,* in Eliot's *Family Reunion,* in O'Neill's *Lazarus Laughed,* and O'Casey's *Within the Gates.* A single individual, speaking alone or with other characters, may also perform the functions of the classic chorus in a more or less informal manner, as do Seth and the townspeople in O'Neill's *Mourning Becomes Electra.*

A unique formalist device appeared in a modern psychological context when O'Neill restored the old-fashioned "aside" as a recurrent feature of his redundant but successful nine-act drama *Strange Interlude.* The aside was used here as interior monologue, so that it is actually soliloquy. O'Neill's fluent use of this device is comparable to Joyce's employment of stream-of-consciousness writing in *Ulysses,* although the playwright's language is decidedly less imaginative than the novelist's. Progress in modern theatre was once associated with the abolition of the aside and the soliloquy; when this had been achieved, however, progress soon came to be associated with the recovery of these devices for playwriting. Writing in 1910, Clayton Hamilton, in *The Theory of the Theatre,* deplored the aside, especially because the actor delivering it had to step out of the proscenium frame and annihilate the fourth wall. Hamilton was kinder to the soliloquies, distinguishing two kinds: objectionable "constructive soliloquies," in which the plot is explained (as at the beginning of the last act of *Lady Windermere's Fan*) or by which off-stage events are reported, and acceptable "reflective soliloquies." The latter were permissible to the modern playwright, he said, because they reveal a character's train of thought. Hamlet's speeches, for instance, could be made to seem natural because they were psychologically motivated.

Writing in 1939, Clayton Hamilton said that the asides in *Strange Interlude,* which did not at all disturb the public of that highly successful Theatre Guild production, were "reflective soliloquies," for the actor was not "forced out of the stage picture."[29] These analyses of the aside and the soliloquy are likely to be helpful only to someone who cares about the preservation of the "stage picture"—that is, the preservation of the environment established by means of the proscenium arch and the fourth-wall convention. For a mode of theatre in which the illusion of reality is not a desideratum, the playwright and the director may very well *intend* to force the actor out of the stage picture. They may not want to "motivate" the soliloquy, but to startle and stimulate the audience by violating illusion. They will therefore replace psychology with theatricality, and make use of the power (or the charm, or the comic possibilities) of direct address to the spectator. When the theatricalist writers and directors recovered the soliloquy for modern theatre they were certainly not interested in making it "natural"; they wanted it to be "unnatural" —that is, theatrical. Giraudoux obviously had this intention when he wrote his *Electra* in 1937.

Formalism was also well served, of course, by the return of the narrator, who came to be used in a variety of imaginative ways. In *Our Town,* for instance, the narrator (called the Stage Manager) is not merely a townsman of Grover's Corners, New Hampshire; he is the informal master of ceremonies who addresses the audience directly. In Cocteau's modernist retelling of the Oedipus myth, *The Infernal Machine,* the narrator is a disembodied voice. The Voice formally summarizes the plot in advance of the action, as if to say to the audience, "Now that you know the story, I can proceed with demonstrating it to you psychologically and intellectually—and, to be sure, *theatrically*." And this, in fact, is what the narrator declares, starting with the statement, "He will kill his father. He will marry his mother," and commenting further on, "For the gods really to enjoy themselves, the victim must fall from a great height." The introductory narration concludes with an undisguised public address: "Spectator, this machine you see here wound up to the full in such a way that the spring will slowly unwind the whole length of a human life, is one of the most perfect constructed by the infernal gods for the mathematical destruction of a mortal."

[29] *The Theory of the Theatre* (New York, 1939), pp. 48-51.

An especially candid formalism is achieved by the use of a narrator in Tennessee Williams' delicately written play *The Glass Menagerie*. Here the narrator is an older edition of the boy Tom, who is one of the three important characters in this four-character play. Tom, as the narrator, opens the play by looking back into the past—a past that he now sees in perspective. Dressed as a merchant sailor, he appears out of the darkness, strolls across the front of the stage, and stops at the fire-escape entrance of his remembered home.

Tom becomes, like the narrator in *Our Town*, a man addressing his public in plain violation of the realistic fourth-wall convention. He announces candidly: "Yes, I have tricks in my pocket. I have things up my sleeve. But I am the opposite of a stage magician. He gives you illusion that has the appearance of truth. I give you truth in the pleasant disguise of illusion." After commenting on the depression period of his boyhood and thus establishing the social background of the play, he explains to the audience that it will now see a "memory play." Then, as if the formalism of the work were not already sufficiently apparent, Tom the narrator changes roles; he enters the house and becomes the boy he once was. Finally, at the conclusion of the last vignette of remembered home life, the young Tom once more becomes the narrator. He again addresses the audience as he stands "outside," while the action "inside" is pantomimed by Tom's mother and his sister Laura. His speech ends with his addressing Laura as he watches her across the years. As she bends over the candles in the parlor, Tom says, "Blow out your candles, Laura, and so good-bye. . . ." She does so, and the memory play ends.

From these examples it will be seen, then, that formalism has played an important part in modernist stylization, very much as it did in the great prerealistic periods of the past in which soliloquies, asides, choruses, and narrators were accepted as stage and dramatic conventions. Theatricalism has not, therefore, been merely a swirl of whimsies and fads whipped up in the theatre of our century. It has been a series of revolts and innovations involving alterations of dramatic form and theatrical style. And whether or not these have succeeded completely, they have achieved some liberation of theatrical art, some release of poetic imagination.

The full importance of such changes (or, at least, the fact that they are changes in form) can be realized when we contrast theatricalized dramas with simple fantasies such as *Outward Bound* and *On Borrowed Time*, in which supernatural occurrences are rendered realistically both in the writing and the stage production. Conventional fantasy has been deliberately written and staged as though it were "true," the purpose being to provide the same illusion of reality that common realism affords. At the same time we tend to believe, in the "eat-your-cake-yet-have-it-too" school of commercial theatre, that fantasy will call attention to itself more strongly when the unnatural events occur in an everyday manner and in an environment in which only humdrum occurrences are to be expected. When the present writer produced a Welsh fantasy, Richard Hughes' *Minnie and Mr. Williams,* on Broadway, he debated the question of using either a realistic background distinguished by local color or a predominantly fantastic setting. The latter would have enabled one of the main characters, an imp of Satan, to enter a Welsh preacher's house through the walls. The back wall was to be omitted from the set in at least one scene, and the imp was to appear out of nowhere, as it were, in a blaze of supernatural light laid down by the stage electricians. A realistic style was ultimately selected on the grounds that the presence of an imp of Hell in a preacher's home was eery enough. Eddie Dowling, the stage director of the production, argued that Hell in the shape of an innocent-looking little girl would be considerably more impressive in a natural environment than in a supernatural one.

Not merely imagination, but imagination directed toward the formalization of theatre and drama, has been a decisive factor in the theatricalist revolution. The premise that theatre is art and that art is a tissue of conventions is inherent in the formalistic approach. The aim of theatricality is to create a new reality —*a reality of art*—on the stage. Tennessee Williams, by no means the first writer to favor this view, worded it well in his production notes for *The Glass Menagerie:*

> Everyone should know nowadays the unimportance of the photographic in art: that truth, life or reality is an organic thing which the poetic imagination can represent or suggest, in essence, only through transformation, through changing into other forms than those which were merely present in appearance.

And this definition of art as truth, life, or reality represented in essence and "through changing into other forms" applies as well as any to the artistic reality of great non-naturalistic drama such as *Antigone* or *Hamlet.* Williams' explanation brings us close to Alexander Bakshy's illuminating, though necessarily oversimplified, differentiation between the realistic-naturalistic and the theatricalist ideas of theatre, expressed as a distinction between "representational" and "presentational" art. Representational theatre, said Bakshy, aims for the illusion of actuality, whereas presentational theatre does without that illusion. Dramatic realism, then, can be called "a mode of actuality," and dramatic presentationalism can be called "a mode of theatre."

The Possibilities of a Modern Synthesis

That the makeshift theatricalism of ordinary showmen should have led nowhere except to riches or bankruptcy in the market place is understandable. That the extravagances of abstraction-haunted visionaries should have fizzled out instead of supplying a steady light for creative endeavor is also understandable. The extreme stylizers made promises they could not have kept without either smothering the dramatic medium in symbolism or exploding it with expressionism. But why has not sound and moderate theatricalism, clearly understood and tastefully guided by able stage directors, achieved more than minor renovations of the modern stage? This much is apparent: Although retheatricalization of the theatre after the triumph of realism has been a highly commendable aim, theatricalism has not yet endowed the modern theatre with the power and significance it had when it was served by the pioneering giants of realism.

It is possible, to be sure, to list many charming, imaginative productions in the theatricalist mode, ranging from Vakhtangov's production of *Princess Turandot* in the early 1920's to the Peter Brook production of *Ring 'Round the Moon* in London in 1950. It has been possible to derive much civilized entertainment and stimulation from one or more of the successful plays of Cocteau, Pirandello, Giraudoux, Anouilh, and other writers in the theatricalist mode. Many of the playwrights even give the impression of having felt and thought with some intensity. Yet they have rarely made the theatre seem important to the modern public except when their theatricalist aims have been augmented by others quite distinct from that of presenting "theatre for theatre's sake." We may refer to *The Dybbuk,* which is made "real" by the folk-spirit of Chassidic fantasy; to *Liliom,* which begins as the naturalistic portrait of a misfit; to *Six Characters in Search of an Author,* which derives its dramatic power from the paradoxically real emotions of fanciful characters as well as from the polarization of life and theatre in the text; to *Our Town,* which has the quality of a genre painting of an actual New England town; to *The Madwoman of Chaillot,* in which fantasy is treated in a matter-of-fact fashion and has the immediacy of social drama; or to Jean Anouilh's drama *The Lark,* which consists of realistic episodes from the life of Joan of Arc and is, at the same time, "theatricalist" in treatment—mainly in the formalism of the frame of the play and the unchronological sequence of its episodes.

Theatricalism has made—or has given a realistically disposed public the impression of making—significant contributions to the modern drama mainly in association with some quality of realism. Good theatre has, however, also been frequently defeated by the serious intentions that accompany realism, and the theatre of our century has been littered with the lumpy wreckage of imaginations that should never have been required to carry much freight. I believe I am not alone in considering Ugo Betti's brooding fantasy *The Gambler,* one example of overextended theatricality, a far less satisfactory work of art than such pieces of frivolous legerdemain as Molnar's *The Play's the Thing* or, for that matter, any number of farces from *Charley's Aunt* and *The Importance of Being Earnest* to *Private Lives* and *Blithe Spirit.* And the reverse has also been true—the theatricality of a work has negated or diminished its claims to significant meaning. Theatricality made many a German play, from Hauptmann's *And Pippa Dances* in 1906 to Wolfgang Borchert's *Outside the Door* forty years later, embarrassingly frantic rather then genuinely serious, and brought confusion into even the urbane French theatre in the work of Paul Claudel and Armand Salacrou. Giraudoux, too, was not always immune to an undulant fever of theatricality, as in *Ondine* and in two mythological scenes omitted from the New York production of *Tiger at the Gates;* and *The Lark,* as written by Anouilh rather than as adapted by Lillian Hellman, was made more specious by Anouilh's fondness for jumping through theatrical hoops than most New York reviewers realized.

Theatricalists have generally been most secure when governed by a sure sense of comedy and least secure when impelled to write "seriously." The tact and urbanity of Giraudoux have been rare among theatricalist playwrights. Nor is the taste of a Jouvet or Barrault commonly to be found in the field of stage production. Some artists have known how to be playful, and that knowledge is indispensable for anyone who elects to be theatrical. A clodhopper should not dance in ballet, and a dray-horse should not run in the Kentucky Derby. Some subjects and moods, moreover, do not usually lend themselves to successful theatricalization or formalization. The brassy theatricalism of John Howard Lawson's *Processional* suited the materials of the play and served the author's satirical purpose. A charade such as the Fry-Anouilh *Ring 'Round the Moon* is comic and frothy, and theatricality is appropriate in both the writing and performance of such a play. But theatricality was curiously inappropriate in *Camino Real,* Tennessee Williams' fantasy on the failure of modern society and the miseries of modern man. Theatricality, indeed, ran amok in the busy Broadway production of this work when actors pranced about in the auditorium, even up to the box seats. Eddie Dowling, the producer of Williams' earlier play *The Glass Menagerie,* was better advised when he dispensed with the author's rather redundant theatricalism which the reader will find incorporated in the stage directions of the published play.

Formalism, too, has often betrayed its devotees, who have been mostly poets bent upon avoiding contamination by the commercial theatre. Yeats, the most gifted of modern mandarin playwrights, staged his Japanese-inspired pieces in his own or a friend's living room with all the ceremoniousness of a ritual. One such performance of the formalist little play *The Hawk's Well* made O'Casey nostalgic for his own boozy character Fluther in *The Plough and the Stars:* "What headlines his visit would make in the morrow's newspaper! Fluther runs wild in Yeats's drawing room." O'Casey reflected farther that "the people's theatre can never be successfully turned into a poetical conventicle," and he put his finger on a major limitation of any formalism created by fiat or by imitation—the danger of sterile artificiality:

Yeats had read in a big book all about the Noh Plays . . . and had seized on the idea that he could do in an hour what had taken a thousand years to create. And so . . . Yeats' idea of a Noh Play blossomed for a brief moment, then the

artificial petals faded and dropped lonely to the floor, because a Japanese spirit had failed to climb into the soul of
a Kelt.[30]

The conventions of modern nonrealistic theatre have not
developed in a stable cultural context. In earlier ages, the development of presentational or formalistic theatre had paralleled a development toward cultural climaxes; this was true in
Periclean Athens, in Elizabethan England, and in France in the
age of Louis XIV. The course of our century's nonrealistic theatre
has paralleled only a flux of tensions, passions, and reactions.
Modern theatricalism has not been, perhaps could not have
been, an organic style. The theatricalist form of theatre has not
grown up naturally. It has been invented or willed into existence
by talented idealists like Craig and Copeau and talented op-
portunists like Reinhardt. On the one hand, then, we have had
much routinized realism; on the other, much footless theatricality. It is not surprising that at the midcentury we have found
ourselves in Matthew Arnold's uncomfortable situation of wan-
dering between two worlds—one dead, the other powerless to be
born.

At first glance there seems to be no possibility of breaking
this impasse. Yet the situation is not at all desperate wherever
the theatre artist and the playwright can create without intimida-
tion and official control. Realism has survived as a vital mode of
theatrical art in our century precisely because theatricalism has
challenged it continually and because the realists have been able
to learn from the theatricalists. The great realists of the past
were antitheatrical, after all, only to the degree that they opposed false and question-begging drama and empty showmanship.

There appears to be a way out of the artistic impasse in
which the contemporary theatre finds itself. It is for the realists

[30] *Inishfallen, Fare Thee Well* (Macmillan, 1949), p. 373.

to tap the dramatic resources of theatricalism, but to use them in order to *advance essential realism*. And this would demand integrity, not opportunism. There can be no real gain in merely tidying up or prettifying realism, as the British especially have been trying to do for decades. We must respect the fact that not all things have to be fluent, graceful, and glossy in order to attract and stimulate. The true artist and the intelligent critic can only endorse Santayana's statement in the preface to his poems: "The owl hooting from his wintry bough cannot be chanticleer crowing in the barnyard, yet he is sacred to Minerva."

Imagination is the link between all schools of modern art. It is clear that there need be no conflict between the leading realists and their opponents over the importance of imagination. This is made evident by such developments as the crystallization of Stanislavsky's so-called system, which had for its objective the stimulation of the actor's imagination or "magical, creative *if*," and the rise of the Musical Studio of the Moscow Art Theatre, which startled the Western world with superb productions of Charles Lecocq's *The Daughter of Madame Angot,* Offenbach's *La Périchole,* Aristophanes' *Lysistrata,* and Bizet's *Carmen,* the last presented in the memorable gypsy version entitled *Carmencita and the Soldier*. It is noteworthy that these imaginative contributions to the lyric theatre came not out of the *avant-garde,* antirealistic theatres, but out of the Moscow Art Theatre, that center of realism. Also, the director of the Musical Studio was none other than Stanislavsky's celebrated cofounder and codirector of the Art Theatre, Vladimir Nemirovich-Danchenko. To historians of modern theatre it may indeed seem ironic that the greatest service to the romantic or Wagnerian ideal of "synthetic theatre" made since Wagner's day should have come in the twentieth century from the theatrical organization that gave the realistic stage its highest status. Far from allowing experience with the realistic stage to lead him into "the barren field of realistic opera," [31] Danchenko turned to the great fusion that has

[31] *Inside the Moscow Art Theatre,* by Oliver M. Sayler (New York: Brentano's, 1925), p. 148.

been dreamed of by Western artists ever since they began, during the Renaissance, to look back to the Greek theatre as a lost ideal of synthesis. We may certify it, as Wagner did in his *Art Work of the Future*, the "great united art-work," in which the play is regarded as only one element of a totality which is theatre. Wagner described this synthesis as one that must embrace all the genres of art *and in some degree undo each of them in order to use it as a means to an end*.[32] It is plain, then, that one of the great theatres of realism, if not indeed the greatest, was entirely willing to accept the *theatrical nature* of theatre by 1919.

Only at the Moscow Art Theatre, declared Danchenko,[33] could he have achieved the results he had visualized, because there "the atmosphere of triviality is an utter impossibility." But he also understood a more important point, of which he made use in practice—namely, that a productive merger, so to speak, is possible when the realistic and the theatricalist approaches to theatre are allowed to *complement* rather than destroy each other. "It would be the greatest mistake, and disastrous for the music, to construct an operatic performance according to the naturalistic methods of the drama," declared his associate Sergei Berthensson, the Musical Studio's acting director in 1924.[34] Without a doubt, however, it is possible to establish a link between the presentational form of music-drama and that quintessence of realistic performance which Stanislavsky and his followers called "inner justification." Berthensson declared that "if a wonderful singer is not first of all an actor" he should not be used except at a concert; only a singer-actor "can create a performance instead of a concert." He expressed the possibility of a merger of realism and theatricalism when he spoke as follows:

A singer must not, like a dramatic actor, live his role realistically. A singer cannot cry because a sincere tear would

[32] *Ibid.*, p. 146.
[33] *Ibid.*, p. 54.
[34] *Ibid.*, p. 55.

FORMALIST PLATFORM STAGE FOR A SHAKESPEAREAN PRODUC-
TION *Teo Otto designed this setting for a Zurich Schauspielhaus production of* Romeo and Juliet *in 1950. Teo Otto's own statement may
serve as both justification and unintentional self-criticism: "Naturalism
may be bad as a programme, but it can be an excellent means of expression. So can abstract representation, though carried to the point
of a system it will kill art." From* World Theatre *magazine.*

THEATRICALIST USE OF THE PLATFORM STAGE *An extreme example of the theatricalist approach to staging a play was furnished by
the Zurich Schauspielhaus production of* The Taming of the Shrew *in
1952, designed by Teo Otto.* Photograph: W. E. Baur, from *World
Theatre* magazine.

THEATRICALIST DÉCOR, OR "ELEGANT THEATRICALISM" *The 1950 American production of the Anouilh-Fry "charade"* Ring 'Round the Moon *was a replica of the British production directed by Peter Brook and designed by Oliver Messel. The playful theatricalist quality of the production, marked by an elegance not inappropriate to the social background, is particularly apparent in the skeletal form of the hothouse and the free—that is, "theatrical"—treatment of the striped awnings at the right and the left.* Photograph: Eileen Darby for Graphic House. A Gilbert Miller production; courtesy of the producer.

contract his larynx; he cannot laugh without the risk of spoiling his tone. But with a flexible artistic fantasy, he can detect an inner problem, embracing the musical foundations of the subject matter, the psychological background and the plastic form. Without the "inner justification," all so-called "play" results in nothing but stencils, frauds—all that which creates tasteless and unconvincing "theatricality." [35]

It should be added here only that, as Danchenko declared concerning his work on Charles Lecocq's opera, "music helps to make immense psychological leaps." And ballet, when properly associated with drama, also introduces psychological leaps. In *Oklahoma!*, for example, the superb ballet created by Agnes de Mille for the end of the first act expressed the heroine's mental conflict far more impressively than a dramatic discussion could have done. The realistic theatre's ideals of analysis, motivation, and conviction were attained here by the expressive employment (or shall we say deployment) of music and the dance. "Realism," as understood in terms of these ideals, becomes impossible only when, as in ordinary practice, there is no true interfusion of arts, but a haphazard or routine mingling of elements; for musical theatre and opera are usually treated as "an omelet of the arts of the theatres." [36] Inner justification of action certainly can appear only when considerations of theatrical spectacle or musical virtuosity do not prevail so strongly that human motivation above the kindergarten level is eliminated.

It was the striving for a theatricalism that agrees with essential realism, instead of conflicting with it, that kept the aims of the two original leaders of the Moscow Art Theatre from clashing. Stanislavsky was never an enemy of the imagination: he staged Maeterlinck's fantasy *The Blue Bird*, as well as some of the Belgian writer's early symbolistic one-act pieces, before World War I and indeed had a symbolist phase himself, as did many leaders of Russian literature, between 1905 and 1916.

[35] *Ibid.*, p. 55.
[36] A. Kugel, a Russian critic, quoted in Sayler, *Inside the Moscow Art Theatre*, p. 139.

Stanislavsky's concern was with making the imagined action real for theatrical purposes through the proper use of the actor. After a quarter of a century of intensive work, Stanislavsky spoke clearly enough on this particular point in 1924 when he described his "system" as a means for promoting "the creation of the creative mood," or producing "a favorable condition for the appearance of inspiration by means of the will, that condition in the presence of which inspiration was most likely to descend into the actor's soul." Stanislavsky added that he came to understand that the actor becomes a creator by virtue of the "magical, creative *if*." The actor believes in this "imagined truth" more ardently than he believed in "practical truth": "From the moment of the appearance of *if*, the actor passes from the plane of actual reality into a plane of another life, created and imagined by himself. Believing in this life, the actor can begin to create." [37]

Stanislavsky and the imaginative realists could require no less of the actor than Wordsworth required of the poet, who was in turn Wordsworth's romantic hero:

> . . . a disposition to be affected more than other men by absent things as if they were present; an ability of conjuring up in himself passions, which are indeed far from being the same as those produced by real events, yet . . . do more nearly resemble the passions produced by real events than anything which, from the notions of their own minds merely, other men are accustomed to feel in themselves. (Preface to *Lyrical Ballads*, 1800.)

We may conclude that the creative act was one of *imagination* for Stanislavsky, whether he was concerned with realistic or nonrealistic plays. It is nonsense to say that realistic artists have been unimaginative. If they had been unimaginative, they would not have been artists. And this is true whether the individual happened to write, stage, design, or act in a play. It would be

[37] Sayler, *op. cit.*, pp. 176-177.

absurd, for example, to say that there is no imagination at work in *Ghosts, Rosmersholm, The Wild Duck,* and *John Gabriel Borkman,* or that this imagination is of a lower order than that which created, let us say, *Cyrano de Bergerac.* I am surely not alone in attributing a stronger imagination to Ibsen than to Rostand. And taking our cue from Coleridge's distinction between imagination and fancy, we could profitably pursue the question of whether good realistic writing, staging, or acting is not more profoundly imaginative than a great deal that has passed for imagination in the nonrealistic theatre.

By no means has a feeling for theatre been the exclusive attribute of those who like to play at making theatre or those who elect to perform literary or nonliterary legerdemain in dramatic writing and on the stage. There is surely as much sense of theatre (and, indeed, a *power* of theatre) in *Hedda Gabler* as in, let us say, Molnar's *The Play's the Thing,* or, for that matter, *Liliom.* Maxwell Anderson's *Joan of Lorraine* is an ingenious theatricalist play about an actress rehearsing in a play about Joan of Arc and learning to understand the role. Thus Joan's idealism is elucidated for the audience in discussions of scenes with the stage director, who is also a character in the play. It does not follow, however, that *Joan of Lorraine* is more dramatically and theatrically effective than Shaw's *Saint Joan,* which is just a play about Joan of Arc herself that calls no attention to the theatre, or to itself as make-believe, until we reach the epilogue. And surely Shaw knew as well as Maxwell Anderson that what he was writing about Joan of Arc would be performed in the theatre and would not be merely studied in the reading room of the British Museum. Stanislavsky, in staging *The Lower Depths,* was just as concerned with making Gorki's play vibrate as an experience of theatre as in making us feel that the characters lived and suffered. And the great actor Ivan Moskvin, who played the pilgrim Luka in this masterpiece of naturalism, was triumphantly *both* that character and an actor bent upon giving theatrical definition, rhythm, and accent to the performance. We may say, then, that in so far as realists and naturalists were supremely effective in the theatre, they were distinctly theatrical as well as imaginative. Strictly speaking, we should not call their work realism or naturalism, but *theatrical realism* and *theatrical naturalism.*

How richly theatrical some essentially realistic productions of the past have been cannot be conveyed to anyone who did not see the Moscow Art Theatre's productions of *The Cherry Orchard* and *The Lower Depths* in New York in the mid-1920's, or for that matter, the Group Theatre's production of *Awake and Sing!* in the mid-1930's. How supremely theatrical, without being specious, some realistic plays have already been will be evident to anyone who takes the trouble to give careful study to O'Casey's *Juno and the Paycock* and *The Plough and the Stars,* written in the 1920's, or to Chekhov's *The Three Sisters,* written at the beginning of this century. And a more immediate example is *A Streetcar Named Desire,* which actually contains considerably more theatre in its fabric of characterization, atmosphere and action (this in spite of Williams' naturalism) than many nonrealistic plays, not excluding poetic ones such as *The Cocktail Party* and *The Lady's Not for Burning.*

That self-consciously sensational jumping of the fourth wall, trick effects, and other kinds of theatricalism that are destructive of conviction and depth in playwriting are unnecessary to the production of powerful theatre by a playwright was, surely, best demonstrated by Chekhov, in whose works realism and the sense of theatre merged perfectly. Not only is the structure of *The Three Sisters* superbly symphonic, not only do the action and speech of the characters appear in continual counterpoint, but the pantomime and sound effects, a fire in the town, the playing of a military band, and other nonliterary details produce the crackle of theatre in this drama. Theatre is constantly created, moreover, in details of action that are at once *characterizing* in a realistic mode and *symbolic* in a theatrical mode. One cannot fail to realize this in considering the character Solyony, who wantonly kills the youngest sister's fiancé at the end of the play. Throughout the play, Solyony pours perfume on his death-dealing hands; this mentally twisted man cannot stand the smell of mortality that he imagines them to have. Throughout this play, objects are used theatrically—that is, as theatrical extensions and symbols of Chekhov's realistic action and characterization. And, of course, there is nothing more honestly theatrical in Chekhov's work, as well as more realistically characterizing, than the ridiculous ball in that other Chekhovian masterpiece, *The Cherry Orchard*—a ball staged so inappropriately just when the family has lost its estate. That dramatic realism can fuse with theatricalism and can thereby increase rather than lose its persuasiveness is, indeed, too apparent to justify despair of prospects for revitalizing the realistic theatre.

The leaders of theatrical stylization, too, can play an increasingly effective role in facilitating a merger of the rival modes. In 1941, after having staged *My Heart's in the Highlands*, Robert Lewis, who later directed other fanciful productions such as *Brigadoon* and *The Teahouse of the August Moon*, was moved to protest that there had been a mistaken distinction between so-called stylization and naturalism—"the implication being that the former has problems of form and the latter hasn't." Any satisfactory production, as well as any play, whether it is satisfactory or not, must have form. "To be sure," Mr. Lewis declared, "*realism*, too, is a form; one of the theatrical forms. In realistic drama and theatre, too, the life presented on the stage has been arranged—that is, 'formed.'" But from his experience as a member of the Group Theatre and as teacher of acting, he went on to remind us that in the realistic mode the emphasis is more markedly on the "inner movement" of the play. Everything important in it is determined by what the character wants—that is, by psychological justification.[38] A fusion of theatricalism and realism was, besides, the aim of Jacques Copeau, the most dedicated leader of the theatricalist movement of Western Europe, whose disciples kept theatrical art alive in France. Copeau formalized

[38] Gassner, *Producing the Play*, pp. 294-300.

his scenery because he wanted to simplify it; and he simplified it in order to prevent the décor from overshadowing the dramatic text. Nor did Copeau want to slight character creation. He gave close attention to acting style at his theatre and school with a view to making the actor achieve convincing characterization. Copeau cultivated the histrionic sensibility of the actor as thoroughly as possible, teaching him to *act out* and underscore or punctuate characterization. But he also expected the actor to enact his role with virtually the same "inner realism" that Stanislavsky cultivated at the Moscow Art Theatre. (See pp. 197-202, and pp. 202-205.)

The mixed effect on playwriting of Copeau's work is perhaps best exemplified by André Obey's biblical play *Noah,* written in 1931 for the Company of Fifteen directed by Copeau's talented nephew and disciple Michel Saint-Denis, who became head of the Old Vic School. In Obey's play will be found both universality of theme and concreteness of characterization. In *Noah,* theatricalism is advanced by means of spectacle, pantomime, and dance. And, at the same time, the major requirement of realism is met by orderly sequences of credibly motivated human behavior. (Pierre Fresnay in New York and John Gielgud in London found the title role a thoroughly gratifying one in 1935.) Both the poetry and prose of the human condition are evoked in this work. And Obey requires the actors to provide both realistic portraiture and theatrical action—the latter in the miming of animal roles (for Obey makes charming use of the animals in the ark), and in the dancing of a primitive "earth-greeting" when Noah's children emerge from the ark and touch land at last.

Noah is fundamentally a piece for the little art theatre, and is incapable of affording a gripping experience or sustaining a keen adventure or combat of the mind. Obey, who reached his apogee with this play, has remained a distinctly minor figure in the modern theatre. I believe that even his sturdier colleagues, including Giraudoux and Anouilh, who also emerged from the Copeau-influenced French theatre, have lacked stature commensurate with their talents, not to say with their reputation. Political and financial weather permitting, we may expect a renascence of modern theatre as a result of the intelligent synthesizing of realism and theatricalism. But we shall have only the shadow of a renascence unless there is also a *revitalization* of the drama itself. Imaginative and theatricalized dramatic writing will have to attain at least some of the depth and force with which Ibsen and the other pioneers modernized the drama. By itself, neither the poetic simplicity of an Obey nor the theatrical sophistication or finesse of an Anouilh, nor any of the other histrionic and formalistic qualities to be found in theatricalist writing, can create a very vital stage.

Glimmerings of a renascence of modern theatre have been discovered from time to time since the 1930's whenever a Giraudoux, Anouilh, Brecht, or O'Casey has married theatricalist dramaturgy to contemporary reality or to contemporary realizations of legend and history, as in Giraudoux' *The Trojan War Will Not Take Place*[39] and Brecht's best work. If a vital, noncoterie theatre is to be created it is, however, still imperative that we overcome the tendency to associate theatrical imagination predominantly with absolute emotional states (as in Yeats's *The Player Queen* and *A Full Moon in March*) or with exquisite poetic experience (as in Obey's *Venus and Adonis*) rather than with commitments to the contemporary world. It is especially important to go beyond commitments to theatricality alone even when these are as entrancing as Anouilh's youthful play *Le Bal des voleurs* (*Thieves' Carnival*). So far as significant theatre for the twentieth century is concerned, theatricalism for its own sake, or theatre-for-theatre's sake, is a blind alley. It is the blind alley of amateurism, on the one hand, and of decadent sophistication on the other.

[39] Now to be known in English forever as *Tiger at the Gates,* the title of Christopher Fry's excellent translation and Harold Clurman's superb London and Broadway productions in 1955.

In the theatricalist-realist synthesis there must be a suitable mediation between *immediacy* and *universality*, between the specificity of a subject and the imaginative projections that lead us out of time and place into the realms of essence. And at the same time, the synthesis must be predicated on a sense of the present. For effective drama we need a grasp of events, emotion, and thought transpiring in an environment rather than in the vast inane that romanticism began to sanction after 1770. If we disavow topical or journalistic realism as an ideal, we must also repudiate the idealization of absolutes and the dream of arriving at universals by means of inspired leaps into the void.

Before 1919, Julien Benda sensibly warned writers about "this aesthetic of the elementary soul" which tends to lead to exploitation of the simplicities until art becomes vacuous. Idealized naiveté, the special passion of the sophisticated, has littered the stage with fragile women possessed of inexpressible yearnings, pure Mélisandes and Mary Roses, as well as with "between-wars" Magdalens like the prostitutes of Simon Gantillon's *Maya* and the amoral heroine of John Van Druten's *I Am a Camera*. And inevitably, of course, with beatified degenerates and idiots. *Der reine Tor,* the Wagnerian "pure fool," is a romantic creation; the "impure fool" of our own times, who exhibits the surface naturalism that outrages censors, is merely the obverse side of the same idealization of mindlessness. He is produced by the romanticization of the dungheap, whereas his counterpart emerged from the flower garden. The overvaluation of the "instinctive life" results in the depiction of the same character feeling the same things over and over again, yet understanding nothing but his own impulse.

Without contesting the right of the purely instinctive to a place among the materials of art,[40] Benda protested against the

[40] Julien Benda, *Belphégor* (New York, 1929), pp. 77-85. The essays in this abrasive volume, published in French in 1919, were written before 1914.

doctrine that it is "sole material of art, the material *par excellence. . . .* As though intelligence were not just as great a reality. As though Goethe's soul were less real than Mélisande's." Goethe's soul would, of course, reintroduce complexity, take us beyond primitive levels of sensation, and point in the direction of the "drama of ideas" which first invigorated realistic theatre.

All these caveats are especially needed in view of the insubstantiality of the writing of many playwrights, even tough-fibered ones, when they leave their realistic moorings. And warnings may be in order, too, against the search for profundity through indistinctness—the profundity-fetishism which, unlike the cultivation of the "play of ideas," is a foe to light and a friend to darkness. The obscurities of the soul, the inscrutability of fate, the mystery of faith may well provide matter for meditative poetry, but, unless aided by strong plot and characterization, they are likely to prove soporific on the stage. "Profundity" is the special delusion of poets and poetasters of the theatre that makes an effective fusion of realism and theatricality particularly difficult. This delusion was first powerfully fostered by Maeterlinck and Andreyev, those sentimentalists of the universal and hierophants of an unintelligible universe. The mirage of profundity, however, has become particularly seductive in recent decades for those who write in English; Fry and Eliot are only the best known, they are not the worst, of the deluded. Nor do all the deluded write formal poetry, as O'Neill proved in *Dynamo* and *Lazarus Laughed* and as Williams did in *Camino Real*. In the theatre, it would seem, the imagination outruns, and sometimes overwhelms, the creative faculty.

Our reasonable expectations for a realist-theatricalist synthesis by no means place dramatic poetry under interdict, however. Indeed, the full resonance of dramatic art will have to come from more than a mere *poésie de théâtre*. However greatly indebted the playwright who makes use of such a synthesis may be to his own theatrical imagination and that of his stage director, he will need language. The art of the mime, the subtleties of stage movement, the most expressive scenery and stage lighting, all technical and histrionic skills, may well be deplored if they should tend to reduce the artist of words to a cipher in the theatre. Visions of a fusion of realistic and theatricalist art, indeed, light ultimately upon a poetic drama that is the creation of the writer rather than the technician, the mere showman, and the play-carpenter. Dramatic poets cannot of course be created by fiat from a critic's pen or by a general clamor for songbirds in the modern playhouses. But a theatre that gives the poet an opportunity to develop his skill may ultimately be rewarded with a vital poetic drama.

A Chronology of Meyerhold's War Against Realism

A blow-by-blow account of Meyerhold's assault on realism as recounted by Huntly Carter (*The New Spirit in the Russian Theatre, 1917–1928*) is instructive. It indicates that (1) Meyerhold's nonrealistic experimentation started long before the Russian political revolution of November 1917; (2) his art, like that of the dramatic and nondramatic writers of the prerevolutionary period (Andreyev, Evreinov, Sologub, Blok, Pasternak, Ivanov, and others), was not exclusively Russian but was part of a wave of the antinaturalistic, symbolist, and formalistic movement diffused throughout Europe; (3) the revolution in Russia merely accelerated his imaginativeness and theatricalizing disposition; (4) constructivism, as noted previously, was only one phase of his career and one that he had abandoned by the middle 1930's, so that "formalistic" excesses could no longer honestly be charged against him when he fell afoul of Stalinist reaction in the arts; and (5) constructivism was not simply a naive form of mimesis, a response to industrial architecture and modern machinery, but a fairly self-sufficient program for arriving at esthetic ends. Also, Meyerhold's arbitrary treatment of the classics was not barbarity or mere whim on his part. He had to take drastic liberties with the text in order to assert his own time-conditioned creativeness. Nor was Meyerhold alone in tailoring the text to the director's creative vision or to his political passion. In support of this statement, we need only recall the free handling of plays by Reinhardt, Piscator, and Orson Welles.

Below is an abbreviated chronology of Meyerhold's search for form in the years 1898–1920.

1898   Meyerhold joins the Moscow Art Theatre at its formation and becomes steeped in realism, creating the roles of Treplev in *The Sea-Gull* and Baron Tusenbach in *The Three Sisters*.

1902   Meyerhold leaves the Moscow Art Theatre and goes in search of new forms of theatre in opposition to Stanislavsky's realistic doctrine of ignoring the audience—*i.e.*, of observing the fourth-wall convention. He travels to Italy next year.

1904–1905   He adopts "conventionalism," then called "conditionalism" in Russia. He strives to punctuate his productions with some ruling accent or notion of a somewhat abstract character.

1905   He tries to create a "mystic theatre" and responds to Maeterlinckian symbolism in producing Maeterlinck's nebulous drama *The Death of Tintagiles*.

1906   Staging plays in Tiflis, he uses some indefinite kind of formalism, apparently under the influence of Greek theatre. "He now turned to develop the idea of music applied to dramatic form . . . [producing Maeterlinck's mystic drama *Sister Beatrice* and Schnitzler's *The Call of Life*]. . . . He sought to make the actors' movements resemble those of a dance." In a provincial theatre, Meyerhold next removes the proscenium and the act-drop in producing *Ghosts,* which had been written for representational, "fourth-wall" performance. "Take away the act-drop and the spectator is immediately saturated by the stage and its contents, and is thus prepared for the act of dramatic communication," says Carter, approvingly.

(November) Meyerhold becomes associated with the successful actress-manager Vera Fedorovna Komisarjevskaya (1864–1910), who had come under the influence of the symbolist movement. His aim in directing *Sister Beatrice* for her in St. Petersburg was "to dematerialize [sic] the stage in order to express the mystery . . . in the play. So he gave it the air of a religious service." To abolish the separation of the actor and the spectator, he used the shallow-stage technique (as used in the Künstlertheater in Munich) "by playing on the forepart of the stage against flat decorative church-like scenery." He also used "melodic speech, and plain, precise, carved-out gesture." He showed the actor "carved, as it were, in relief" against the flat decorative scenery.

Meyerhold successfully produces, in association with Komisarjevskaya, Andreyev's symbolist morality play *The Life of Man.* "The make-up of the actors was mask-like. Their beards were as though sculptured. Here the aim was to communicate the sentiments and feelings of a dream."

1907 Meyerhold goes to Berlin with Komisarjevskaya and studies the work of Reinhardt there. He now moves toward giving the actor the roundness of sculptural form in space, treating the actor like free-standing sculpture instead of presenting him against the scenery like a figure in relief.

1907   (*Continued*)

Back in Moscow, Meyerhold stages Wedekind's natural-ist-expressionist drama of adolescence *The Awakening of Spring*, using different stage levels for presenting the ac-tor in the round. He also introduces stairs across the stage that raise the actors to different heights.

1908   After Meyerhold's rupture with Komisarjevskaya, because (as she alleged) she opposed his interest in marionettes and his tendency to turn the actors into puppets, he stages plays in Minsk. He continues his theatricalist experimen-tation, using screens instead of sets and using full light on the audience, because he thought "it heightened the mood of the spectator, while enabling the actor to see, as in a looking-glass, the effect which he was communicating." Also, in staging opera, he uses the actor more and more sculpturally on bare levels, emphasizing the contours of the body, arms, and legs. This practice probably marks the beginning of Meyerhold's celebrated principle of "bio-mechanics" in acting.

1910   He develops other theatricalist methods, as well as those sketched above, especially in staging Molière's *Don Juan* as a spectacle and in using masks for another production. Japanese and Greek influences are strongly present in his work as a director at this time. He also produces a harle-quinade.

1912–1913   He goes to Paris and stages a play by D'Annunzio with décor by the celebrated Léon Bakst. He also organ-izes a studio for the teaching of the technique of the *commedia dell' arte*.

1914   In producing the poet Alexander Blok's symbolistic-poetic play *The Unknown*, he uses a "construction," instead of "decoration," for the first time. This marks the beginning

ECLECTICISM—A SYMBOLIST THEATRICALIZATION OF REALISM

This multiple setting was designed by Jo Mielziner for the 1948 Broadway production of Tennessee Williams' realistic drama Summer and Smoke. *The production made use of simultaneous mansion-like settings (an extension of medieval staging) for the homes of the principal characters, with symbolism introduced in the centered statue of Eternity. The steps in the center were serviceable as playing levels, but they were not used as a major production element. The screen-like skeletal flats at the right and left provided a lyrical tracery of exteriors. Imaginative design settings have been greatly admired in the English and American commercial theatre even when the story, as in this case, has possessed strong naturalistic elements.* Photograph: Eileen Darby for Graphic House. Courtesy of Margo Jones.

DYNAMIC ECLECTICISM—SIMULTANEOUS REALISM AND STYLIZA-
TION *The 1955 Elia Kazan production of Tennessee Williams' naturalistic drama,* Cat on a Hot Tin Roof, *was designed by Jo Mielziner.
The photograph indicates the neutral character of the background and
the suspension of the action in space, as it were. That is, the actors
seemed to be performing on an apron stage while actually playing the
scene with inner realism—if not indeed also with external naturalism.
(For further comment see pages 124-125.)* Photograph: Zinn-Arthur.
Courtesy of William Fields for the Playwrights' Company.

1914 (*Continued*)

of his break with the symbolist technique of esthetic unity or "synthesis." Now begins his use of open theatricalization: "eccentric accessories, jugglers, Chinese boys throwing oranges among the audience, quaint things and human figures were interwoven in a fantastic manner."

1918 With the Bolshevik revolution, Meyerhold begins a search for dynamic form that will express collectivist aims and the industrialization of society along with a depersonalization of the individual.

1919 He stages open-air productions of such works as the poet Mayakovsky's revolutionary rhapsody *Mystery-Bouffe,* which was presented as a "mass spectacle." He develops the technique of "construction" or "constructivism," which represents an evolution of his use of levels and plastic acting. He had at first used acting levels for the purely esthetic or Appian purpose of liberating the actor from décor and giving him sculptural dimensionality. But now the scenic construction has the mechanical qualities of a machine, for Meyerhold brought "the ideas of the builder, the engineer, the mechanic into the theatre . . . a new conception of the surroundings of social life."

1920 Meyerhold now fully develops his acting system of bio-mechanics or bio-dynamics, which tends to turn the actor into an athlete, acrobat, and animated machine; the system showed the influence of behaviorism and of Pavlov's studies of conditioned reflexes. He also begins to use vertical constructions—frames divided into floors and compartments joined by platforms, staircases, and gangways, which made it possible for a large number of scenes to be played without pause. He also begins to use film strips with stage productions, as Piscator and Brecht were to do later in their style of epic theatre. Next, he uses movable constructions, and begins to employ movable walls and a revolving stage divided into concentric rings which move separately, so that many scenes can follow in rapid suc-

1920   (*Continued*)

cession: "he was able to stage the 35 or more scenes into which he divided a play with a film-like speed and continuity"—a system of producing a play for which, indeed, perhaps only acrobatic acting was appropriate.

Meyerhold continued his experiments for another 17 years. Of his later productions, the most notable for its bold inventions was his brilliant staging of Gogol's *The Inspector-General*. The scene presenting the return of the hero from a drunken spree while people appeared at the numerous doors of the background and rustled paper money at him was particularly outstanding. The scene was plainly a projection, on a fantastic scale, of bribery under the old Czarist regime.

The variety of this director's creative output taxes the imagination and makes adequate description impossible. A director's creations exist only on the stage, and Meyerhold's work was so completely of the theatre that the text of a play, even of a classic like Gogol's comedy, was to him only the libretto for an essentially nonverbal creation. Charles Dullin, Copeau's disciple and a great stage director himself, paying homage to Meyerhold in 1931, called him a creator of form and a poet of theatre—"un créateur de formes, un poète de la scène"—who wrote with gestures, rhythms, and a theatrical language invented for his needs, and who addressed himself to the eyes as much as the text of the play addressed itself to the ears: "Il écrit avec des gestes, des rhythmes, avec toute une langue théâtrale qu'il invente pour les besoins de sa cause et qui parle aux yeux autant que le texte s'addresse à l'oreille." [1] Without doubt this master of *la poésie de théâtre* entranced all who saw his productions, even if they could not be entirely certain he was not confounding art with artifice and making them connive in his misdemeanor.

This brief review of Meyerhold's ventures up to 1920

[1] Charles Dullin, *Souvenirs et notes de travail d'un acteur*, Paris, 1946.

should be sufficient to indicate the nature of his quest, which epitomized the search for antinaturalistic form that has characterized the theatre in our century. Perhaps this summary will also serve as a reminder that virtually every device or system of theatrical stylization has been tried, so that the problem is no longer one of *inventing* theatricalist methods, but of using them organically and meaningfully.

Theatricalism and the Actor

Competent acting is, indeed, essential to truly gratifying theatricalism. Thus, a great deal of the theatricalist staging in our college and university theatres is unsuccessful, despite admirable work by the directors and designers, because the performance of individual roles is inadequate. Few students have succeeded in creating characters rather than character types, animated cartoons, and automatons, and even among the best of the student actors and amateurs will be found few who are capable of sustaining a long role. Understandably, then, the directors endeavor to compensate for the deficiency by tolerating, if not indeed encouraging, such mechanical tricks as gesticulating, stamping, shouting, leaping, and mugging.

Encouraged by local success, the directors may think up more and more ways of turning their actors' inadequacies to theatrical advantage. And being persons who are in general better educated than most professional producers and directors, they have no difficulty in finding esthetic justifications for their practices. They are, understandably, the most ardent exponents of theatricalism, to which they are greatly indebted for tolerable productions, just as they are greatly beholden to Gordon Craig. With him, they place reliance on "directors' design" and give it priority over acting. Their productions are usually superior in design to Broadway and Shaftesbury Avenue productions. But the productions rarely penetrate to the living core of a good play precisely because they are based on design rather than on character realization. Nor is the result appreciably better when the play to be staged stems from a historically conventional theatre, such as that of Louis XIV, the Restoration period, or the eighteenth century—that is, when the play is "artificial" by historical sanction. The tendency, in some academic dramatics, is to assume that a production of *Love for Love, She Stoops to Conquer, The School for Scandal,* or *The Importance of Being Earnest* needs only to be theatrical in order to be successful. The resulting productions are often full of clever stage business, including such extraneous feats as an actor's pretending to light candles in chandeliers or in eighteenth-century footlights, but often leave an impression of style pursued for the sake of style rather than employed as a means to some further end.

If plays are to survive theatricalist treatment, they need acting that is *better* rather than worse than that required by ordinary realistic drama; they need character building *and* style. We ought not to forget that comic characterization is still characterization, and that a Molière and a Congreve stand out among numerous forgotten playwrights not because they were "artificial" but because they had something to say through such character-creations as Millamant, Mirabell, Alceste, and Harpagon. When John Gielgud produced a memorable *Importance of Being Earnest* and played John Worthing in it, he showed his awareness of the importance of comic characterization even in farce by supplying a John Worthing who had more substantiality and was more "real" than a run-of-the-mill performer's realistic portraits. Gielgud's Jack had reality *with* style. The mediocre realist thinks that he can be real without style; the mediocre theatricalist, that he can have style without reality. The results are equally inadequate for both realism and theatricalism. A theatricalism of pat and transparent artifice, far from being "progressive," is retrogressive; it brings us back to the bankrupt prerealistic theatre of pasteboard dramatics and ham acting.

It is not surprising, then, that some leaders of stylization have paid close attention to the training of actors. Copeau, at the height of his fame, gave up producing in order to establish a school for acting; and his associates and their disciples—Jouvet, Dullin, and Barrault—gave most of their attention to the creation of character within the ambience of a particular style and the limits of a particular type of play. It is characteristic of their regard for character realization that Christian Bérard's setting for the celebrated Jouvet production of *L'École des femmes* was a highly theatricalist, toylike construction (Arnolphe's house was surrounded by a collapsible fence), but that Jouvet's Arnolphe was a total creation—a foolish and obsessed but *complete* man. One could even feel somewhat sorry for him.

Brecht, too, has formulated a theory of acting. It has been set forth in his *Kleines Organon für das Theater* and other writings, including "A Short Description of a New Technique of the Art of Acting Which Produces an Effect of Estrangement," written for the International Theatre Institute's quarterly publication, *World Theatre* (Vol. LV, No. 1). The views of Brecht, like those of Meyerhold, Barrault, and other proponents of stylization, can mislead the inexperienced. There are pitfalls in his writings for those who might adopt his anti-Stanislavskian methods without realizing that Brecht, like other leaders of the European theatre, assumes that his actors will be competent enough to create character and get *inside* a role. Having made that assumption, he then considers how he can teach the actor to get *outside* the role as well. There is, of course, no point in training an actor to get out of his role if he cannot get into it. In playwriting, too, Brecht's principle of breaking the illusion is meaningless for the playwright who is not capable of creating an illusion, just as there isn't much point in telling a playwright or actor to guard against emotionalism if he lacks a capacity for feeling.

The mature Brecht has created true characters in his plays perhaps more frequently than he himself has realized. A character, of course, is not a reproduction of a person in the street, but a playwright's and actor's creation, which makes him a work of art. This involves selectivity, intensification, special perspective, composition or design, and a certain abstractness along with the obvious attention to creating a resemblance to persons. At one time Shaw was accused of failing to create characters, too; yet today few dramatic characters are as well known as Shaw's in the English-speaking world. It was a mistaken view of both realism and character reality that inspired the charge against Shaw, who became the modern theatre's greatest "realist-theatricalist." But we can make the same mistake about the work of older playwrights if we fail to realize that the effective theatricalism of the great ages has been memorable for its characterizations: Otherwise the great actors and dramatists of the pre-realistic stage could never have attained their reputation for carrying conviction ("holding up a mirror to nature"), and all the famous dramatic characters from Antigone and Oedipus to Hamlet would have been mere two-dimensional cartoons. In a sense, acting *is* characterization, and the soundest theatricalist artists know only what realists also have known—namely, that there are both "round" and "flat" characters in a play, just as in novels. The theatricalist merely deploys the characters, especially the flat ones, more "theatrically"—with more or less "theatricalist" objectives in mind.

It is this deployment that is implicit in the introduction written by Michel Saint-Denis for the publication of Arthur Wilmurt's translation of Obey's *Noah*. On the one hand, Saint-Denis stresses the importance of having a good actor for Noah and "a sensitive actress of wit and personality" for Mrs. Noah; on the other hand, he calls for the "theatrical" treatment of Noah's children and the animals. The important thing in producing the play is to make them act as choruses: "There is nothing complex about their individual psychology—it is the movement which they do together which must be thought out and combined so that they give shape and rhythm to the action."

And he is right in sounding a warning against "complex psychology," which tends to be overused as a result of misapplied realism and misunderstood Stanislavskian training until each actor plays his part as though he were a case history.

Saint-Denis defines a vivid histrionic method when he writes that "it is through their movements together that the children mime the rain as it begins to fall, that they make us feel the roll of the boat during the storm . . . , that they enable us to follow the flight of the dove in the sky; and finally, before going their separate ways, it is together they first set foot on dry land and fight to possess it." It is work of this kind that is soundly threatrical, and Saint-Denis gives a good description when, in writing of his Compagnie des Quinze, he declared that the actors were capable of "showing life rather than explaining it, relying more on sound and physical movement than on talking, used to singing and dancing, able to build up from choral work to the invention of simple, clearly defined characters." Nevertheless, it is plain that even the best ensemble of this kind would have little power to engross our attention for an evening of theatre in the absence of character creation by the chief actors, as *Noah* wouldn't be much of a play if it were all chorus and no character. It is possible, indeed, to prefer Odets' not entirely clear version of the biblical theme *The Flowering Peach* precisely because less "artiness" stands in the way of characterization.

The Realists, Copeau, and the Possibilities of Synthesis

We can readily understand that some rapprochement between realistic and theatricalist views of theatre should have taken place in our century. Even Antoine had not intended to make his *Théâtre Libre* an exclusive citadel of naturalism. Stanislavsky sought theatrical effects wherever he could attain them without sacrificing truth of environment and truth of character.

About forty years after he had founded it, the Moscow Art Theatre could make a theatrical romp out of a dramatization of *The Pickwick Papers* without feeling that it had betrayed its ideals. (This celebrated production even combined painted and three-dimensional scenery, and used both live actors and painted figures.) Nor is there any evidence that Stanislavsky was in the least disturbed when his favorite pupil, Eugene Vakhtangov, gave the modern theatre two of its most famous early theatricalist productions, *Princess Turandot* and *The Dybbuk*, after World War I. Stanislavsky, who staged several plays by Maeterlinck and exercised patience and humility in working with Gordon Craig on the latter's Moscow Art Theatre *Hamlet* production in 1911, had indeed given abundant proof of his regard for theatrical imaginativeness before 1918, as had other pioneers in realism. For example, it was none other than the pioneer of German naturalistic theatre, Otto Brahm, who gave Craig his first opportunity to design a production on the Continent. Craig was utterly stalemated in England in 1904 when Brahm, then managing the Lessing Theatre in Berlin, invited him to design the Hugo von Hofmannsthal version of Thomas Otway's *Venice Preserved*.

A greater fusion of realism and theatricalism east of the Rhine was made difficult, however, by the turbulence of the theatre after World War I. The revolutionary postwar situation in Central Europe favored the wild excesses of the expressionists which made the gulf between realism and theatricalism altogether too wide to be bridged. And in Russia during the 1920's and early 1930's the Moscow Art Theatre came to be regarded as a stodgily academic organization by those who combined political revolutionism with revolutionism in the arts. Vakhtangov, who could have perhaps mediated between Stanislavskian realism and extreme theatricalism, died in 1922.

In Western Europe, the possibilities of mediation depended largely upon the teachings and example of Copeau. These bore fruit in some highly regarded productions by Dullin, Jouvet, and others, and in plays by Giraudoux and a few other playwrights. Copeau, unlike some other Parisian *avant-garde* producers, could esteem the work of Antoine, Becque, and Stanislavsky while at the same time developing his art of simplified and theatricalized acting and staging. Unfortunately, however, Copeau's career in the Parisian theatre was interrupted by World War I and then disorganized by his own temperament—or, rather, by the defects of his virtues. He succumbed to religio-esthetic mysticism and to that last infirmity of noble minds called perfectionism. His Théâtre du Vieux Colombier had closed its doors by 1924. He was no longer a practicing producer-director during the last decades of his life except for a few disturbed years between 1936 and the fall of Paris when he had limited scope as one of four stage directors at the Comédie Française. Copeau died at the age of seventy in 1949, but the important part of his career in the public theatre was over by the time he had reached his forty-fifth year. Gide noted, regretfully, in the third volume of his *Journals,* that "Copeau, though claiming not to do so, was working for a select few," and wanted "to lead to perfection, to style, to purity, an essentially impure art." Gide charged Copeau with having allowed himself to be deluded into inactivity by a vision of holiness "which misleads only the holiest."

It was with good reason, too, that Granville-Barker pleaded with Copeau in 1928 "to spend no more time kissing the earth [Copeau had retired to the countryside in order "to kiss the soil" and regain spiritual strength] or laying foundations, but to go ahead with your building; that is to say, with the interpreting of one good play after another, letting the art of one beget the better art of the next." He warned Copeau that "all the virtue goes out of simplicity that is guarded too carefully and too long. . . ." [1]

Waldo Frank, referring to Copeau's refusal to perform many successful modern plays at the Vieux Colombier, reported in

<hr>

[1] Harley Granville-Barker, "A Letter to Jacques Copeau," *Theatre Arts Monthly* (October 1929), p. 755.

1925 that a "legend grew that Copeau's purity was a Puritan madness against living merit." [2] Copeau allowed the work of Pirandello, O'Neill, Crommelynck, and other candidates for his attention to pass out of his hands. The men he encouraged most, Gide and Jules Romains (and he lost the latter, too) were chiefly novelists by vocation.

More than other men, Copeau could have reconciled the aims of realism and antirealism. But a man who rejected the possibility of having a strong, immediate effect on living playwrights could not resolve the conflict between styles. To influence stage production and the training of actors, as he unquestionably did, was not enough.

[2] *Theatre Arts* (September 1925), p. 586.

The Duality of
Theatre

In dramatic art the eye is more easily
deceived than the mind.—JULES JANIN

. . . the aim and object of all true art
is the skillful blending of the real
and the ideal.—WILLIAM CHARLES MACREADY

I am for nature and against naturalism.
—CONSTANT COQUELIN

The stage is a lie; make it
as truthful as possible.—VOLTAIRE

A work of art which serves life
cannot at the same time be independent
of life.—ALEXANDER BAKSHY

. . . the theatre, as Huysmans said of schools of literature,
is neither realistic nor poetic;
it is only good or bad, true or false.—STARK YOUNG

THE COMBINATION OF REALISTIC AND THEATRICALIST TECHNIQUES IN the writing and staging of a play or the acting of a part can never be a simple matter. It requires a great deal of understanding, taste, and tact at all times, and the *ad hoc* decisions that have to be made (and often revised) cannot be discussed abstrusely. Certainly, there is no rule of thumb by which the playwright, the actor, and the *régisseur* can infallibly mingle realism and theatricalism. It is important, however, to make it possible for them to function without inhibition and with a minimum of confusion; and to this end, it is essential to formulate principles upon which their creativity in the theatre can rest securely. In other ages these principles apparently did not need to be formulated, but clarifications of theory are generally desirable in a self-conscious age like our own, and they are especially needed by self-conscious contemporary students of theatre who have been exposed to the seductions and obfuscations of the rival theatrical programs of our century. The fuzzy acceptance of eclecticism so often associated with decadence in art and the "anything-goes" attitude so characteristic of show business cannot satisfy the needs of responsible artistry. These needs will be met only by a view of theatre that recognizes the ambivalent character of all representation on the stage. It is a view that cannot accept any rigidly monistic attitude toward the making and experiencing of theatre.

Since the vogue of the symbolists, we have been greatly under the influence of the unity-minded, design-minded leaders of the Craig-Appia school. These leaders have felt that one central design or style of treatment must bring all elements of a given stage production into a single focus, that one tone must dominate it, and that one vision must rule it if the theatre is to be taken seriously as an art. This prescript agrees so well with esthetic principle in general, and has indeed been so effective in preventing many productions from disintegrating into chaos, that the principle of *design* should not be rashly discarded. Nor has esthetic unity been challenged in our time except on special principle, Erwin Piscator, Bertolt Brecht, and their associates in epic theatre having violated it only on the grounds that unbroken identification with stage characters and complete immersion in an emotional situation can work on the mind of the spectator as a soporific.

Nevertheless, it does not follow that the *sense of reality* must be violated by theatricality, for the play in the theatre can be served by a factor that operates strongly in theatrical practice and in the response of audiences—namely, a factor of *duality*. Duality of experience exists to some degree in every theatre and for both the performer and his audience: action in the theatre is both make-believe and actual for them.

As spectators in the theatre, we make use of a built-in mechanism comparable to a shuttle, which enables us to move back and forth between the planes of reality and theatre. Or this faculty may be described as double vision, which enables us to experience a stage performance in such a way that it is both reality and theatre at the same moment. We can focus on "real life" (that is, succumb to the *illusion* of reality), at one point in the performance, and soon thereafter respond to a thoroughly theatrical effect which we *know* to be "theatre" rather than "real life." Also, we can have the experience of feeling an action to be "real" and "theatrical" *at the same time*, just as we are simultaneously aware of "real" time and "theatrical" time, which may be much longer and may even consume decades during the actual lapse of minutes.

When theoreticians of play production speak of "esthetic distance" they surely imply such a fusion of the real and the unreal, of reality and theatre. When esthetic distance has been established at a performance of *Hamlet*, I may feel the death of Hamlet deeply, tragically; but I do not feel it with the immediacy (or, if you like, reality) that would make me want to run up onto the stage and administer first aid. I sympathize with Hamlet as though he were more real to me than most people, but I also know that I am in the theatre.

One may go somewhat further and maintain that the esthetic distance was there from the moment the curtain rose because the mechanism that established the distance already existed in my sensorium. I came to the theatre prepared to give myself up to the experience on the stage, but also wary of total involvement. I was prepared to *detach* myself from the experience lest it engross me to the point where my capacity for criticism, my physical safety, or my sense of personal dignity might suffer. There is much to be said for Samuel Johnson's assertion "the spectators are always in their senses, and know, from the first act to the last, that the stage is only a stage, and the players are only players." The spectator can turn his empathy on and off, so to speak. He can derive gratification both from identification with the actor as a momentarily real person in a real-life action, and from observation of the actor as the performer of a feat of acting. (Almost, indeed, as though the actor were supplying the intellectual-emotional equivalent of bareback riding and of acrobatics on a flying trapeze.) Our response to many a favorite of the stage has been of this nature: We wait for Alfred Lunt and Lynn Fontanne to deliver an inflection "just so," for Helen Hayes to establish a character detail with her characteristic piquancy, and for Mary Martin to "put across" a certain song. These things belong legitimately to the experience of theatre. Moreover, enjoyment of this sort need not hamper appreciation of characterization. At all times, the good actor functions both as an *actor* and a *character,* and there is no reason to believe that histrionic duality was ever absent, even when the actor was a masked Greek protagonist or a masked *commedia dell' arte* harlequin.

The experience of the theatre is always a dual one, if for no other reason than that the playgoer brings with him his double consciousness or focus, his ability to experience theatre on two planes. Therefore, it is always possible for the stage to achieve a satisfactory synthesis of realism and theatricalism. Audiences (at least today's audiences) are remarkably ready to feel themselves into the major roles, to identify themselves with the characters. Vicariousness seems to be the particular passion of entertainment in our century. And the ability to achieve identification makes the playgoer and the player much alike. To some degree, they both employ "affective memory." There is probably no immoderate manifestation of naïveté to be discovered in all this illusion-seeking, which intellectual and formalist artistry has endeavored to moderate or "cool down." Perhaps even the urbane playgoer is never completely "out" of illusion except while functioning as a specialist whose business it is to judge the performance technically. (As is the case, for instance, when a producer and his associates go "out of town" with the show with a view to improving it during the try-out period.) Perhaps it is even more accurate to say that the playgoer is usually both "in" and "out" of a stage production at the same time, and that the play is an *extratheatrical* and a *theatrical* experience for him at the same time.

It is noteworthy how easily an effect that is distinctly realistic or naturalistic can be converted into its opposite, into something grotesque or symbolic. On the basis of this fact, we may postulate for the theatre the existence of some sort of *law of conversion*. Extreme effects have a tendency to undergo some transformation for the spectator into an effect of a different, perhaps opposite, character.

A case in point is *Tobacco Road*, as produced on Broadway in 1933. For those whom its sensualism and brutish naturalism repelled, the production, of course, lost effect. For other play-goers, the naturalism tended to be transformed into social comment; the play induced pity and aroused the social conscience, and so the brutishness of the production underwent a transformation. That was the present writer's experience, and it induced him to include the play in one of his anthologies of American plays.[1] The reasons for including *Tobacco Road* could probably never have been made clear to the elderly Louisiana lady who burned the book because she was outraged by the "indecency" of the play; she could not have understood that for playgoers who had been conditioned by the depression of the 'thirties to look for "social significance" *Tobacco Road* was no more pornographic than a scalpel stuck in a tumor.

At the other extreme, there was the response of an older and wiser critic, Joseph Wood Krutch, for whom the naturalism of *Tobacco Road* underwent conversion into grotesque humor. Mr. Krutch attributed this humor to Erskine Caldwell's novel, upon which the play was based; however, one may wonder whether it was not actually the stage production that sharpened this distinguished theatre critic's awareness of the grotesque. Caldwell's "peculiar effects" were made possible for Mr. Krutch

only by the assumption of an exaggerated detachment from all the ordinary prejudices of either morality or taste and a consequent tendency to present the most violent and repul-

---

[1] *Twenty Best Plays of the Modern American Theatre* (New York: Crown Publishers, 1939), now a volume in *John Gassner's Library of Best American Plays*.

sive scenes with the elaborate casualness of a careful pseudo-naïveté . . . the mood which dominates his writing is the mood of a grotesque and horrible humor.[2]

He could have said of Caldwell's story what W. C. Brownell once wrote about some of Maupassant's work: "Every detail is real, but the implication of the whole is fantastic."[3] I should go on to say that Mr. Krutch, who considered the play "scarcely more than a parody on humanity," nevertheless found the work entertaining and expressed considerable approbation for it. And so it happened that the two drama critics of the 1930's who approved, in the main, of *Tobacco Road* were critics who would normally have been least inclined to do so. The flagrantly naturalistic production became transmuted into a mordant poem of pity for the present writer and into a sort of comedy of the grotesque for Mr. Krutch.

Perhaps the best example of the working of this process of conversion—or of the ease with which reality may become unreality in the theatre—is provided by Mordecai Gorelik's comments on the Broadway production of *Street Scene*. Although Alan Downer could call Elmer Rice's play "selective realism at its best,"[4] the slum tenement setting would ordinarily impress us as a naturalistic one. But a curious transmutation takes place as one studies that setting: (1) we start with an *artifice*—namely, the artificially constructed setting, a thing mainly made up of frames and canvas to simulate a brownstone tenement house; (2) the first result is the naturalistic illusion of the house, a dreary achievement of verisimilitude, of fidelity to ugly fact; (3) we end up experiencing this scenic construction as a "theatrically immediate," rather than "actual," reality, and as a symbol of sorts. Gorelik's view was that

> while the setting for *Street Scene* is at first glance almost in the style of Belasco, it shortly becomes evident that the

[2] *The American Drama Since 1918* (New York: Random House, 1939), pp. 122-128.
[3] *William Crary Brownell: An Anthology of His Writings* (New York: Scribner's, 1933), p. 150.
[4] *Fifty Years of American Drama* (Regnery, 1951), pp. 63-65.

apartment house façade is first of all a theatrical convention which permits the play to be staged in a new and arresting way. *The longer the setting remains on the stage* (in this case it remains throughout the play), *the less an audience identifies it as an actual place.* Instead, the audience sees and accepts it as *a sheer theatrical device.*[5]

Those who have had much experience in the theatre could undoubtedly report many arresting instances of conversion, although one must concede, of course, that conversion is a subjective phenomenon. John Mason Brown found the horrifying laundry scene in Sidney Kingsley's play *The World We Make* objectionably naturalistic. For the present writer, however, the steam laundry was an effective theatrical realization of the reality the rich young heroine of the play must learn to accept before she can be freed from her neurosis. But surely the point need not be labored; it is sufficiently familiar to artists in diverse fields. It is perhaps necessary only to remind ourselves that the law of conversion works both ways: not only may the apparently real become the apparently unreal or symbolic, but the reverse may happen—the apparently symbolic may become the apparently real, and the theatrical construction may take on (or give off) an effect of naturalistic verisimilitude.

A symbolist-impressionist setting, such as Mielziner's famous Williamsburg Bridge design for *Winterset,* may well convey the reality of New York's East Side more convincingly than a photograph. It may be said, then, that *environment,* too, is not at all as simple a thing as it seemed to be when the naturalists gave painstaking attention to realizing it on the stage with solid settings and the symbolists to dissolving it with space stages and atmospheric lighting. The environment may become a symbol, and the symbol may become an environment, once the total experience of theatre begins to be sought by writers and directors. Many a constructivist setting used by such theatricalist

[5] "The Conquest of Stage Space," *Theatre Arts* (March 1934). Italics mine.

director-producers as Tairov and Meyerhold underwent transformation in the spectator's mind from theatrical abstractness into the reality of factory catwalks, girders, bricklayers' scaffolds, and other structural elements.

Meaningless, finally, becomes the idea of "presentational" staging as the panacea for modern dramatic art. Unless the producer is prepared to make a carnival out of every modern play, or unless the playwright has included a narrator, choruses, and soliloquies or other presentational elements, the audience may well turn the presentational production into a representational or realistic one. Let us suppose we staged Shaw's *Don Juan in Hell* interlude "presentationally." What does this really mean? Unless the director orders each actor to carry on the Shavian conversation while hanging head downwards from a trapeze, isn't it likely that the audience will soon feel itself into the situation by identifying itself with the characters? (The spectator does not identify himself with a character's ideas; he identifies himself with the *character,* once he is sufficiently interested in the thoughts.) The actors performed on a bare stage and faced the audience directly in the Paul Gregory "reading" that was successfully given in the early 1950's. How long did it take the audience to make persons out of the actors and push them into a "real" environment (a little corner of Hell), instead of saying to themselves how delightfully unreal, how charmingly theatrical, everything is? And conversely, suppose *Don Juan in Hell* were staged, as was Sartre's existentialist conversation-piece *No Exit (Huis Clos),* in a realistic environment. In view of the character of Shaw's interlude, isn't it highly probable that the spectator would at times resist fourth-wall illusionism to the extent of receiving various portions of the dialogue, such as Don Juan's great apologia, as rhetorical displays or arias out of an "opera" by that Mozart of the spoken theatre, Shaw? (In this connection, it is perhaps wise to quote what Shaw said about casting plays: "The four principals should be soprano, alto, tenor, and bass . . . take care that every speech contrasts as strongly as possible in speed, tone, manner, and pitch with the one which provokes it, as if coming unexpectedly as a shock, surprise, stimulant, offense, amusement, or what not." [6]) The audience, then, may *restore* the fourth wall to the presentational production and abolish it in the representational production. A *law of conversion* or transmutation in the theatre, it is apparent, discourages an "either-or" effect. It induces fluctuations between presentationalism and representationalism, illusionism and theatricalism.

A "theatricalist-realist" or "realist-theatricalist" synthesis indeed must have always been experienced by audiences because of the spectator's capacity for adjusting himself to stage convention and yielding to an illusion of reality, and the actor's capacity for creating and nourishing that illusion. The actor has always been a powerful maker of illusion, whether masked or not, and whether standing on the platform of the Globe Theatre or under a chandelier on the abbreviated forestage of a seventeenth- or eighteenth-century playhouse. He has the two indispensable qualifications for engendering an illusion of the real— namely, the actuality of the human body in posture, gesture, and movement, which not all the pomp and stylization of costume can nullify, and the actuality of the human voice, that penetrating *vox humana* that comes out of a mask as well as out of the uncovered face. Where illusion is maintained, however, there convention also prevails: the illusion is illusion only because it is maintained within some artificial framework of art. And the frame-of-reference of dramatic reality, as well as its physical framework, can only be the theatre. We may say, then, that in the theatre an experience is not reality unless it is, first of all, theatre. Mrs. Alving's story, no less than the great debate between philanderer and devil in Shaw's *Don Juan in Hell* interlude, has existence only as theatrical reality—and the greater the theatrical reality of play and performance, the greater the illusion of reality.

[6] *Theatre Arts* (August 1949), p. 9.

Bearing in mind such an obvious fact (not obvious, however, to doctrinaire theatricalists any more than to doctrinaire naturalists), we can find it easy to understand why fidelity to nature has been claimed for favorite playwrights and players from the time of Shakespeare. No one received more praise than Garrick for introducing naturalness in acting on the English stage; yet Garrick's naturalness, which obviously carried a great deal of conviction for audiences in 1750, was theatrically realized at Drury Lane on an apron stage extending 13 feet from the proscenium arch and the front lines of the stage setting. And Garrick's "realism" was lit by chandeliers suspended from the ceiling of the playhouse. "The candles once lit at the beginning of each act remained so for all its scenes, and thus suspended in the midst of a moonlit grove, a dark forest, or a street at midnight, were always inevitably those six chandeliers in the foreground." [7]

In all periods, playwrights and players have been realistic *for their times* and within dramaturgic and theatrical conventions —that is, within limits more or less agreed to by their audiences. A present-day American audience would not agree with an Athenian audience of the fifth century B.C. that the making of theatre must be limited by the requirements of open-air production, by taboos, and by vestiges of ritual. The theatre we use as a frame of reference makes demands for the sake of "reality" that radically distinguish our plays and performances from those of the Greeks. In the twentieth century, the "realism" of Garrick's age would be either valueless or it would be incongruously "theatricalist." And if the "realism" of another period is theatrical in ours, it cannot function as the nontheatricalist element in a realist-theatricalist synthesis.

It follows, then, that such a synthesis requires a full realization, rather than any adulteration, of truly modern realism, and especially of the inner realism with which the actor is concerned.

[7] Mary Barton, *Garrick* (Macmillan, 1949), p. 81. I say nothing here about the incongruous costuming in that century. "The subjects of Queen Anne saw nothing incongruous in the full-bottomed wig worn with breast-plate and helmet by Booth as a noble Roman" (p. 82).

Realism and theatricalism should serve as checks on each other, but the greater check should be exerted by the former, for conviction remains the main desideratum in the dramatic experience. Chicanery and skittishness are the particular dangers of any theatricalist mode that is not rooted in national culture; Athenian theatricalism was so rooted, because the mask, the chorus, and the epiphany, or *deus ex machina,* were inherited from ritualism.

With respect to creating suitable stage settings there has been no serious difficulty ever since selective realism came into vogue as a result of the revolt against naturalism inspired by Appia and Craig; and today acting performances that are both realistically and theatrically based can be developed further. Even so Stanislavskian a school as the Actors' Studio of New York was able to turn out young actors after World War II who could create convincing characterizations and at the same time play their parts in a pattern of theatrical presence, pose, and movement. The present writer was particularly aware of this duality in the performances of Ben Gazzara, who played leading roles in *End as a Man* and *Cat on a Hot Tin Roof* between 1953 and 1955. The actors in Copeau's and Vakhtangov's type of theatre were particularly noted for this double faculty of creating a convincing character and theatricalizing it at the same time. Some remarkable notes in Vakhtangov's diary[8] present Stanislavsky's own teachings with exceptional clarity. They indicate that the Stanislavskian-trained actor would by no means be unfitted for a "theatricalist" performance. Critics of Stanislavsky, according to Vakhtangov, tended to neglect "the statement which takes first place in the system"—namely, "that the actor should not be concerned about his feeling during a play." Feeling will come of itself, if the actor thinks first of all about what he, as a character, wants to obtain. The diarist re-

[8] *Acting: A Handbook of the Stanislavski Method* (New York: Lear Publishers, 1947), pp. 116-124.

calls that Stanislavsky said to his pupils, "Don't wait for emotions —act immediately," and there is surely no better advice for the actor serving a theatre unfettered to naturalism. But it is plain, of course, in Vakhtangov's notations, that Stanislavsky did not dream of fostering mechanical acting. The attentive pupil, who was later going to develop his own style of production, made such familiar notes as "you must proceed from yourself . . . place yourself in the position or the situation of the character. . . . To create and not to be oneself is impossible."

In developing the style required by the synthesis we seek it is necessary to guard against extravagant Stanislavskian (or, shall we say, pseudo-Stanislavskian) overmotivation, on the one hand, and overtheatricalization on the other. The former is usually apparent in the work of earnest professionals, which is likely to be hobbled by a finicky treatment of characterizing detail. It is a serious error to overextend characterization greatly beyond the needs of a scene and so withdraw attention from the dominant dramatic action, thus retarding the evolution, obscuring the point, and dulling the edge of a play. So talented an actor as John Garfield, for example, played an early scene in *Peer Gynt* with such twisting of his body and such constant rubbing of his haunches on a ladder that he subverted the style and spirit of the play. The overconscientious actor was bent on giving us a total characterization at a point at which it was vastly more important to get ahead with Ibsen's symbolic and satiric fable. The error of overtheatricalization is more characteristic of the untrained or ill-trained nonprofessional actor who has learned to spark his movements with all the kinetic energy of an athletic young body and all the lack of restraint of ignorance. In one university production, the performer's footwork was so energetic that the present writer watched it with trepidation, expecting the young man to slip and break his neck at any moment. So efficient was his stamping that he came through the performance with nary a mishap. But if the footwork was excellent, the "face-work" was virtually unnoticeable. It would have been better to clap a mask on this actor's face, so that the spectator would have stopped expecting more than one carved expression from him.

Even in professional performances, however, the theatricalizing impulse can easily get out of hand. The actor may elect to play the virtuoso, and the result may be the superficiality and thinness that can keep a theatre solvent without making it significant. Some distinguished performers of our time have succumbed to the temptation of dramatizing *themselves* rather than the part. And the temptation to strive for effect alone has been even greater for those virtuoso directors who impose a theatrical style on the play instead of letting its "theatre" grow out of its dramatic substance and idiom. European directors such as Reinhardt, Jessner, and Meyerhold tended to take liberties that amounted to drastic adaptation.

At the very source of these dangers will be found an imperfect understanding of the theatre's duality. This misunderstanding comes from failure to realize the fact that there is no "either-or" principle at work in dramaturgy and stage production, that the theatrical experience can be both real and stylized, both real and theatrical. Only when this possibility is clearly realized or deeply sensed can a play be written, as well as staged of course, so that it will be most notably real when it is most theatrical, and most notably theatrical when it is most real. The ability to achieve both the illusion of reality and the ideality of art, both realism and theatricalism, in the same play has characterized the greatest playwrights of all previous ages. This dual power is the glory of Sophocles and Shakespeare. It was never entirely absent in the best work of such modern dramatists as Ibsen, Strindberg, Shaw, Chekhov, O'Casey, and O'Neill.

It is not suggested that a gratifying synthesis is to be achieved by combining incompletely realized elements—that is, by taking a pinch of adulterated realism and a pinch of diluted theatricalism and then shaking well. On the contrary, a fruitful synthesis can come only from realizing fully the possibilities inherent in both realism and stylization, within the limits of the author's intent and the conditions that rule the theatre for which the play was written. This is illustrated by such masterpieces as *Oedipus the King, Phèdre,* and *Macbeth.* In the first mentioned, the personal anguish of Oedipus and Jocasta, on the one hand, and the formal collective role of the chorus, on the other, are never inhibited or offered stingily in order to effect a compromise between the realistic (I should say, rather, naturalistic) situation of the characters and the formal dramatic pattern. In *Phèdre,* the neoclassic formalism of the writing is not in the least incompatible with the convincing reality and obsessive urgency of the Queen's emotions. In *Macbeth* the quality we nowadays call "psychology" is never sacrificed to the theatrical atmosphere and action, and neither are theatrical atmosphere and action stinted in order to thrust the psychological element into the foreground. Shakespeare moves here from "psychology" to "theatre," back and forth; there is no evidence that he was aware of any incompatibility between the two. There are, in point of fact, very great scenes, such as the murder of Duncan and the appearance of Banquo's ghost, in which the "psychology" of the work (the state of mind of Macbeth and his wife) is "theatre," and conversely, the "theatre" of the work (what we should otherwise call melodramatic action) is "psychology." It can be seen, therefore, that the word "psychology," used in so many discussions of modern theatre, has little meaning. Great drama (great performance, too) is neither psychological nor unpsychological.

The blending of realistic characterization and formal or informal theatricality also produces a good deal of the charm, dramatic scope, and imaginative vigor of plays regardless of their dramatic magnitude. This mingling of modes of presenting a dramatic story produces vivid contrasts of formalism and feeling, pageantry and pain, preciosity and naturalness in *Romeo and Juliet.* In *Richard II* there is an especially noteworthy contrast of styles of presentation in the difference between the actuality of the scene before Flint Castle (Act III, Scene 3), in which

Richard yields to Bolingbroke, and the morality-play effect of the very next scene, in which the Duke of York's Gardener, addressing his helpers, delivers his formal speech on good kingship:

> Go bind thou up yon dangling apricocks,
> Which, like unruly children, make their sire
> Stoop with oppression of their prodigal weight.
> Give some supportance to the bending twigs.
> Go thou and, like an executioner,
> Cut off the heads of too fast growing sprays
> That look too lofty in our commonwealth.
> All must be even in our government. (III, 4, 29-36)

In the celebrated abdication scene (Act IV, Scene 1) there is, besides, a provocative blending of psychological and rhetorical elements or qualities. Realism in the characterization of Richard and Bolingbroke and theatricalism in the ceremonialism of the scene are superbly interfused here.

Richard the character, besides, is his own actor, so that there is a fusion of characterization and theatricality in the hero himself. It can be noted, indeed, that other Shakespearean characters are intrinsically actors. Richard III, Iago, Benedick, Beatrice, Mercutio, Falstaff, Hotspur, and Henry V, not to mention Hamlet, are some of these. Shakespeare, like every true dramatist, wrote for actors; and to express humanity in the theatre, he needed "actor-characters" in his plays—characters who are highly articulate, histrionic, self-dramatizing. Henry V is the "actor-as-character" in Act IV, Scene 1, when he walks through the English camp at night casually conversing with the common soldiers, and primarily the "character-as-actor" or as "actor-orator" in the Saint Crispin's Day address to the troops two scenes later (IV, 3). The first scene is heightened realism (the key to it, perhaps, is the line "I am afeard few die well that die in battle"), and the later scene is motivated theatricalism, since the king's aim is to inspire his followers.

We may make similar observations concerning modern

plays. The mad countess in Giraudoux' *Madwoman of Chaillot* is a good example of the character that exists simultaneously on the planes of reality and theatricality. And the scene of weird discourse with her mad cronies, too, is surely both a theatrical *tour de force* and a scene full of the spontaneity and immediacy of life.

All things point to the possibility of advances in modern dramatic art along the lines of a realist-theatricalist fusion. The greatest promise lies in the nature of theatre itself—that is, in its dual aspects as illusion and theatre. The principle of duality —of bifocality or double functioning—appears in all aspects of theatre. It appears in the spectator's double vision or dualism of response, so that a performance can be simultaneously or alternately reality *and* theatre. It also exists in playwriting and play production. And there is, of course, considerable interaction between the kind of playwriting and the kind of stage production that develops at any particular time. Whether the first moves are made by playwrights or stage directors, the results are likely to be the same.

We have been moving for some time toward a realistic-theatricalist theatre. In the century's rarely satisfactory, usually inconclusive search for new dramatic forms, nothing else has held out so much promise. We may, then, hope for a resolution of the crisis in dramatic art that has existed ever since nineteenth-century realism began to show diminishing returns. It cannot be true that the modern drama has lost the power to develop, and we have had ample evidence that modern stagecraft *has* developed. Realism without theatrical intensification generally has proved dull. And theatricality without a realistic foundation frequently has proved trivial. But a judicious fusion of the potentialities of both modes of theatre may legitimately arouse the highest expectations. In order that the possibilities of success may be increased and the possibilities of failure reduced, it is imperative to resolve, once and for all, the conflicts between realism and theatricalism. These were never esthetically necessary; and if they were once historically necessary, they are so no longer in any modern theatre of the West.

A Chronology
of Modern Theatre

I HAVE PREPARED THIS CHRONOLOGY UP TO 1950 IN THE HOPE THAT IT will provide a bird's-eye view of important developments in the theatre. The reader will note that the striving after new forms of dramatic art has been continuous and that the issues presented in the preceding essays have been of interest and of practical consequence for many years. This chronology will also, I hope, supplement the text by presenting the background of plays and stage productions upon which the argument of this book is based.

1486   Discovery of *De architectura*, Vitruvius' Latin treatise on architecture, containing a section on classic theatre (architecture, stage machinery, etc.) which proved influential in the Italian Renaissance.

1545   Sebastian Serlio's *Architettura*, containing his celebrated drawings of perspective settings for comedy, tragedy, and pastoral drama or "satyr plays." Important in the diffusion of illusionism and the use of perspective scenery in the European theatre.

227

1584   The Teatro Olimpico, designed by Palladio and completed by Scamozzi, built at Vicenza. This theatre was a Renaissance adaptation of the Roman stage, providing vistas through five arches; these were filled with scenery in perspective.

1605   Inigo Jones first uses changing scenery, in the form of a revolving screen "in the Italian manner," at Oxford University.

1618 (1619)   Completion of the Teatro Farnese at Parma. This theatre, which contained a well-defined proscenium arch, marked the appearance of the picture-frame stage, since scenery was placed behind the proscenium. The proscenium arch also masked any scene-shifting that might occur during the course of the play, so that changes of scenery without destruction of illusion could now be attempted. However, there remained a forestage in front of the proscenium arch that was used by the actors.

1638   Publication of Nicola Sabbatini's *Pratica di fabricar scene e machine ne' teatri* (*The Practice of Making Scenes and Machines*), a description of how scenery may be changed.

Masque at Salisbury Court in London, noteworthy for the use of five changes of scene, effected behind a drop-curtain.

1656   Inigo Jones's noteworthy use of mobile scenery for the production of William Davenant's *The Siege of Rhodes*, considered the first English opera.

1731   Drury Lane production of George Lillo's early "middle-class tragedy" *The London Merchant; or, the History of George Barnwell*.

1773–1784   "Storm and Stress" movement in the German theatre breaks down the barriers of neoclassicism, produces early Romantic plays such as Goethe's *Goetz von Berlichingen* (1773) and Schiller's *Die Räuber* (*The Robbers*) (1781), and anticipates the "liberation" of the European theatre by Victor Hugo.

1808   *Penthesilea,* Heinrich von Kleist's pathological drama of sexual passion—an anticipation of realistic, naturalistic, and expressionist ventures into psychopathology such as Strindberg's *The Father* and *Miss Julie* and Wedekind's "sex tragedies."

1811   *The Prince of Homburg*, Heinrich von Kleist's remarkable psychological Romantic drama. (Psychological interest in the romantic theatre antedated realistic psychological drama.)

1824   Founding of the Maly ("Little") Theatre in Moscow, notable for its promotion of realistic satire in the 1840's with productions of *The Inspector-General* and *Woe from Wit*, and for its promotion of the middle-class realism of Ostrovsky from about 1855 to 1885. (The Maly became known as the "House of Ostrovsky" as a result of the long association of the author and the theatre.)

Theatrical realism introduced into England by J. R. Planché's authentic-costume production of *King John* at Covent Garden, Jan. 19, 1824.

1827   Victor Hugo's preface to *Cromwell*, which was a rejection of vestigial neoclassic principles of dramatic art, a program for Romantic theatre, and a charter of freedom for all subsequent playwriting.

1830   The "Battle of *Hernani*." The French classicists in the theatre are routed by the Romanticists under the leadership of Hugo, Gautier, and others.

1831   Madame Vestris assumes the management of the Olympic Theatre in London and inaugurates scenic changes leading to surface realism in English décor.

1835   Georg Büchner's seminaturalistic, semiexpressionistic historical drama *Dantons Tod* (*Danton's Death*); first published in 1873 and first produced in 1916 by Max Reinhardt. (Produced at Orson Welles's Mercury Theatre in New York in 1938.)

1836   Büchner's remarkable naturalistic, yet also expressionistic, fragment *Woyzeck*. First published in 1879; first staged in 1913. Best known as basis for Alban Berg's modernist opera *Wozzeck*, 1925.

Russian Court Theatre première of Gogol's celebrated early social satire *Revizor* (*The Inspector-General*).

1841 A box set is used in the production of Boucicault's *London Assurance* at the Olympic Theatre in London under the management of Madame Vestris. "Instead of representing an interior scene by a series of wings set one behind the other, the scene shifters now built the side walls of a room solidly from front to rear; and the actors were made to enter, not by walking through the wings, but by opening actual doors that turned upon their hinges." (Clayton Hamilton, *The Theory of the Theatre*, Henry Holt, 1939, p. 46). But the apron stage still remained.

1844 Friedrich Hebbel's realistic middle-class tragedy *Maria Magdalena*.

1850 Charles Kean takes over the management of the Princess Theatre in London and provides pictorial realism in England throughout the decade.

1855 *Le Fils naturel* (*The Illegitimate Son*), the first of the younger Alexander Dumas' sermonizing realistic "problem plays."

1865 The production of T. W. ("Tom") Robertson's *Society*, the early semirealistic social drama at the Prince of Wales Theatre. The production of this play and of Robertson's *Caste* (1867) successfully introduced realistic stage practice into England.

1867 *Peer Gynt*, the climax of Ibsen's Romantic phase and the high point of social criticism in his *poetic* writing.

1868 Preface to *A Prodigal Father* by Dumas *fils*. A ringing call for an "engaged" drama rather than dramatic legerdemain in the manner of the midcentury's most successful playwright Scribe, called by Dumas a shadow-Shakespeare "expert at manipulating characters that had no life." Dumas called for a dramatist "who knows *man* as Balzac did, and the theatre as Scribe did."

1871 Rimbaud's Letter of May 15, which may be considered an anticipation of surrealism. Among Rimbaud's points in that letter were that poets should not try to *explain* experience, and that words are to be regarded as *myths*—they are "not understandable in any ordinary sense."

1873   Émile Zola's Preface to *Thérèse Raquin,* the first important manifesto of naturalism for the theatre, predicting that "the experimental and scientific spirit of the century will enter the domain of the drama," and calling for an inquiry into "the two-fold life of the character and its environment."

1873–1893   Development of naturalism in the major European theatres.

1874   The Meiningen Company (1874–1890), pioneering in realistic scenic detail and in ensemble performance, especially in the realistic management of crowds, succeeds in Berlin with productions of *Julius Caesar* and *As You Like It.*

1875   Henry Becque's naturalistic drama *Les Corbeaux* (*The Vultures*), first produced in 1882.

Edward William Godwin (1833–1886), architect, archaeologist, and designer, father of Edith and Gordon Craig, designs the production of *The Merchant of Venice* in which Ellen Terry played Portia. In this production Godwin introduced solid architectural settings, platforms, and steps.

1876   Wagner's Bayreuth Theatre established, with emphasis upon provision for Wagner's "mystic gulf" between the stage and the audience; this was accomplished by putting the pit for the opera orchestra in front of the stage. The "mystic gulf" was intended to "distance" the stage action and so promote the ideality of Wagnerian music drama. Romanticism in this instance helped to promote the picture-frame theatre and to separate the actor from the auditorium and the spectator from the stage.

The Meiningen Company produces Ibsen's historical tragedy *The Pretenders* in a historically realistic manner in Berlin.

1877   *The Pillars of Society,* the play with which Ibsen began his social criticism in prose drama.

1878   Henry Irving starts his management of the Lyceum Theatre, where even Shakespeare's plays were subordinated to scenic realism.

1879   Eleonora Duse makes her debut at the Teatro Fiorentini in Naples and scores a great success in Zola's naturalistic drama *Thérèse Raquin*.

Ibsen starts his influential realistic phase with *A Doll's House* followed by *Ghosts* in 1881 and *An Enemy of the People* in 1882.

Augustin Daly's New York production of *L'Assomoir* (*Drink*) the early and unsuccessful venture in naturalism in the American theatre; and David Belasco's successful production of the same play in San Francisco.

(Nov. 1)   Henry Irving's Lyceum Theatre production of *The Merchant of Venice*, a milestone in "picturesque realism."

1880   Production of Ibsen's *The Pillars of Society* in London, at the Gaiety Theatre, in a translation by William Archer.

Steele MacKaye uses an elevator stage for changing settings at the rebuilt Madison Square Theatre in New York.

1880–1887   Electricity installed in the most important theatres of Europe and America, increasing the effectiveness of lighting for both naturalistic and atmospheric purposes.

1881   The Meiningen Company visits London.

Zola's collection of essays, *Le Naturalisme au théâtre* (*Naturalism in the Theatre*), which set down a naturalistic program for the stage.

1883   The first German translation of *Ghosts*.

Establishment of the Deutsches Theater in Berlin under Adolf L'Arronge.

Henry Irving goes to America, introducing his realistically set productions which apparently influenced Augustin Daly and David Belasco.

1884   Ibsen enters upon a more or less "symbolist" phase with *The Wild Duck*. This play was followed by *Rosmersholm* (1886), *The Lady from the Sea* (1888), *The Master Builder* (1892), *Little Eyolf* (1894), *John Gabriel Borkman* (1896), and *When We Dead Awaken* (1897–1899).

1885 Becque's naturalistic comedy, *La Parisienne*.

1886 (April 14) First production of *Ghosts* in Germany at the Stadttheater in Augsburg.

1887 *The Father*, the beginning of Strindberg's realistic work in the theatre.

André Antoine establishes the first outpost of naturalism, the Théâtre Libre, in Paris. The theatre ends its career in 1894 and Antoine carries his influence first into the commercial Théâtre Antoine and then into the state-subsidized theatre, the Odéon.

1888 Strindberg's naturalist drama *Miss Julie*. The author's foreword to that play is an important document in the development of realism and naturalism. Strindberg declared that "the psychologic process is what interests people most today."

1889 Die Freie Bühne founded in Berlin along the lines of the Théâtre Libre; designed as an outpost of realism and naturalism by Otto Brahm and prominent associates.

First successful English production of a realistic drama by Ibsen: *A Doll's House* presented at the Novelty Theatre, London.

1890 James A. Herne's *Margaret Fleming*, the first American realistic drama.

Beginning of Max Burckhard's term (lasting until January 1898) as director of the Burgtheater in Vienna; this period was distinguished by productions of both naturalistic and symbolist plays by Ibsen, Hauptmann, and Schnitzler.

The beginning of the Volksbühne, the German People's Theatre, supported chiefly by the German trade-union movement— an indication that modern realism had made the theatre matter to the forward-looking social movements. In 1930, the Volksbühne had 500,000 subscription members and had membership groups in about 300 German cities.

(May 30) *Ghosts* produced at the Théâtre Libre, with Antoine playing the role of Oswald.

1891   Publication of Shaw's *Quintessence of Ibsenism*, providing a Shavian exegesis of Ibsen's plays, important not only for its championship of Ibsen's realism but for interpreting that realism as "critical" or "intellectual" rather than as the realism of photographic detail. First delivered as a lecture for the Fabian Society of England on July 18, 1890. Enlarged for republication in 1913.

Théâtre d'Art founded at the Salle Montparnasse in Paris for the promotion of antinaturalism; more or less symbolist drama was produced. Antoine's comment: "a good thing, for the Théâtre Libre is not enough . . . I don't see any competition there, but a complement in the evolution which is going ahead." (Diary, Jan. 17, 1891.)

(April 27)   Antoine produces Ibsen's *The Wild Duck* at the Théâtre Libre, declaring, "Just as I was the first to open my doors wide to the Naturalist drama, so I shall open them wide also to Symbolist drama." (*See entries for 1907 and 1908*, Moscow Art Theatre, *below*.)

1891–1897   Duration of J. T. Grein's pioneering small subscription theatre, the Independent Theatre, in London, which produced such naturalistic plays as Zola's *Thérèse Raquin* and Shaw's *Widowers' Houses*.

1892   Adolphe Appia's designs for *The Valkyrie*, exemplary for modern scenic art because of their achievement of "plastic unity of effect in space."

Berlin production of Hauptmann's *Die Weber* (*The Weavers*).

The Independent Theatre stages Shaw's first play, *Widowers' Houses*.

An Italian version of *Ghosts* is played in Florence by Ermete Zacconi.

Production of José Echegaray's pseudo-Ibsenite play about hereditary venereal disease in terms of Spanish life, *El hijo de Don Juan* (*The Son of Don Juan*).

1893   First performance of an Ibsen play in Spain; *An Enemy of the People* produced in a Castilian version, *Un enemigo del pueblo*, in Barcelona.

(May)   The successful London production of Pinero's quasi-Ibsenite drama *The Second Mrs. Tanqueray*.

Antoine's productions of Strindberg's *Miss Julie* and Hauptmann's "mass drama" *The Weavers* at the Théâtre Libre.

Otto Brahm, leader of German naturalism and founder of the Freie Bühne, becomes director of the Deutsches Theater, the foremost theatre in Berlin.

Hanneles Himmelfahrt (*The Assumption of Hannele*), Hauptmann's synthesis of naturalism and symbolism.

Shaw's *Mrs. Warren's Profession*, the first marked synthesis in English theatre of naturalism and discussion drama.

Lugné-Poë, a former actor for Antoine at the Théâtre Libre, takes charge of the Théâtre d'Art, renaming it the Théâtre de L'Oeuvre. Its first production was Maeterlinck's crepuscular love-tragedy *Pelléas et Mélisande*.

1893–1897   William Archer's dramatic criticism for *The World*, in which he championed the modern realistic theatre and the "new drama" of Ibsen and other realists.

1894   Brahm becomes manager of the Deutsches Theater, the leading theatre in Berlin—a victory for realism and naturalism in Central Europe.

William Poel's founding of the Elizabethan Stage Society, which gave non-naturalistic, more or less presentational, "Elizabethan" productions under Poel's direction from 1895 to 1905.

1895   Adolphe Appia's *La Mise en scène du drame Wagnérien* (*The Staging of Wagnerian Music-Drama*), published in Paris.

1895–1898   Shaw's dramatic criticism written for *The Saturday Review*, now collected in *Our Theatre in the Nineties*, noteworthy for Shaw's championship of critical realism, chiefly Ibsen's; for his attack on the old-fashioned drama of intrigue (as exemplified by Victorien Sardou—"Sardoodledom") and pseudo-Ibsenism (as exemplified by Pinero's *The Second Mrs. Tanqueray* and *The Notorious Mrs. Ebbsmith*), and on the

Henry Irving and Beerbohm-Tree method of producing Shake
speare's plays with solid realistic scenery while butchering th
text in order to reduce the number of scene changes.

1896   The revolving stage is introduced into the German theatr
by Karl Lautenschläger. As a result, it became possible to pro
duce multi-scened plays with ease.

Production of Jacinto Benavente's *Gente conocida* (*In So
ciety*), marking the beginning of his career as the leader o
Spanish social realism.

The founding of the Teatre Independent in Barcelona and th
production of *Ghosts* in a Catalan translation.

William Poel's production of *Doctor Faustus* at St. George Hall
London, on a reproduction of the stage of the Fortune Theatre
of Elizabethan times.

Miguel Unamuno's *La regeneración del teatro español* (*Th
Regeneration of the Spanish Theatre*), a plea for the develop
ment of a "drama of ideas" in Spain.

Adolphe Appia's designs for *Parsifal*.

Maurice Maeterlinck's symbolist "static drama" manifesto, *Le
Tragique quotidien* (*The Tragical in Daily Life*): "Here we
are no longer with the barbarians, nor is the man now fretting
himself in the midst of elementary passions . . . *he is at rest.*
. . . It is no longer a violent, exceptional moment of life that
passes before our eyes—it is *life itself.*" Maeterlinck also
stressed the importance of "unnecessary dialogue" (that is, dialogue that is valuable even if it does not advance action): "a
poem draws the nearer to beauty and loftier truth in the measure that it eliminates words that merely explain the action."

(Dec. 10)   Production at the Théâtre de L'Oeuvre in Paris of
Alfred Jarry's presurrealistic parody of conventional tragedy,
Ubu Roi, a product of the symbolist movement in the field of
comedy and satire. (King Ubu, the hero of the play, is a sort
of super-marionette of the comic stage in his coarse "bourgeois"
typicality.)

1897   Schnitzler's naturalistic drama dealing with "the death-dance of love," *Reigen* (*Hands Around; La Ronde*).

Antoine establishes the Théâtre Antoine in Paris.

Cyrano de Bergerac. Neoromanticism wins a major victory in the theatre with the elder Coquelin's Paris production of Rostand's play.

1898   The Teatre Intim, an *avant-garde* theatre, founded by Adrián Gaul in Barcelona.

The Moscow Art Theatre founded by Konstantin Stanislavsky (1865–1938) and Vladimir Nemirovich-Danchenko (1859–1943).

Strindberg's *To Damascus,* marking the beginning of his expressionist phase in playwriting, as well as the beginning of expressionism in the modern theatre.

The beginning of Chekhov's association with the Moscow Art Theatre as a result of its successful production of *The Sea-Gull.*

1899   Appia's *Die Musik und die Inszenierung* published in Munich. ("Music and the Scene" does not translate the original title satisfactorily, since *Inszenierung* means the total staging.)

The Stage Society of London, organized by leaders of English literature and theatre, opens with a production of Shaw's *You Never Can Tell.* (1938–1939 was the last season of this progressive group.)

The beginning of the Irish Literary Theatre in Dublin; later becomes successively the Irish National Dramatic Company, the Irish National Theatre Society, and the Abbey Theatre.

(March 20)   *Ghosts* produced in Spain by the Teatre Intim in Barcelona.

1901–1906   Mrs. Fiske's management in New York of the Manhattan Theatre, where she produced *Hedda Gabler, Rosmersholm,* and other important plays.

1902 The Moscow Art Theatre's celebrated production of Gorki's naturalist drama *The Lower Depths*.

(April 2–4) First productions of the Irish National Dramatic Company, headed by W. G. Fay, in Dublin. The program consisted of A.E.'s *Deirdre* and Yeats's *Kathleen ni Houlihan*, with Maud Gonne playing Kathleen.

Stephen Phillips' neoromantic verse drama *Paolo and Francesca*, believed to mark the beginning of a renascence of poetic drama in England which failed to materialize.

The Dream Play, Strindberg's important symbolist-expressionist drama, published in Stockholm; first produced there in 1907.

Meyerhold breaks with Stanislavskian realism and leaves the Moscow Art Theatre, where he had been an actor from its beginnings.

Reinhardt starts his career at the Kleines Theater in Berlin with works by Strindberg, Wedekind, Gorki, and Wilde.

1903 Gordon Craig's designs for Ellen Terry's production of Ibsen's romantic drama *The Vikings*, in which Craig first succeeded in putting his theories into practice.

Reinhardt stages Maeterlinck's symbolist drama *Pelléas et Mélisande* at the Neues Theater in Berlin.

Guillaume Apollinaire's *Les Mamelles de Tirésias* (*The Breasts of Tiresias*), which Apollinaire, denouncing realism in his preface to the work, called *un drame surréaliste*. This was possibly the first use of the term "surrealism."

1904 (Dec. 27) The curtain is rung up for the first time at the Abbey Theatre in Dublin. The program included premières of Yeats's neoromantic one-act verse drama *On Baile's Strand* and of Lady Gregory's one-act peasant farce in Irish dialect, *Spreading the News*.

Reinhardt starts his experiments in stylized production at the Deutsches Theater in Berlin.

The Abbey Theatre's production of John Millington Synge's *Riders to the Sea*.

1904–1907 The Barker-Vedrenne management at the Court Theatre in London, where important modern productions of plays by Shakespeare, Shaw, Galsworthy, and other modern writers were given under the direction of Harley Granville-Barker (1877–1946).

1905 Publication of Gordon Craig's first influential essay, "The Art of the Theatre."

(Oct. 31) Arnold Daly presents *Mrs. Warren's Profession* in New York for one evening before the production is forced to suspend by the police. The play is denounced in the New York press; Norman Hapgood of the New York *Herald* declares that "You cannot have a clean pig stye . . ."

Max Reinhardt's spectacular Berlin production of *A Midsummer Night's Dream*. Reinhardt is made director of the Deutsches Theater.

1906 Meyerhold joins the actress-manager Komisarjevskaya in St. Petersburg and directs poetic productions for her, such as Andreyev's symbolist drama *The Life of Man*. In this year also, Meyerhold removed the front curtain from the stage for an antinaturalistic production of *Ghosts*.

Mrs. Fiske's production of Langdon Mitchell's "modern" comedy on divorce, *The New York Idea*, in New York.

Reinhardt opens an intimate "chamber-theatre," the Kammerspiele, for experimental productions; he produces Frank Wedekind's naturalist-expressionist drama *The Awakening of Spring* there.

1906–1916 Antoine's directorship of the state-subsidized Odéon theatre.

1907 The Abbey Theatre's production of Synge's *The Playboy of the Western World*.

The Moscow Art Theatre stages Leonid Andreyev's decidedly "symbolist" allegory *The Life of Man*. (The citadel of modern realism responds to the vogue of symbolist drama.)

The Ghost Sonata (also translated as *The Spook Sonata*), Strindberg's famous expressionist drama, published in Stockholm; produced there in 1908.

The Intimate Theatre (Intima Teatern) established by August Strindberg and August Falck in Stockholm for modernistic experimentation; controlled by Strindberg until 1910. (Strindberg wrote *The Ghost Sonata* for this theatre.)

1907–1913   The Pilgrim Players, an amateur company in Birmingham, England, produces experimental plays.

1907–1917   The vogue of "Belascoism," or sensationally pictorial naturalism, in the American theatre.

1907–1921   The Manchester Repertory Company: Miss A. E. F. Horniman maintains an important company at the Gaiety Theatre in Manchester for the production of provocative realistic plays. Among the productions were Stanley Houghton's *Hindle Wakes* (1912), St. John Ervine's *Jane Clegg* (1913), and Harold Brighouse's *Hobson's Choice.*

1908   Jaroslav Kvapil, translator of Ibsen, but also a Shakespearean producer, becomes chief director of the Czech National Theatre in Prague for a decade.

The Moscow Art Theatre stages Maeterlinck's fantasy *The Blue Bird*. "Those who think that we sought for Naturalism on the stage are mistaken," wrote Stanislavsky, complaining that the Art Theatre inclined toward naturalism because "spiritual technique was only in its embryo stage among the actors of our company." It is quite clear from Stanislavsky's (and also Antoine's) attitude, expressed as early as 1890, that the specialists in naturalistic drama would have become symbolists if symbolism had given birth to plays capable of sustaining a vital theatre.

(May 17)   Opening of the Munich Künstlertheater (Artists' Theatre), founded by the critic Georg Fuchs in association with the architect Max Littman and the scene designer Fritz Erler. Designed for formal and imaginative presentation of plays rather than for peepshow theatre, with some presentational stylization assured by bringing out the acting area—a narrow shelf for presentational stage production rather than a deep area that would lend itself to the representation of environment.

Gordon Craig settles in Florence and starts his magazine *The Mask*.

1908–1923   George Jean Nathan writes drama criticism for *Smart Set* magazine, combats "Belascoism," and champions imaginative and stimulating theatre.

1909   Production in Rome of Sem Benelli's successful neoromantic drama *La Cena delle beffe* (*The Jest*).

Diaghilev takes the Ballets Russes to Paris, introducing the Western theatre to the possibilities of the dance for dramatic effect and exhibiting an impressive synthesis of the arts of dancing, music, and painting.

Belasco's naturalistic production of Eugene Walter's *The Easiest Way*, an unusually naturalistic American drama.

1910   Stravinsky's *L'Oiseau de feu* (*The Firebird*) is presented by Diaghilev's Ballets Russes; and Léon Bakst's painted scenery wins the acclaim which starts a reversal of the theatre's hostile attitude toward the use of painted scenery ever since the advent of realism.

Max Reinhardt's productions of *Oedipus the King* and the pantomime *Sumurûn*, for which Reinhardt, having noted the use of runways in the Japanese Kabuki theatre, used them to break the fourth-wall convention and reunite the actors and the audience.

First German expressionist group in the theatre, the Sturmbühne, starts giving matinees of expressionist plays by August Stramm, Lothar Schreyer, and Oskar Kokoschka.

1911   Gordon Craig designs the Moscow Art Theatre production of *Hamlet*, using a combination of abstract convex screens of great height. These, according to Stanislavsky, "hinted at architectural forms, corners, niches, streets, alleys, halls, towers, and so on."

Publication of Gordon Craig's book *On the Art of the Theatre*. Presentation of Stravinsky's *Petrouchka*, the masterpiece of the Ballets Russes.

The beginning of the Liverpool Repertory Theatre, especially noteworthy as a school of acting.

The Max Reinhardt production of *The Miracle*, for which the interior of the Olympia Theatre in London was redesigned as a cathedral.

1912   Lugné-Poë's Parisian production of Paul Claudel's symbolist drama *L'Annonce faîte à Marie*. Produced 10 years later in New York by the Theatre Guild as *The Tidings Brought to Mary*.

Constructivist sculpture (by Pevsner, Gabo, and others) makes its appearance; it is nonrepresentational and consists chiefly of a balance of planes.

A venture in Oriental stylization in the popular American theatre—the production of the Hazelton and Benrimo play *The Yellow Jacket*.

George Pierce Baker starts the 47 Workshop at Harvard. (Baker subsequently, in 1925, establishes the Yale School of Drama.)

The Chicago Little Theatre, devoted to dramatic experimentation, is founded by Maurice Brown and Ellen Van Volkenburg.

Reinhardt's production of the Oriental pantomime *Sumurûn* is brought to New York; an introduction to modern theatricalist style.

The experimental Toy Theatre established in Boston.

1913   Benavente's naturalistic psychological drama *La malquerida* (*The Passion Flower*), an important work of naturalism in the Spanish theatre.

(Feb. 5) Opening of the Birmingham Repertory Theatre, which continued the experimental work of the Pilgrim Players.

Collaboration of Appia and Jacques Dalcroze at the latter's school in Hellerau, near Dresden, where Appia was able to make use of some of his ideas on scene design in simplified productions of Gluck's *Orpheus* and Claudel's *The Tidings Brought to Mary*. The stage, which had hardly any furniture, was simply a three-level platform with connecting steps. There was no distinction between the lighting of stage and auditorium.

Vittorio Podrecca establishes his famous marionette theatre, the Teatro dei Piccoli, an important theatricalist venture, in Rome. Puppets were used at first.

Winthrop Ames's Broadway production of the symbolist play *Prunella*, by Granville-Barker and Laurence Housman.

Louis Jouvet joins the Théâtre du Vieux Colombier as actor and stage manager.

Publication of Gordon Craig's *Towards a New Theatre*.

Choreography by Nijinsky of Stravinsky's *Le Sacre du printemps* in Cubist style.

)13–1916 Shaw writes *Heartbreak House*, a notable fusion of social realism and symbolism.

)14 The Kamerny (Chamber) Theatre established by Alexander Tairov for the creation of a "synthetic theatre" combining all the arts. It was rebuilt in 1930 and made larger.

)15 (Jan. 27) Robert Edmond Jones presents an influential anti-naturalistic setting for the Granville-Barker production of *The Man Who Married a Dumb Wife*, by Anatole France, in New York City.

Manifesto of the Futurist Synthetic Theatre in Italy.

(Feb. 19) The Washington Square Players open the first season of their art theatre at the small Bandbox Theatre in New

York under the leadership of Edward Goodman, Lawrence Langner, Philip Moeller, Rollo Peters, Lee Simonson, and Helen Westley. The *pièce de resistance* of their first program, made up of *avant-garde* one-acters, was Maeterlinck's mood-piece *Interior*.

The Provincetown Players give their first production on a wharf in Provincetown, Mass., where they continue to stage plays during the next two summers. The group is headed by George Cram Cook, Susan Glaspell, Robert Edmond Jones, and Eugene O'Neill.

The Neighborhood Playhouse is founded in New York's East Side district by the Misses Alice and Irene Lewisohn. This notable experimental theatre existed until 1927.

D. W. Griffith's film *The Birth of a Nation*. The pictorial possibilities of the cinema soon made stage naturalism seem inadequate and superfluous.

1916   John Williams' successful Broadway production of Galsworthy's *Justice*, with John Barrymore playing the lead—a triumph for realism in the American theatre.

The founding of the Arts and Crafts Theatre by Sam Hume in Detroit, and of *Theatre Arts Magazine* as a quarterly dedicated to the propagation of advanced ideas of dramatic art. Symbolist design receives special attention in this periodical.

First production by Max Reinhardt of Georg Büchner's *Dantons Tod* (*Danton's Death*), written in 1835.

From Morn to Midnight, Georg Kaiser's celebrated expressionist drama of a bank cashier's blind search for freedom and sympathy in a hollow and meretricious society.

Luigi Chiarelli's *La maschera e il volto* (*The Mask and the Face*) produced in Rome—an important step in the development of the "school of the grotesque" which became internationally important through the more or less theatricalist plays of Pirandello.

Alexander Bakshy's manifesto of theatricalism *The Theatre Unbound*, published in 1923.

First manifesto of dadaism issued at Zurich.

The Cleveland Playhouse starts its course of experimental theatre under Raymond O'Neill; later, after 1921, it is directed by Frederic McConnell.

The Washington Square Players produce Maeterlinck's symbolist play *Aglavaine and Sylvette* and Chekhov's realistic masterpiece *The Sea-Gull* in New York.

1917 The Washington Square Players present Andreyev's symbolist drama *The Life of Man* in New York.

Founding of the Pasadena Playhouse, a progressive community theatre in California, by Gilmor Brown.

Founding in Moscow of the Hebrew company, the Habima, famous for its grotesque theatricalist style, especially in the production of *The Dybbuk* (1922), staged by Vakhtangov. The company has been resident in Palestine since 1931.

Production of Guillaume Apollinaire's *Les Mamelles de Tirésias* (*The Breasts of Tiresias*), a surrealist "play," in Paris.

Parade, Jean Cocteau's surrealist ballet, with music by Satie and designs by Picasso.

1917–1919 Copeau, Jouvet, and the Théâtre du Vieux Colombier company appear in New York for two seasons.

1917 (Dec.)–1920 Reinhardt produces expressionist dramas such as Reinhard Sorge's *Der Bettler* (*The Beggar*) and Reinhard Goering's *Seeschlacht* (*Sea Battle*) for the *avant-garde* group called Das junge Deutschland (Young Germany).

1918 The Washington Square Players produce *Mrs. Warren's Profession* in New York without running into difficulties with censorship.

The Provincetown Players take over a disused stable on Macdougal Street in Greenwich Village and name it the Provincetown Playhouse.

The Carolina Playmakers, founded by Frederick H. Koch at the University of North Carolina, starts its noteworthy career in creating regional theatre.

1918–1920   Kaiser's expressionist drama *Gas I* and *II*, a nightmare picture of the industrialization of society.

1919   *The Cabinet of Dr. Caligari*, a German film which represents the peak of expressionism in scene design and plot. (Followed by *The Golem*, 1920, and *Metropolis*, 1926.)

(Nov. 28)   The opening of Reinhardt's Grosses Schauspielhaus, a circus-like theatre in Berlin adapted for presentational stage-production on a large scale.

Founding of the Theatre Guild in New York.

1919–1925   Leopold Jessner directs the Berlin State Theatre and promotes expressionism with dynamic productions of Schiller's *Wilhelm Tell* and Wedekind's *Marquis of Keith*, staged, in the main, on steep ramps of stairs (*Jessnertreppen*).

1919–1926   The Phoenix Theatre of London becomes notable for its revival of Elizabethan and Restoration drama.

1920   *Le Boeuf sur le toit, ou The Nothing Happens Bar*, a surrealist pantomime on which Cocteau, Milhaud, and Dufy collaborated. Played by the Fratellini clowns at the Comédie des Champs-Elysées. (Clowning in any form has been highly acclaimed by the *avant-garde*, which has revolted against the rationalistic and practical-minded theatre of realism. Clowning was especially attractive to surrealists as an incursion of the irrational into the theatre. They favored the circus and had their unofficial headquarters in Paris near the Cirque Medrano.)

The Provincetown Players' production of O'Neill's *The Emperor Jones*, especially noteworthy for its expressionistic technique and the use of sound (the sound of the tom-toms) in the creation of tension.

The Hopkins-Barrymore *Richard III* in New York, with symbolist designs by Robert Edmond Jones.

First production of the music studio of the Moscow Art Theatre, Lecocq's satire *The Daughter of Madame Angot*.

The founding of the Salzburg Festival by Max Reinhardt, opened by the production of Hofmannsthal's *Jedermann* on a platform in front of the Salzburg Cathedral, whose portals and baroque statuary served as the main background.

1921 Adolphe Appia's *L'Oeuvre d'art vivant* (*The Work of Living Art*) published in Geneva and Paris.

Karel Hugo Hilar (1884–1935), an important expressionist and theatricalist, becomes director of the Czech National Theatre. Among his associates was the famous constructivist scene-designer A. Heythum.

Pirandello's theatricalist masterpiece *Sei personaggi in cerca d'autore* (*Six Characters in Search of an Author*).

Vakhantagov's famous theatricalist production of *Princess Turandot* in ironic harlequinade style, with actors introducing themselves to the audience and costuming themselves in public, with settings shifted in public by stagehands who burlesque the play. An example of "joyous" or "gay" theatricalism, and of Oriental stylization.

Famous expressionist production of Ernst Toller's *Masse-Mensch* (*Man and the Masses*) by Jürgen Fehling at the Volksbühne in Berlin, with designs by Hans Strohbach. Produced later by the New York Theatre Guild with direction and settings by Lee Simonson.

Meyerhold's production of the Belgian poet Verhaeren's symbolist drama *Les Aubes* (*Dawn*), written in 1898, in a constructivist style. (Constructivism had been anticipated by Meyerhold in 1914 in his production of Alexander Blok's poetic drama *The Unknown*.)

The Arthur Hopkins and Robert Edmond Jones symbolist production of *Macbeth*, in which environment was dissolved into a black background, with masks and arches used as scenic properties mainly to suggest the "soul" of the play.

1922   *The Dybbuk* (written in 1914) performed in grotesque, Oriental theatricalist manner by the Habima Theatre in a production directed by Vakhtangov.

Théâtre de l'Atelier established in Paris by Copeau's celebrated associate Charles Dullin (1885–1949).

Pirandello's theatricalist psychological drama *Enrico IV* (*Henry IV*); produced in New York in 1922 as *The Living Mask*.

Karel and Josef Capek's *Insect Comedy* (literally, "the comedy of insects").

The Provincetown Players' production of O'Neill's *The Hairy Ape*, characterized by symbolist and expressionist techniques.

The Theatre Guild's complete production of Shaw's *Back to Methuselah* at the Garrick Theatre in New York.

Reinhardt converts an imperial ballroom into a little theatre, the Redoutensaal, for formalistic intimate productions.

Cocteau's *Antigone*, performed in Renaissance costume, with music by Honegger and designs by Picasso; the text, a trimmed-down, "cooled-off," deliberately dry version of Sophocles' play.

1923   *Saint Joan*, in which Shaw proved that the impossible was possible by turning discussion drama into high tragedy.

The Theatre Guild production of Elmer Rice's expressionist fantasy *The Adding Machine*, with famous expressionist settings by Lee Simonson. Also, John Howard Lawson's expressionist social drama, *Roger Bloomer*, produced in New York.

The successful and apparently influential Pitoëff production of *Six Characters in Search of an Author* in Paris.

Tairov's playful use of constructivist theatricalism in the production of *The Man Who Was Thursday*, adapted from a novel by G. K. Chesterton.

Production by the Moscow Art Theatre Musical Studio (not an opera company, but a theatre whose actors sang) of Aristophanes' *Lysistrata*, with "musical theatrical realism."

1924   Arthur Hopkins' celebrated realistic production of *What Price Glory?* by Laurence Stallings and Maxwell Anderson.

The Winthrop Ames production of *Beggar on Horseback* by George S. Kaufman and Marc Connelly—the first popular Broadway adaptation of expressionism in the American theatre. Production of *Desire Under the Elms,* in which O'Neill fused naturalism and symbolism, in New York.

The Moscow Art Theatre Musical Studio production of *Carmencita and the Soldier* in the style of "musical theatrical realism" instead of in the operatic manner usually employed in staging *Carmen.* (The Hammerstein Negro version *Carmen Jones* in the 1940's was an adaptation of "musical theatrical realism" as inaugurated in Nemirovich-Danchenko's studio.)

(March 3)   The Abbey Theatre production of O'Casey's *Juno and the Paycock,* a modern mingling of comedy and tragedy, and also a distinguished example of the fusion of naturalism and poetic dialogue.

André Breton's first Manifesto of Surrealism, with emphasis on "pure psychic automatism" requiring the elimination of intellectual, moral, and esthetic factors from the creative process.

1924–1934   Louis Jouvet is actor-manager at the Comédie des Champs-Élysées.

1925   The Theatre Guild production of John Howard Lawson's theatricalist *Processional,* a "jazz-symphony" of social conflict and confusion. A notable feature of this production was Mordecai Gorelik's theatricalist setting, the main element of which was an extravagantly painted vaudeville backdrop of a mining town.

Art Theatre at the Teatro Odescalchi founded by Pirandello in Rome.

Hallie Flanagan Davis becomes director of the Vassar Experimental Theatre, noted for its work in stylization. (Her administration lasted until 1935, when she became director of the Federal Theatre.)

Alban Berg's opera *Wozzeck,* based on Büchner's dramatic fragment *Woyzeck* (1936).

(Oct. 30) The opening of the Gate Theatre in London; this "private" (hence uncensored) theatre, under Peter Godfrey's leadership, produced modernistic experiments, such as Kaiser's *From Morn to Midnight,* Toller's *Hinkemann,* and Evreinov's *The Theatre of the Soul,* until 1940.

1926 (Feb. 8) The Abbey Theatre production of O'Casey's *The Plough and the Stars,* an important group, or mass, drama.

The Pitoëff production of Cocteau's surrealist drama *Orphée* at the Théâtre des Arts in Paris, with Georges Pitoëff as Orpheus and Ludmilla Pitoëff as Euridice. It should be noted that the meaning of a play like *Orphée* cannot be unraveled— it is, indeed, not supposed to be unraveled: "In symbolism, the chemistry was too conscious of its means and ends. Surrealism tries to go beyond the elaborate consciousness of symbolism . . . to the very sleep in which the myths of man are preserved" (Wallace Fowlie, *The Age of Surrealism,* Denver, A. Swallow, 1950, p. 140).

The New York production of O'Neill's *The Great God Brown,* especially noteworthy for the formalistic use of masks to symbolize modern man's dual personality.

Constructivist and theatricalist productions of O'Neill's *The Hairy Ape* and *Desire Under the Elms* at Tairov's Kamerny Theatre.

Meyerhold's famous theatricalist production of Gogol's satire *The Inspector-General*—a combination of constructivism, expressionism, and naturalism with a semicircular permanent setting and a smaller movable stage.

The Cambridge Festival Theatre founded in England by Terence Gray, who declared: "We are the theatre theatrical. We don't want the wisest or the most foolish member of our audience to play at visual make-believe or ever to forget that the stage is only the stage." Gray dispensed with the proscenium—"the width of the stage was the width of the auditorium itself."

1926–1933   Eva Le Gallienne's Civic Repertory Company in New York. It became noted for productions of plays by Ibsen, Chekhov, Martinez-Sierra, and other Europeans.

1927   Jacques Copeau stages his dramatization of *The Brothers Karamazov* for the Theatre Guild in New York.

The Theatre Guild production of Dorothy and Du Bose Heyward's *Porgy*, staged by Rouben Mamoulian. An important step in the retheatricalization of the "serious" theatre.

Erwin Piscator takes over the management of the Theater-am-Nollendorfplatz in Berlin for productions in "epic theatre" style.

1927–1928   Reinhardt's season in New York.

1928   The association of Giraudoux and Jouvet starts with Jouvet's production of Giraudoux' anti-war (and somewhat Pirandellian) drama of *Siegfried*. Then followed Jouvet's productions of *Amphitryon 38, Judith, The Trojan War Will Not Take Place, Electra,* and *The Madwoman of Chaillot*.

Erwin Piscator's production of *The Good Soldier Schweik* at the Nollendorf theatre in Berlin makes use of drawings for film projection by George Grosz, and scenery unrolled on a treadmill in comic "conveyor-belt" manner. This "epic" satire on World War I militarism and bureaucracy in Central Europe was a dramatization of Jaroslav Hasek's Czech novel.

The production of *The Three-Penny Opera* in epic-theatre style (book and lyrics by Brecht, music by Kurt Weill, décor by Caspar Neher) at the Theater-am-Schiffbauerdamm in Berlin.

O'Casey turns to expressionistic theatre and starts his departures from naturalism with the writing of *The Silver Tassie*. He breaks with the Abbey Theatre because it rejects the play.

The founding of the Dublin Gate Theatre, a modernist or theatricalist counterpart of the Abbey Theatre.

The Theatre Guild's production of Stefan Zweig's theatricalist *commedia dell' arte* adaptation of Ben Jonson's *Volpone*.

Louis Aragon's *Traité du style*, his essay on surrealist art.

The high point of the surrealist movement is reached when it is joined by Salvador Dali. (First important defection when Aragon resigns, 1931.)

The Arthur Hopkins Broadway production of Sophie Tread-well's *Machinal*, with expressionist treatment of a popular murder case. Later staged in Europe, notably by Tairov at the Kamerny Theatre.

The Theatre Guild production of O'Neill's *Strange Interlude*, staged by Philip Moeller. Especially notable for the management of "interior monologue" and for playing on both realistic and formalized "stream-of-consciousness" levels.

"Dadaist" production of E. E. Cummings' *him* at the Provincetown Playhouse, New York City.

1929   Stage Society of London produces R. C. Sherriff's *Journey's End*, a landmark in British realism.

William A. Brady's production of Elmer Rice's *Street Scene*, a notable appearance of naturalism in the American theatre.

The establishment of the Malvern Festival, noted for numerous productions of Shaw's plays, by the founder and patron of this annual summer festival, Sir Barry Jackson.

The production of Denis Johnston's Irish expressionist drama, *The Old Lady Says "No,"* by the Dublin Gate Theatre. Also, the production of O'Casey's expressionist drama *The Silver Tassie* in London, October 11, 1929. Shaw, the champion of Ibsenite realism four decades earlier, gives enthusiastic endorsement to the production.

1930   Second manifesto of surrealism, including an extension of surrealist principles.

1931   García Lorca writes the poetic fantasy *The Love of Don Perlimpín and Belisa in His Garden*, partly surrealist and partly formalistic.

1931–1941   The Group Theatre in New York; the development of social drama and of modified Stanislavskian acting in the

American theatre under the leadership of Harold Clurman, Cheryl Crawford, and Lee Strasberg.

1932   Jean Cocteau's surrealist film *Blood of a Poet*. (Mordecai Gorelik refers to surrealism as "Romanticism pushed to the logical limit of unreason." But it was the tension between realistic and fantastic elements in works such as this that produced the dramatic effect. It is, in the words of Herbert Read, "a continual state of opposition and interaction between the world of objective fact . . . and the world of subjective fantasy . . . [creating] a state of disquietude.")

The first developed theatre-in-the-round or arena style production in America is presented by Glenn Hughes at the University of Washington.

1932–1936   Nikolai Okhlopkov's flexible arena-style, distinctly theatricalist, staging at the Realistic Theatre in Moscow.

1933   Establishment of the Mercury Theatre by Ashley Dukes. This *avant-garde* little theatre in London gave some early productions to Eliot's *Murder in the Cathedral* and to other poetic dramas by Fry, Ronald Duncan, Ann Ridler, and others.

Sensationalist naturalism in the American theatre: the extremely successful Broadway production of *Tobacco Road*.

A second wave of modernism at the Old Vic starts with the association of Tyrone Guthrie, John Gielgud, and Laurence Olivier.

1933   García Lorca's poetic tragedy *Bodas de sangre* (*Blood Wedding*), with formalistic allegorical elements: the Moon and Death appear as characters.

1934 (Feb. 7)   London production of O'Casey's *Within the Gates*, in which the former realist employed choruses in the theatricalist manner, although his social sympathies were no less evident here than in his early naturalistic plays.

Cocteau's theatricalist treatment of the Oedipus legend in *The Infernal Machine.*

Louis Jouvet starts his management of L'Athénée theatre in Paris.

Production by Margarita Xirgu of García Lorca's theatricalist tragedy *Yerma,* in Madrid.

Broadway production of Gertrude Stein's dadaist-surrealist *Four Saints in Three Acts.*

Sidney Howard's *Yellowjack,* in which epic-theatre dramaturgy was employed by one of the American theatre's most successful realists.

First Convention of the Soviet Writers, noted for the semi-official introduction of the style of so-called "Socialist Realism"; the start of a rigorous dictatorship over dramatic art which favored utilitarian lesson-setting, and propagandistic theatre and disapproval of theatricalist "formalism."

1935   Idealistic naturalism—one could call it "didactic naturalism" or "sociological realism"—wins great success in the American theatre: the Broadway production of Sidney Kingsley's *Dead End,* with naturalistic scenery by Norman Bel Geddes.

New York production of Clifford Odets' *Waiting for Lefty,* the leftist agitational (so-called agit-prop) one-acter that introduced Odets as a playwright. Important in the history of modern dramatic form, along with Irwin Shaw's *Bury the Dead* (1936) and Marc Blitzstein's *The Cradle Will Rock* (1937), for its application of theatricalism to social drama.

Winterset, Maxwell Anderson's major effort to create poetic tragedy in the American theatre, produced and directed by Guthrie McClintic, with settings (including the famous symbolist Williamsburg Bridge setting) by Jo Mielziner.

T. S. Eliot's *Murder in the Cathedral* given productions at the Chapter House of Canterbury Cathedral and at Ashley Dukes' small Mercury Theatre in London.

1935–1939   The government-subsidized Federal Theatre, the first (and thus far only) "state theatre" in the United States, noted for "epic" productions, called "living newspapers," such as *Power* and *One-third of a Nation,* as well as for other types of theatricalist experimentation with productions of *Murder in the Cathedral, Pinocchio, Doctor Faustus,* and a Negro *Macbeth.*

1936   Federal Theatre production of *Triple-A Plowed Under* (in New York City), the first of the "living newspapers."

Paul Green's "epic-theatre" antiwar satire *Johnny Johnson* produced by the Group Theatre in New York.

Louis Jouvet becomes one of the stage directors of the Comédie Française.

García Lorca writes his poetic-naturalist tragedy *The House of Bernarda Alba.*

1936–1937   Meyerhold's production of Dumas' *Camille* (*The Lady of the Camellias*) in a lyrical and simple style which differed sharply from his earlier extremist stylization.

1937   The Federal Theatre "living newspaper" *Power.*

The notably theatricalist Orson Welles production of *Doctor Faustus* for the Federal Theatre; use of an apron stage; highly theatricalist use of pools and columns of light by A. Feder.

Orson Welles' Mercury Theatre modern-dress production of *Julius Caesar* on a space stage. (By taking liberties with the text, Welles was able to present Shakespeare's drama in terms of the then current conflict of democracy and fascism; Brutus, played by Welles himself, represented the "plight" of the liberal in the 1930's.)

The Lost Colony, Paul Green's pageant-play or "symphonic drama," produced at Manteo on Roanoke Island, North Carolina, on the approximate site of the first English settlement in America. *The Lost Colony* became the prototype of many American pageant-plays given outdoor production in specially built theatres.

A reaction against nonrealistic stylization is in full swing in the Russian theatre; Meyerhold's theatre is attacked as "a foreign theatre" and theatrical formalism is denounced as "decadent."

1938   Arrest of Meyerhold, who subsequently disappeared. "The conversion of the Soviet Theatre to socialistic realism [i.e., commonplace, utilitarian realistic playwriting and play production] was complete." (Juri Jelagin, *Taming of the Arts* [Dutton, 1951]. For Meyerhold see pp. 153-174.)

(Aug. 6)   Death of Stanislavsky.

The Federal Theatre "living newspaper" production of *One-third of a Nation.*

The Jed Harris theatricalist production of Thornton Wilder's theatricalist drama *Our Town.*

1939   The Broadway production of Lillian Hellman's *The Little Foxes,* social drama with naturalistic, *comédie rosse,* qualities that invite comparison of the play with Becque's *Les Corbeaux.*

1939–1941   The "Saroyan period" in the American theatre. Such plays as *My Heart's in the Highlands, The Time of Your Life,* and *The Beautiful People,* whether given a "poetic" production (as was *My Heart's in the Highlands,* staged by Robert Lewis) or a "realistic" one (as was *The Time of Your Life*), represented a vogue of moderate theatricalism in the American drama.

1940–1950   Erwin Piscator's management of the Studio Theatre at the New School in New York City and "March of Drama" repertory at the President Theatre: the longest experience of the American public with "epic-theatre" style. Among plays given "epic" production were Piscator's own dramatization of *War and Peace,* Dan James' *Winter Soldiers,* Jean-Paul Sartre's *The Flies,* and Robert Penn Warren's *All the King's Men.*

1942   André Breton's reaffirmation of surrealist principles in his *Situation du surréalisme.*

Elia Kazan's production of Thornton Wilder's imaginative theatricalist drama *The Skin of Our Teeth.*

1943   Sartre's existentialist drama *Les Mouches* (*The Flies*) produced in Paris by Charles Dullin.

1944   The Theatre Guild production of *Oklahoma!* presented the first modern ballet (with choreography by Agnes de Mille) in American musical comedy.

1945   The Eddie Dowling and Margo Jones production of Tennessee Williams' *The Glass Menagerie* on Broadway.

Louis Jouvet's production of Giraudoux' poetic fantasy and social satire *La Folle de Chaillot* (*The Madwoman of Chaillot*) in Paris.

An arena theatre opened by Margo Jones (1913–1955) in Dallas, Texas. The first successful professional "theatre-in-the-round" in the United States.

1947   François Poulenc's opera based on Guillaume Apollinaire's surrealist play *Les Mamelles de Tirésias* produced in Paris.

Elia Kazan's production of Tennessee Williams' *A Streetcar Named Desire,* an example of poetic naturalism.

1949   The London production of Christopher Fry's romantic verse play *The Lady's Not for Burning.*

The Elia Kazan production of *Death of a Salesman,* with scenery by Jo Mielziner. A notable example of the synthesis of realism and theatricalism in the American theatre.

T. S. Eliot's *The Cocktail Party* given its first production at the Edinburgh Festival.

1950   The first arena theatre in the Broadway area opened at the Hotel Edison.

Bibliographic Note

Index

A COMPLETE BIBLIOGRAPHY WILL NOT BE INCLUDED IN THIS VOLUME because an adequate one would be disproportionately long. A few comprehensive works, however, may be mentioned because of their special appropriateness. They are Mordecai Gorelik's *New Theatres for Old;* Lee Simonson's *The Stage Is Set;* the compilations *Actors on Acting* and *Directing the Play,* both edited by Toby Cole and Helen Krich Chinoy; Kenneth Macgowan and Robert Edmond Jones's *Continental Stagecraft* (an indispensable volume of direct observation of the theatre at the beginning of the 1920's); Macgowan and William Melnitz's lucid book *The Living Stage;* A. M. Nagler's *Sources of Theatrical History;* Thomas H. Dickinson's *The Theatre in a Changing Europe;* Barrett H. Clark's *European Theories of the Drama* (the 1947 Crown Publishers edition containing an American supplement); Hiram Kelly Moderwell's *The Theatre of Today;* Anna Irene Miller's *The Independent Theatre in Europe;* Bertolt Brecht's *Sinn und Form* (containing his *Kleines Organon für das Theater,* trans-

261

lated as "A Little Organum for the Theatre" by Beatrice Gottlieb in *Accent*, Winter 1951); Norris Houghton's *Moscow Rehearsals;* H. D. Albright, William Halstead, and Lee Mitchell's *Principles of Theatre Art;* Francis Fergusson's *The Idea of a Theatre;* Eric Bentley's *The Playwright as Thinker* and *In Search of Theater;* and perhaps my own books, *Masters of the Drama, Producing the Play,* and *The Theatre in Our Times.*

For an extensive bibliography the student may consult *Masters of the Drama* (1954 Dover edition), pages 805-840.

Works listed in the Bibliographic Note, pp. 261–262, have not been indexed.

Räuber, Die, 228
Read, Herbert (1893–   ), Br. poet and critic, 253
realism, 3–50, 229, 230
   and acting, 25–30, 42, 55–56, 57–60, 90–91, 92–93
   and antitheatricalism, 46–47
   Appia on, 21–22
   and classicism, 79–97
   conflicts over, 81–83
   and convention, 218
   critical, 83, 84
   criticism of, 48, 49–50, 83, 86
   and dialogue, 37, 38–40
   discussion in, 40–46
   environment in, 17–25, 26–29, 54–65
   and forensic drama, 84
   Ibsen and, 31–32, 39–40, 64, 65, 66
   and illusionism, 87–88
   inner, 29, 187
   Meyerhold's war against, 192–198
   and mimesis, 46–47
   modernity of, 5, 17–18, 19
   in motion pictures, 62–63
   and naturalism, 50, 66–70
   and neoclassicism, 31–33, 34
   pre-Ibsenite, 5, 25–26
   and prose, 37–38, 39–41, 70, 71, 72–73
   Shaw and, 64–66
   "socialist," 12, 254, 256
   Strindberg and, 233
   and structure, 30–35, 39
   "theatrical," introduction of, 229
   and theatricalism, 138, 139–140, 181–191, 202–206, 209, 217
   and verse, 70–76
   (*see also* epic theatre)

Realistic Theatre (Moscow), 253
Regeneración del teatro español, La, 236
Reigen (La Ronde), 34, 68, 237
Reinhardt, Max (1873–1943), Austrian producer, actor, and stage manager, 55, 94, 112, 159–160, 229, 238, 239, 241, 242, 244, 245, 246, 248, 251
   staging of *Jedermann* by, 168, 247
   staging of *A Midsummer Night's Dream* by, 239
   staging of *The Miracle* by, 55, 160, 242
   staging of *Oedipus Rex* by, 160
   use of theatricalism by, 159–160
representationalism, 175, 216
retheatricalization, 149–152, 153, 161–162, 251
retrospective action, 31–32
Revenge of Bussy d'Ambois, The, 39
Revizor (The Inspector-General), 5, 197
revolving stage, introduction of, 236
rhetoric, and drama, 38–39
Rice, Elmer (1892–   ), Am. playwright, novelist, and director, 85, 248
Richard II, contrasts of style in, 222–223
Riders to the Sea, 64, 100, 238
Right You Are (If You Think So!), 13
Rimbaud, Arthur (1854–91), Fr. symbolist poet, 230
Ring of the Nibelungs, 80n.
Ring 'Round the Moon, 134, 176, 178